Jonathan G. Campbell
The Use of Scripture in the
Damascus Document 1–8,19–20

Beihefte zur Zeitschrift für die alttestamentliche Wissenschaft

Herausgegeben von
Otto Kaiser

Band 228

Walter de Gruyter · Berlin · New York
1995

Jonathan G. Campbell

The Use of Scripture in the
Damascus Document 1-8,19-20

Walter de Gruyter · Berlin · New York

1995

♾ Printed on acid-free paper which falls within the guidelines of the ANSI
to ensure permanence and durability

Library of Congress Cataloging-in-Publication Data

Champbell, Jonathan G. (Jonathan Goodson). 1964–
   The use of Scripture in the Damascus document 1–8,19–20 /
Jonathan G. Campbell.
      p.   cm. – (Beihefte zur Zeitschrift für die alttestamentliche
Wissenschaft ; Bd. 228)
      Revision of the author's thesis (Ph. D.)–Oxford University. 1991.
   Includes bibliographical references.
   ISBN 3-11-014240-6   (lib. binding)
      1. Damascus document.   2. Qumran community.   3. Bible. O.T.-
Extra-canonical parallels.   4. Dead Sea scrolls. 40–Criticism.
Interpretation, etc.   I. Title.   II. Series: Beihefte zur Zeitschrift für
die alttestamentliche Wissenschaft : 228.
BS410.Z5   vol. 228
[BM175.Q6]
296.1'55–dc20   95-5898
                                                                      CIP

Die Deutsche Bibliothek – Cataloging-in-Publication Data

[Zeitschrift für die alttestamentliche Wissenschaft / Beihefte]
Beihefte zur Zeitschrift für die alttestamentliche Wissenschaft. – Berlin ;
New York : de Gruyter.
   Früher Schriftenreihe
   Reihe Beihefte zu: Zeitschrift für die alttestamentliche Wissenschaft
NE: HST
Bd. 228. Cambell, Johanthan G.: The use of scripture in the Damascus
document 1–8, 19–20. – 1995
Campbell, Johanthan G.:
The use of scripture in the Damascus document 1–8, 19–20 / Jonathan
G. Campbell. – Berlin ; New York : de Gruyter, 1995
   (Beihefte zur Zeitschrift für die alttestamentliche Wissenschaft ; Bd.
228)
   Zugl.: Oxford, Univ., Diss., 1991
   ISBN 3-11-014240-6

ISSN 0934-2575

Printed in Germany
Printing: Arthur Collignon GmbH, Berlin
Binding: Lüderitz & Bauer-GmbH, Berlin

Acknowledgements

I would like to thank my former supervisor, Prof. Geza Vermes, as well as Dr. Martin Goodman, Dr. George Brooke, and Prof. Joseph Baumgarten, for the help and information they gave me during the original preparation of this study as a doctoral thesis in the University of Oxford. Moreover, I am very grateful to Prof. Vermes, Ms. Mary Betley, and Dr. Richard Crowe for the support and feedback they provided during the painstaking process of revision for publication.

Thanks are also due to Prof. Otto Kaiser who, as editor of the *BZAW* series, accepted my analysis of the Damascus Document into the series, as well as to the University of Wales, Lampeter, for granting me a term's study leave to work on this project.

Finally, it should be stated that I alone am responsible for the final shape of the examination of the Admonition which follows.

JGC

ושבחתי אני את השמחה
אשר אין טוב לאדם תחת השמש
כי אם לאכול ולשתות ולשמוח
והוא ילונו בעמלו ימי חייו
אשר נתן לו האלהים תחת השמש

קהלת ח טו

Preface

This book constitutes a revision of a dissertation accepted for the degree of Doctor of Philosophy in the University of Oxford in September 1991. It has sought to incorporate, where relevant, additional information and changes in perspective that have resulted from the release of previously unpublished Dead Sea Scrolls in late 1991, while at the same time avoiding a complete rewriting of the original study.

Essentially, it is argued that the Damascus Document 1-8 and 19-20 consistently draws upon a select body of scriptural contexts by way of citation and allusion. It is at this level that the unity of the text can be found. Moreover, this feature of the work may enable scholars to re-evaluate the historical problems that are usually associated with the Admonition and its relevance for reconstructing Qumran origins. It also raises important methodological questions about how ancient texts from the Second Temple period should be 'read'.

It may be helpful here to draw attention to a few simple points by way of explanation. Firstly, 'bible' is a term used to designate the open-ended scriptural collection of Second Temple Judaism, while 'Hebrew Bible' is reserved for the three-fold canon of later times. Secondly, the following Hebrew, Aramaic, and Greek editions have been employed: K. Elliger, W. Rudolph, *Biblia Hebraica Stuttgartensia*, Stuttgart (1967-83); A. Sperber, *The Aramaic Bible*, I-III, Leiden (1959); A. Rahlfs, *Septuaginta*, Stuttgart (1979); K. Aland, *Novum Testamentum Graece*, Stuttgart (1979). It should be pointed out that, given their small number, quotations in Greek appear in unaccented form. As for citations in English, the New Revised Standard Version, as well as J.H. Charlesworth, *The Old Testament Pseudepigrapha*, I-II, London (1983-5), have been drawn upon, unless otherwise stated. Thirdly, the text of the Damascus Document itself has been taken from M. Broshi (ed.), *The Damascus Document Reconsidered*, Jerusalem (1992).

Finally, it should be noted that verses within independent quotations from the Masoretic Text in the body of our study are closed with a colon (:), while the Tetragrammaton is represented by ה׳.

Contents

Acknowledgements V
Preface IX

1	**Introduction**	**1-10**
1.1	The Damascus Document	1
1.2	The Difficulty with the Damascus Document	4
1.3	Scripture in the Damascus Document	8
2	**The Bible at Qumran**	**11-32**
2.1	The Bible and the Dead Sea Scrolls	11
2.2	The Use of Scripture at Qumran	19
2.3	Schwarz on Scripture in the Damascus Document	25
2.4	The Damascus Document and Scripture	27
3	**The Damascus Document and the Historical-Critical Method** . . .	**33-48**
3.1	Understanding Ancient Texts	33
3.2	Poetry in the Damascus Document	35
3.3	An Address to the Sons of Light	41
3.4	Literature and Culture	43
4	**Scripture in the Historical Sections**	
	of the Damascus Document	**49-102**
4.1	The Historical Sections	49
4.2	Scripture in CD 1:1-2:1	51
4.2.1	Torah in CD 1:1-2:1	57
4.2.2	Nevi'im in CD 1:1-2:1	60
4.2.3	Ketuvim in CD 1:1-2:1	63
4.2.4	Summary	65
4.3	Scripture in CD 2:14-4:12a	67
4.3.1	Torah in CD 2:14-4:12a	72
4.3.2	Nevi'im in CD 2:14-4:12a	79
4.3.3	Ketuvim in CD 2:14-4:12a	84
4.3.4	Summary	86
4.4	Scripture in CD 5:15a-6:11a	88
4.4.1	Torah in CD 5:15b-6:11a	91
4.4.2	Nevi'im in CD 5:15b-6:11a	96
4.4.3	Ketuvim in CD 5:15a-6:11a	98
4.4.4	Summary	99
4.5	Scripture in the Historical Sections	100

5	**Scripture in the Midrashic Sections**	
	of the Damascus Docuent	**103-174**
5.1	The Midrashic Sections	103
5.2	Scripture in CD 2:2-13	106
5.2.1	Torah in CD 2:2-13	109
5.2.2	Nevi'im in CD 2:2-13	112
5.2.3	Ketuvim in CD 2:2-13	114
5.2.4	Summary	115
5.3	Scripture in CD 4:12b-5:15a	116
5.3.1	Torah in CD 4:12b-5:15a	122
5.3.2	Nevi'im in CD 4:12a-5:15a	127
5.3.3	Ketuvim in CD 4:12a-5:15b	130
5.3.4	Summary	130
5.4	Scripture in CD 6:11b-8:21	131
5.4.1	Torah in CD 6:11b-7:9a	138
5.4.2	Nevi'im in CD 6:11a-7:9a	144
5.4.3	Ketuvim in CD 6:11a-7:9a	146
5.4.4	Torah in CD 7:9b-8:21	146
5.4.5	Nevi'im in CD 7:9b-8:21	148
5.4.6	Ketuvim in CD 7:9b-8:21	150
5.4.7	Summary	151
5.5	Scripture in CD 19:1-33a	152
5.5.1	A Comparison of Manuscripts A and B	153
5.5.2	Torah and Nevi'im in CD 19:1-33	158
5.5.3	Summary	160
5.6	Scripture in CD 19:33b-20:34	161
5.6.1	Torah in CD 19:33b-20:34	163
5.6.2	Nevi'im in CD 19:33b-20:34	167
5.6.3	Ketuvim in CD 19:33b-20:34	169
5.6.4	Summary	170
5.7	Scripture in the Midrashic Sections	171
6	**Conclusions**	**175-208**
6.1	The Damascus Document and Scripture	175
6.2	The Damascus Document and History	189
6.3	Mark 15:22-37 and Scripture	195
6.4	The Damascus Document, Scripture and History	200
6.5	Use of Scripture in the Damascus Document 1-8, 19-20	205
Abbreviations	. . . .	209
Bibliography	. . . .	213

1 Introduction

1.1 The Damascus Document

The Damascus Document (CD) was discovered in Cairo in 1896/97 by Solomon Schechter among a large body of manuscripts (MSS) and fragments in an old synagogue genizah; it was subsequently published in 1910.[1] The work in a different edition(s) was uncovered when texts in caves of the Judaean desert were found between 1947 and 1955 around the site of Khirbet Qumran.[2] The most important copies were the remains of eight MSS retrieved from Cave 4 (4QD^{a-h} or 4Q266-273), although a few fragments were also recovered from Cave 5 and Cave 6.[3] However, due to the unavailability of the 4QD texts to the majority of scholars during most of the past forty-five years, CD, in conjunction with what were viewed to be other sectarian documents from Qumran, came to be read in lieu of 4QD as expressive of the origins, religion and laws of the Essene sect living in the Judaean desert during the final third of the Second Temple period.[4]

---

[1]   S. Schechter, *Documents of Jewish Sectaries: Fragments of a Zadokite Work*, Cambridge (1910); this was reprinted with a prolegomenon and bibliography by J. Fitzmyer in 1970. Photographs of the Cairo Genizah MSS, prepared by E. Qimron, can be studied in M. Broshi (ed.), *The Damascus Document Reconsidered*, Jerusalem (1992), pp. 9-49.

[2]   For details of the results of archaeological work in and around Qumran, see R. de Vaux, *Archaeology and the Dead Sea Scrolls*, London (1973); P.R. Callaway, *The History of the Qumran Community: An Investigation*, Sheffield (1988), pp. 29-51. For a complete catalogue of the Dead Sea Scrolls (DSS), see G. Vermes, *The Dead Sea Scrolls: Qumran in Perspective*, London (1994), pp. 202-225; the same list also occurs in G. Vermes, *Dead Sea Scrolls in English*, London (1994), pp. xxxvi-lvi.

[3]   The small fragments from Caves 5 and 6 were included in M. Baillet, J.T. Milik, R. de Vaux, *Les 'Petites Grottes' de Qumrân*, Oxford (Discoveries in the Judaean Desert, III; 1962), pp. 128-131, 181.

[4]   For an outline of the resultant consensus, see E. Schürer, G. Vermes, F. Millar, *The history of the Jewish people in the age of Jesus Christ*, II, Edinburgh (1979), pp. 555-590. For the main so-called sectarian DSS, see the relevant portions of Schürer, III.1, pp. 380-469, and below, note 11.

There have been numerous variations and permutations on this hypothesis over the years, not least concerning the precise role CD should play in such historical and ideological reconstructions.[5] Moreover, the resultant debate is now set to intensify in view of the new access scholars now have to previously unpublished DSS, including the 4QD material.[6] Given these complexities, it will be useful to describe CD and 4QD in a little more detail.

The Cairo Genizah evidence consists of two medieval MSS, referred to as MS A and MS B. The former is divided into sixteen columns (termed CD 1-16 or CD I-XVI), while the latter is made up of two longer columns (labelled CD 19-20 or CD XIX-XX). Further, in terms of style and content, the material divides naturally into two parts: CD 1-8 and 19-20, which are often called the 'Admonition' or 'Exhortation'; and CD 9-16, which is referred to as the 'Laws' or 'Statutes'.[7] Whilst CD 19-20 in MS B appears to be a continuation of CD 1-8, the fact that 7:5b-8:19,21b overlaps with 19:1-34a is one of the major complications within the Admonition.

As mentioned, the most important of the Qumran copies of the text are 4QD^{a-h} or 4Q266-273.[8] Of these, the oldest and longest is 4QD^a, of some 272 lines and dating to the first half of the first century BCE; 4QD^e is also substantial, although late Herodian in date. When the remains of the eight MSS are coordinated with each other, it appears that 4QD contained all of the Cairo material, along with a number of extra sections not present in the

---

5   See P.R. Davies, *The Damascus Covenant*, Sheffield (1982), pp. 1-47, for a review of scholarly theses pertaining to CD.

6   Photographs of 4QD were made available in R.H. Eisenman, J.M. Robinson, *A Facsimile Edition of the Dead Sea Scrolls*, I-II, Washington (1991). See also B.Z. Wacholder, M.G. Abegg, *A Preliminary Edition of the Unpublished Dead Sea Scrolls: the Hebrew and Aramaic Texts from Cave Four*, Fascicle One, Washington (1991), pp. 1-59, for a reconstruction of the 4QD texts, as well as Baumgarten in Broshi, pp. 57-62, for a description of 4QD^{a-h}.

7   As pointed out by J.T. Milik, *Ten Years of Discovery in the Wilderness of Judaea*, London (1959), p. 151f, the equivalent of CD 15-16 preceded that of 9-14 in 4QD, and this informs the arrangement of the translation in *DSSE*, p. 106f. Note that H. Stegemann, 'Das Gesetzkorpus der <<Damaskusschrift>> (CD IX-XVI)', *RQ* 14 (1990), pp. 409-434, argues that CD 9-16 was originally a work separate from the Admonition with which it is now joined.

8   We follow here the sigla of Baumgarten in Broshi, pp. 57-61. It should be pointed out, however, that 4QD^{a,b,c,d,e,f,g,h} are respectively designated 4QD^{b,d,a,f,e,c,g,h} in WA, pp. 1-59.

medieval edition of the work. This reconstruction of the contents of 4QD can be represented in the following way:[9]

1. Address in the first person singular to the בני אור, exhorting them to obey Moses and separate from the מסיגי גבול (cf. CD 5:20 and 8:3);
2. CD 1-8,19-20;
3. Introduction to the Laws, with a catalogue of transgressions apparently designed to exemplify the laxity of contemporary society and paralleled at points in 11QT and 4QMMT, and an appeal to the יודעי צדק (cf. CD 1:1) to choose life;
4. The role of the priests in the community and regulations concerning priestly disqualifications;
5. The ordeal of the סוטה;
6. Rules about skin disease, fluxes and childbirth;
7. Various agricultural laws;
8. Impure metals employed in pagan cults;
9. Some regulations on marriage;
10. CD 15-16, 9-14;
11. Penal code on discipline in the community (cf. 1QS 8:16b-9:2);
12. Expulsion ritual for use at the annual Renewal of the Covenant ceremony in the third month (cf. 1QS 2:19-25a).

Some 144 lines of the 4QD material relate to the Admonition, while 182 are from CD 9-16; a further 363 lines, not extant in the Genizah texts, are mostly of a legal nature. This means that the Qumran form of the document had an Exhortation approximately half as long as its Laws section.[10]

Further evaluation of 4QD and its relation to CD will require more detailed study of the 4QD data and other hitherto unpublished DSS, which have only been in the public domain for several years. Indeed, the main task of Qumran scholarship will now be to analyse this newly liberated material.[11]

---

9 See Baumgarten in Broshi, pp. 51-57, for the basis of this layout and for the dating of the MSS.

10 Regarding the additional legal material in 4QD, of particular interest are what appear to be parallels with Josephus' description of the Essenes; see J.M. Baumgarten, 'The Cave 4 Versions of the Qumran Penal Code', *JJS* 43 (1991), p. 275, for a possible example in 4QD[e].

11 For a preliminary collection of some of the most important new texts in their original language, together with an English translation, see R.H. Eisenman, M. Wise, *The Dead Sea Scrolls Uncovered*, New York (1992); while the transcriptions in this volume are generally accurate, care should be taken in the use of its

This will be a lengthy task, which will no doubt result in important changes to our perception of the Qumran community, Second Temple Judaism at large and the overall significance of the DSS.

Meanwhile, especially since it seems that 4QD will alter our view of the Laws rather than the Exhortation, we shall be concerned with CD 1-8 and 19-20, as well as the text which preceded this in 4QD in the form of an address, now extant only fragmentarily in 4QD[a,b,c], to the "sons of light". However, the scholarly energy that has been expended on the Admonition since the beginning of the twentieth century is great, and the results are varied. This is shown by the many publications discussing the text that have appeared and by the diversity of approach and hypothesis put forward.[12]   It is, indeed, with not a little hesitation that we embark on another study of CD 1-8 and 19-20, and the remainder of this chapter and the ensuing two chapters are devoted to setting the scene and justifying our approach.

1.2 The Difficulty with the Damascus Document

In recent decades, various competing theories regarding the Admonition and its relation to other DSS and the Qumran community have been proposed, and the student of CD may genuinely be at a loss as to how to discern appropriately between them. The crux of the matter concerns Qumran origins and the role of CD 1-8 and 19-20 in reconstructing them. Largely as a by-product of this debate, some terminological confusion has evolved over designations such as 'Essene', 'pre-Essene', 'proto-Qumran', or 'Qumran', so that scholars use terms with varying nuances, depending on how the connections between the Qumran community, CD and the Essenes are viewed.[13]   Nevertheless, all who attempt to reconstruct earliest Qumran history are obliged to utilize CD, inasmuch as it seems to give important clues to this period, especially in CD 1:1-2:1.

---

interpretative comments. A superior English translation of many of the same new works can also be found in *DSSE*.

[12] For further bibliographical data, see S. Schechter, *Documents of Jewish Sectaries: Fragments of a Zadokite Work*, New York (1970), with a bibliography by J. Fitzmyer, and Broshi, pp. 63-83, containing a compilation of relevant works produced in the period 1970-89.

[13] See P.R. Davies, 'The Birthplace of the Essenes: Where is Damascus?', *RQ* 14 (1990), pp. 503-520, for a helpful discussion on terminology.

Overall, following Davies, we can see a divergence of opinion which presents us with two basic theories:

> "The more long-standing of these, most comprehensively developed by H. Stegemann, is that the Qumran community originally developed from the Hasidim of the Maccabean period and became the Essenes, whereas those Hasidim who rejected the Teacher of Righteousness evolved into the Pharisees....The alternative theory, sustained by J. Murphy-O'Connor, posits an Essene movement prior to Qumran. The arrival of the Teacher provoked a split in this movement; his disciples retreated to the Dead Sea, leaving the larger body of Essenes settled throughout Palestine."[14]

In other words, the view represented by Stegemann and others placed the origins of the Qumran community (which was coextensive with, or the chief and only known exemplar of, Essenism) in the mid-second century BCE, and sought to create a synthesis out of material deemed to be original to the sect - particularly 1QS, the Pesharim, and CD. This, in turn, led to a reconstruction of the community's history and organization, as well as an understanding of its literature and self-identity, which viewed CD as stemming directly from the Essenes, thought to be responsible for all the sectarian DSS written over a 200-year period, at Qumran. While there have been numerous important variations as to the detail of this thesis, in one form or another it had become the consensus view by the 1960s.[15] A second approach, associated with J. Murphy-O'Connor and P.R. Davies, has traced a beginning for the Essenes (or at least a claim to an origin) to some point between the exile and the first half of the second century. The above-mentioned synthesis, they have argued, does not do justice to the individual texts, especially CD, which may even be a document not original to the group among whom it was found. One particular focus of their work has concerned what is to be made of the pre-history of the sect, as narrated in CD 1:4ff, 3:12ff and 6:2ff, before the arrival of the Teacher of Righteousness. These passages seem to place it after the Babylonian exile rather than in the second century BCE, and they sit

---

[14] P.R. Davies, 'Eschatology at Qumran', *JBL* 104 (1985), p. 44.

[15] Associated with it, among others, are names such as J.H. Charlesworth, M. Knibb, J.T. Milik, H. Stegemann, R. de Vaux, and G. Vermes; see note 4 above. It should be remarked, however, that Stegemann has revised his view of Qumran origins in 'The Qumran Essenes - Local Members of the Main Jewish Union in Late Second Temple Times', in J.T. Barrera, L.V. Montaner, *The Madrid Qumran Congress: Proceedings of the International Congress on the Dead Sea Scrolls Madrid 18-21 March, 1991*, Leiden (1992), pp. 83-186.

somewhat uncomfortably with the sort of information usually gleaned from the Pesharim.[16]

To complicate matters further, we may also now speak of a mid-way or third position which has in effect married elements from both of these two theses. As with the theories of Murphy-O'Connor and Davies, this third hypothesis has argued that the Qumran community was a splinter group which formed from a wider Essene movement but, more in line with the consensus view, that broader movement had a thoroughly Palestinian origin in the third or early second century BCE only. This so-called 'Groningen Hypothesis' was formulated by F. García Martínez and A.S. van der Woude and contains several distinctive features of its own.[17]

Of course, this distillation of three main approaches out of the immense scholarly effort that has gone into the study of the Admonition and the related issue of Qumran origins is something of an oversimplification.[18] It is neither practical nor necessary, however, to enter into greater detail at this stage, for a new synthesis is likely to emerge in view of the access which scholars now have to texts released in recent years.[19]

Nevertheless, it appears that, in contrast to the Laws, 4QD changes little of our understanding of the overall shape of the Admonition, apart from the addition of an initial opening address. It will be helpful, therefore, to explain

---

[16]   See J. Murphy-O'Connor, 'An Essene Missionary Document? CD II,14 - VI,1', *RB* 77 (1970), pp. 201-229; 'A Literary Analysis of Damascus Document VI,2 - VIII,3', *RB* 78 (1971), pp. 210-232; 'The Critique of the Princes of Judah (CD VIII,3-19)', *RB* 79 (1972), pp. 200-216; 'A Literary Analysis of Damascus Document XIX,33 - XX,34', *RB* 79 (1972), pp. 544-564; see also Davies.

[17]   See F. García Martínez, 'Qumran Origins and Early History: A Groningen Hypothesis', *FO* 25 (1988), pp. 113-136, for its initial expression and, subsequently, F. García Martínez, A.S. van der Woude, 'A Groningen Hypothesis of Qumran Origins and Early History', *RQ* 14 (1990), pp. 521-542. One element in this thesis, construing 1QpHab 8-12 as portraying six wicked high priests in succession, has been criticized by T.H. Lim, 'The Wicked Priests of the Groningen Hypothesis', *JBL* 112 (1993), pp. 415-425. See below, p. 190, note 35, for further details.

[18]   A number of peripheral hypotheses are untenable, especially in view of the results of radiocarbon dating of the DSS, as reported in G. Bonani *et al*, 'Radiocarbon Dating of the Dead Sea Scrolls', *Atiqot* 20 (1991), pp. 25-32. These include, e.g., J.L. Teicher, 'Die Schriftrollen vom Toten Meer - Dokumente der jüdisch-christlichen Sekte der Ebioniten', *ZRGG* 3 (1951), pp. 153-209; R.H. Eisenman, *Maccabees, Zadokites, Christians and Qumran*, Leiden (1983); B. Thiering, *Jesus the Man: A New Interpretation from the Dead Sea Scrolls*, London (1992).

[19]   See G. Vermes, 'The Present State of Dead Sea Scrolls Research', *JJS* 45 (1994), pp. 101-110, and, more fully, *DSSE*, pp. 1-64, for an expression of how a revised consensus may take shape.

more precisely the reasons for the divergent views mentioned above. As already suggested, the cause lies almost exclusively in the kind of significance given to various passages in CD 1-8 or 19-20, which rehearse the origin of the group being commended in the text. How they relate to each other, to other portions of CD, and to material from other DSS, usually taken as evidence for the sect's beginnings, is also important. The passages are CD 1:1-2:1, 2:14-4:12a, and 5:15b-6:11a, and they mention the מורה צדק, the דורש התורה and contain references, unique among the DSS, to the שבי ישראל and דמשק. Other portions of CD mention the same or seemingly related personages, along with their enemies and associated events (see, for instance, CD 4:19ff, 5:13-15, 7:14-21, and 8:9-13).

At this point, it should be noted that in CD the Teacher is only mentioned in CD 1:11 and 6:11; in the former he is of the recent past, while in the latter he is a figure of the future. Moreover, although most interpreters have equated a second century Teacher with the Interpreter in 6:7, this is difficult if CD 3:12ff and 6:2ff place the community's origin further into the past. As for the nomenclature שבי ישראל, דמשק and the phrase היוצאים מארץ יהודה (see CD 4:6f and 6:5), much depends on the extent to which such terms are viewed as literal or symbolic. Because the metaphorical is certainly involved in some way, however, it is difficult to judge between scholars' views. Thus, שבי ישראל is taken by many as "repentants", ארץ יהודה as second-century Judaism centred on Jerusalem and its temple, and דמשק as a cipher for Qumran. Alternatively, these terms might be seen as referring to "returnees", the actual land of Judah, and Babylon, respectively. These and other factors will be mentioned again in subsequent chapters when the detail of CD 1-8 and 19-20 is discussed.

For now, it is sufficient to note that the main problem in interpreting the Admonition centres on an apparent contradiction between a beginning for the sect which is placed a considerable amount of time after Nebuchadnezzar's destruction of Jerusalem and one set in the intervening period. More concretely, the reader is faced with the task of relating CD 1:1-2:1 to the transition from 3:10b-12a to 3:12ff, and to the similar pattern in 5:20ff and 6:2ff, and then taking into account other portions like CD 7:14-21. There is a similar two-fold picture painted of the wicked; the sins of pre-exilic generations are referred to, as well as the punishment that swallowed them up, but there are also references to more recent wickedness. An ambiguity is present which renders it difficult to make any attempt to distinguish between exilic and later generations in a consistent and precise manner. In short, an examination of CD, especially 1:1-2:1, 3:12b-4:12a, and 5:15b-6:11a, evinces a fluctuation between an origin set in the exile and one placed considerably later on, both set against outside wickedness. While all agree that some group was in existence before the appearance of the Teacher, it is this indeterminate period, before mention of the latter and the "root of planting" in 1:7ff, which different theories have attempted to explain.

All three lines of approach outlined above have points in their favour. On the one hand, it is surely reasonable to expect CD to bear its meaning in relation to the other texts, especially the Pesharim, with which it was presumably meaningfully used by the sect at Qumran, as the synthesis of Stegemann and others has assumed. At the same time, the difficulty of accepting such a theory without compromising the detail of the text must be faced, and it is especially awkward that this problem extends to the internal consistency of the Admonition itself. It may be that, when scholars have had sufficient time to peruse and evaluate the mass of new material now at their disposal and to reassess those sectarian DSS which have been in the public domain for some time, the difficulties considered above will disappear or alter radically. This, however, is by no means certain.

1.3 Scripture in the Damascus Document

In the meantime, we may be sure that the statements of Milik and, subsequently, Baumgarten, that the 4QD texts generally match the Cairo MSS A and B, are correct.[20] This is clear, at least as far as the Admonition is concerned, now that the photographs of 4QD[a-h] are available, although our view of the Laws of CD may change significantly in years to come.[21] Any new approach to CD 1-8 and 19-20, therefore, which bypasses the historical difficulties outlined earlier without preempting the results of future research, is to be welcomed.

---

[20]   See J.T. Milik, *Ten Years of Discovery in the Wilderness of Judaea*, London (1959), pp. 38, 58, 60, and Baumgarten in Broshi, p. 61f.

[21]   Thus, the judgement of P.R. Callaway, *The History of the Qumran Community: An Investigation*, Sheffield (1988), p. 90, was over-cautious:

> "If Milik's reconstructed outline should turn out to be correct, and the still unpublished 4Q material prevents one from checking it, the medieval manuscripts A and B would seem to represent not only a shorter version but also a qualitatively different document from that represented by the 4Q fragments. If CD originally concluded with a liturgy for the Feast of the Covenant Renewal, then one would need to reassess the document according to genre and historical relevance."

Consequently, it is appropriate at this point to turn more specifically to our own reason for embarking on a study of the Admonition, which combines an intuition with an observation by Davies. He maintains that the writer of CD found, or believed himself to have found, his message in the scriptures themselves. It is worth borrowing Davies' own words to express this:

> "...this state of affairs is misconceived if CD is dismissed as a mere 'mosaic' of quotations to which no evidential value may be attached. There are certainly numerous examples of biblical phraseology which must be regarded as unconsidered and even as only part of the author's own biblically saturated vocabulary. But the cumulative force of the numerous quotations and allusions amounts to a statement that the 'plot' of CD can be read in the bible: the community, the time in which it lives, its laws, everything is anticipated, described, regulated in the bible. The conclusion is forced upon one that not only is the bible used by the community to present its appeal, but also that it was in the bible in the first place that the community found its identity".[22]

Davies' conclusion here is itself problematic. What does it mean for a religious group in the second century BCE, or perhaps earlier, to consider its message as stemming from the bible? In one way or another, such would be the case for almost any group of observant Jews of the time, for it is arguable that, from at least the second century onwards, the inner tensions and conflicts within Second Temple Judaism centred largely on competing claims to represent a valid interpretation of the one commonly received corpus of revelation.[23] More practically, approaching an ancient text from a later and different perspective than that of its author, we stand outside the myth of the writer of CD, and it is notoriously difficult to judge in such matters which comes first. In other words, did a consideration of the bible lead to a particular interpretation, now found in CD 1-8 and 19-20, or were the ideas behind this interpretation projected back onto the scriptures?

Nonetheless, a reading of the text of the Admonition may lead us to wonder whether there is more to the use of scripture in the document than appears at first sight, not only as far as the quotations are concerned, but also, and perhaps more interestingly, regarding the many allusions. Indeed, it is difficult not to notice how much biblical allusion is to be found even upon a cursory reading of the work. While some of this may best be described as a superficial web of biblical language, used to impress the hearer or reader, this can hardly be said of a good deal of it. In fact, a closer look at the text shows that certain key passages keep reappearing. From this feature alone,

---

22   Davies, p. 55.
23   This is expressed, e.g., in G. Vermes, *Post-Biblical Jewish Studies*, Leiden (1975), p. 38, and we shall return to it in the concluding chapter.

irrespective of whether it is appropriate to speak of the community finding its
identity in the bible, as Davies has proposed, we may intuitively suspect a
more developed and deliberate use of scripture than scholars have hitherto
reckoned with, notwithstanding the document's apparent inconsistency on the
historical level.

For now, let it be noted that a description of the use of scripture in CD 1-8
and 19-20 will be of value in itself. In any case, since no thorough
examination has yet taken place in the English-speaking world, it appears to
be a worthwhile task on which to embark.[24]

---

[24]   O.J.R. Schwarz, *Der erste Teil der Damaskusschrift und das alte Testament*, Diest
(1965), will be considered in the next chapter.

2 The Bible at Qumran

2.1 The Bible and the Dead Sea Scrolls

In view of the nature of our proposed analysis of CD 1-8 and 19-20, it will be helpful to trace an appropriate background. Firstly, therefore, we shall outline some of the ways in which the biblical MSS from Qumran have contributed to our understanding of the place of the bible within the Judaism of the Second Temple period. Secondly, we shall view summarily the work of scholars on the employment of scripture in the so-called sectarian, non-biblical DSS. Thirdly, such work will be related more specifically to the use of the bible in CD and to our own examination of the document.

First of all, let us describe briefly the biblical finds from Masada, Nahal Hever, Murabba'at and the Qumran Caves. Apart from the discovery of previously unknown sectarian documents, the biblical material from the Judaean desert was itself the most significant discovery relating to the text of the bible for many years.[1] Of course, the group(s) responsible for this material did not leave behind a clearly demarcated collection of authoritative books, but it is likely that all of the contents of the later three-fold canon were counted as sacred writings. It is not so clear whether other additional works were viewed likewise, as might appear to be the case from passages like CD 2:6 and 16:3, which refer to forms of TLev and Jub, respectively, as though they had scriptural status. But in any case, the only part of the Hebrew Bible not in evidence in the Judaean wilderness was Est, the significance of which is not immediately clear, although its shortness could have allowed it to perish in the desert without trace. Similarly, we may suppose that Neh was present, since remains of Ezr and 1,2 Chr were found.[2]

---

[1] Even the relatively old MS behind the standard critical edition of the Masoretic Text (MT), K. Elliger, W. Rudolph, *Biblia Hebraica Stuttgartensia*, Stuttgart (1967-83), is some 1,000 years younger than the MS finds around Khirbet Qumran.

[2] For an inventory of the biblical texts recovered from Qumran, see E. Tov, 'Hebrew Biblical Manuscripts from the Judaean Desert: Their Contribution to Textual Criticism', *JJS* 39 (1988), p. 17, or V. Gleßmer, 'Liste der Biblischen Texte aus Qumran', *RQ* 16 (1993), pp. 153-192.

The overall situation is more complicated than this brief depiction would suggest, however, and necessitates further description.

The Masada, Murabba'at and Nahal Hever material can be dealt with succinctly, because, when compared to the evidence from the Qumran Caves, it is fairly limited. Clearly, the Masada finds date from before 73/74 CE, while texts found at Nahal Hever and Murabba'at must have had an origin before 132-135 CE; *termini a quo* are less determinable.[3]   According to Tov, the remains of bible MSS from these sites can be characterized as proto-Masoretic and consist mostly of the Pentateuch - with Is, Ez, the Twelve Minor Prophets and Pss also attested.[4]

In contrast, the MS evidence from the Qumran Caves is of a more complex nature. This complexity is due to the large number of MSS, combined with their distribution over the several Caves and between three languages. Unfortunately, no logical or consistent arrangement by the sectaries of the material in the Caves is evident, and this problem is exacerbated by the partly accidental nature of what happened to survive in the Judaean desert for 1,900 years. Nonetheless, it is clear that the biblical texts, and their non-biblical counterparts, are to be associated with occupation of the site of Qumran from the second half of the second century BCE until 68 CE; this is demonstrated chiefly by the archaeological links between the MSS and other artefacts found in the Caves, since the latter are in turn connected with the material culture at Khirbet Qumran.[5] The fact that the oldest MS, 4QExod^f, from around 250 BCE, predates this period is not problematic, for we might expect the first settlers at Qumran and its environs to bring with them biblical and other MSS already in their possession.[6]   MSS in the Hebrew language predominate, in particular remains of Dt, Is, and Pss, and it may be assumed that among the texts were both those imported from elsewhere and those copied on site. Further, texts in both square Hebrew and palaeo-Hebrew are in evidence, but the former are more prevalent.   Numerous Aramaic works were also discovered, including targums on Lv (4Q156) and Job (4Q157 and 11Q10),

---

[3]   For the First and Second Revolts against Rome, see J.H. Hayes, J.M. Miller, *Israelite and Judaean History*, London (1990), pp. 636-677.

[4]   Tov, *op. cit.*, p. 16f.

[5]   Despite N. Golb, 'Who Hid the Dead Sea Scrolls?', *BA* 28 (1987), pp. 68-82, whose arguments have been countered by F. García Martínez, A.S. van der Woude, 'A 'Groningen' Hypothesis of Qumran Origins and Early History', *RQ* 14 (1990), pp. 526-536, scholars are right to maintain the connection between Khirbet Qumran and the Caves.

[6]   For further bibliographical information on the oldest MSS - 4QExod^f, 4QSam^b, 4QJer^a, 4QXII^a, 4QQoh^a - see Tov, *op. cit.*, p. 8, note 9,

as well as the well-known 1QapGen; Greek texts were found at Nahal Hever and at Qumran in Cave 4 and Cave 7.[7] Details such as these may lead us to envisage a state of flux regarding the condition and status of the biblical text among the community at Qumran and, probably, elsewhere during the second half of the Second Temple period.

Indeed, closer scrutiny reveals this to be the case in three main respects, as highlighted in a description by Ulrich.[8] The first concerns the orthographic variety to be found in the biblical, as well as non-biblical, texts from Qumran. This phenomenon can be related to the fact that evidence pertaining to the biblical text in the Second Temple period seems to witness to an increasing preference for a longer, *plene* orthography alongside continued use of an older, shorter orthographic system which persisted from monarchic and early post-exilic times. Hence, different copies of the same book at Qumran were written in divergent orthographies, as in the case of 1QIs[a] (*plene*) and 1QIs[b] (short). It makes sense, therefore, to picture the initial founders of the Qumran settlement bringing with them works displaying both sets of characteristics. Subsequently, they would have reproduced those same texts utilizing one or the other of these orthographic systems, depending on whether a particular scribe was acting as a 'copyist' (committed to reproducing a work exactly as found in its *Vorlage*) or 'updater' (modernizing or, perhaps, archaizing a work as was felt appropriate), both of which were acceptable in Second Temple Palestine and elsewhere. As would be expected, moreover, the sectarian documents discovered in the Caves employ the fuller orthography, with only rare exception (as in the case of 4QS[d]/4Q258). If this reconstruction is accurate, it means that Tov's hypothesis that the latter system was in fact specifically the orthography of the Qumran scribal school is incorrect.[9] In fact, there is little significance to be given to the sorts of orthographical variations under consideration here which, for the most part, have no impact on the meaning of a given word or phrase. Normally, they take the form of the presence or otherwise of a *mater*

---

[7]   For these, see R. de Vaux, J.T. Milik, *Qumran Grotte 4: II Archeologie et 4Q128-4Q157*, Oxford (Discoveries in the Judaean Desert, VI; 1977), pp. 86-90; Schürer, III.1, pp. 318-325; and E. Tov, *The Greek Minor Prophets Scroll from Nahal Hever (8HevXIIgr) (The Seiyal Collection I)*, Oxford (Discoveries in the Judaean Desert, VIII; 1990), respectively. A collection of non-biblical Aramaic works is also available in K. Beyer, *Die Aramäischen Texte vom Toten Meer*, Göttingen (1984).

[8]   See E. Ulrich, 'Pluriformity in the Biblical Text, Text Groups and Questions of Canon', in *Madrid*, I, pp. 23-41, on which much of the following discussion is based.

[9]   See Tov, *op. cit.*, pp. 5-37, for this view.

lectionis or suffix in words such as כל (or כול), לא (or לוא), הוא (or הואה) or קטלת (or קטלתה), although there are cases where the addition of a *mater lectionis* can be the result of interpretation.[10]

Secondly, and more significantly, the DSS have provided us with a mass of individual variant readings pertaining to the biblical text.[11] While it is true that before 1947 the extant witnesses to the MT, LXX, Samaritan Pentateuch and other versions presented scholars with copious data in this regard, the Qumran biblical MSS have, nevertheless, radically altered our perception of the state of the scriptures in the late Second Temple period. This is largely because of the unpredictable way in which individual readings in any given Qumran bible MS relate to the MT, LXX or Samaritan. Thus, although a particular text might be described on balance as proto-Masoretic, proto-Samaritan or as reflecting the LXX's *Vorlage*, it may actually contain readings paralleled by two or, as in 5QDt, for instance, even all three of these versions. On the other hand, of the many texts containing LXX readings, only 4QJer[b] has sufficient to be realistically related as a whole to the *Vorlage* of the LXX. Furthermore, there are many independent readings relating to none of the above-mentioned versions, as found in 2QDt[c], 4QDt[l,q], 4QJos[a], 4QSam[a], 5QKi, and 11QpaleoLev. The upshot of such evidence, therefore, is that tripartite theories about the biblical text in the Second Temple period must be abandoned, including the hypotheses of Cross and Talmon, which sought to link the three main ancient versions with geographical or ideological factors, respectively.[12] In point of fact, it is difficult not to agree with Vermes' evaluation:

> "Being so used to the crystallized and finished from of the Masoretic text, we must make a conscious effort to become aware of the elasticity of the Hebrew Scriptures in the Qumran age. Since, with only a small exaggeration, it can be suggested that there are as many editions of a writing...as there are manuscripts".[13]

Indeed, this leads on to a third complicating factor, namely, whether patterns can be detected in the variant readings of Qumran biblical MSS and, if

---

10   See Ulrich, *op. cit.*, p. 30, for an example concerning the ambiguous form תורתי.

11   See Tov, *op. cit.*, pp. 28-32, for an account more detailed than is possible here, as well as his *Textual Criticism of the Hebrew Bible*, Minneapolis-Assen/Maastricht (1992).

12   See F.M. Cross, 'The Evolution of a Theory of Local Texts', and S. Talmon, 'The Textual Study of the Bible - a New Outlook', in F.M. Cross, S. Talmon, *Qumran and the History of the Biblical Text*, Cambridge, MA (1975), pp. 306-315 and 321-400. For a short critique of their theses, see Ulrich, *op. cit.*, pp. 25-29.

13   G. Vermes, 'Bible Interpretation at Qumran', *Eretz-Israel* 20 (1989), p. 185.

so, whether it is then possible to discern familial relationships between those same MSS and the MT, LXX and Samaritan versions. A minimalist position has been taken up by Tov, while Ulrich has argued that it is still helpful to speak of text types and text families.[14] A firm conclusion will not be reached before further analysis, evaluation and debate has taken place but, meanwhile, it is clear that widely differing editions of biblical books existed side by side at Qumran - irrespective of the issue of whether it is an individual MS of a given work, on the one hand, or groups or families of MSS, on the other, that should be deemed to constitute an edition. Unfortunately, however, there is nowhere explicitly stated the attitude of those responsible for preserving the MSS either towards this sort of diversity or to precisely what constituted a set of authoritative texts. For the latter issue, we must turn to other Second Temple literature, which, at least indirectly, may be more forthcoming.

In this regard, a scholarly consensus has emerged, which views the three-fold division of the Hebrew Bible as originating in the Second Temple period. It began with the return of Ezra to Jerusalem in the 440s BCE and his propagation of the Pentateuch or something very like it.[15] Although it is not known under precisely what circumstances the collections of Nevi'im and Ketuvim came together, it is held that they took on a status alongside, albeit secondary to, that of the Torah and with no definitive boundaries set as yet for the Ketuvim. Evidence for this would appear to be present in part of the Prologue to Ecclus, oft-quoted in this regard:

> "Not only this book, but even the Law itself, the Prophecies, and the rest of the
> books differ not a little when read in the original".

A similar outlook may lie behind the words attributed to Jesus in Lk 24:44, referring to the "law of Moses, the prophets, and the psalms...", and the fact that Dn, despite its claim to antiquity, did not gain admission to the Nevi'im shows that this collection was closed by the 160s BCE. Moreover, any imprecision over the limits of the collection of Ketuvim, into which it did gain entry, was clarified by the end of the first century CE, as described by Schürer:

> "Among all Jews, then, the boundaries between canonical and non-canonical
> books had probably remained fluid during the two centuries B.C. and the first
> century A.D. when the canon was finally fixed."[16]

Thus, it is arguable that the Torah stems from the beginning of the Second Temple period. By the mid-second century BCE, a collection of Prophets

---

14   See Tov, *op. cit.*, p. 34ff; Ulrich, *op. cit.*, p. 37-40.
15   This is argued, e.g., in Schürer, II, p. 315.
16   Schürer, III.2, p. 707.

was in existence, while a third grouping of 'writings' was still in the process of formation and not completed till the end of the first, or even into the second, century CE.

Nevertheless, if something approaching the canon finalized after 70 CE was in effect the one used by the religious authorities during the Second Temple period, it need not necessarily have been universally acknowledged by all Jews at the time. The extent to which such a view of the canon prevailed among the masses or within the other Jewish parties contemporary with the pharisaic-like predecessors of the later rabbis is unclear. The latter's may have been only a minority view, especially given the many apocryphal and pseudepigraphical texts recovered from Qumran, at least some of which seem to have been treated as scripture by the sect. Although it is possible that the Qumranites were among those whom officialdom sought to oppose by asserting the fixed nature of their own selection of scriptures, more or less coextensive with the later three-fold canon, a somewhat more radical hypothesis is preferable, as has been put forward by Barton.[17]

Accordingly, the three-fold division of the bible was indeed finalized in the Rabbinic period. This was required in order to ensure the survival of Judaism after the calamity of the destruction of the temple, and it implied a rejection of Second Temple developments from the Maccabees onwards.[18] However, this constituted something of a new departure compared to the situation that prevailed earlier. Thus, it was the Torah which was the foundation of Second Temple Judaism in all its manifestations, so that 'canon' is a term which should only be applied to the Law. That being so:

> "...Scripture outside the Pentateuch formed not two collections with a clear line between them, but one single amorphous pool of material, often called 'Prophets".[19]

In other words, the idea of a closed, fixed standard is applicable to the Torah only. All other scriptures constituted an open-ended, potentially infinite number of works, thought to be ancient and derived from prophetic characters within Israelite history up to the time of Ezra.

It is not possible to explicate Barton's argument in detail but two points can be distilled from his work which make his approach rather compelling. Firstly, and notwithstanding the Prologue to Ecclus and Lk 24:44, a bipartite

---

[17]   J. Barton, *Oracles of God*, London (1986), pp. 1-95.
[18]   This point is made in J. Neusner, *Judaism: The Evidence of the Mishnah*, Chicago-London (1981), p. 171.
[19]   Barton, *op. cit.*, p. 57.

division of the scriptures is the norm, at least in the New Testament (NT). For example, Rom 3:21 states:

"But now, apart from the law, the righteousness of God has been disclosed, and it is attested by the law and the prophets".[20]

Secondly, it appears that Moses was viewed as a prophet and the Torah as the prophetic work *par excellence*, with the corollary that all his godly successors and their writings could be viewed as analogous, if secondary. The latter factor explains the flexibility evident in the terminology employed in the likes of 1 Cor 14:21, citing Is 28:11,12 as part of 'the law'. In any case, it appears that the chief characteristic of a prophetic work was its origination from some godly individual from the period covered by the Deuteronomic history. This would explain references to Daniel and David as prophets, and probably informed Josephus' assertion that, for a book to be viewed as scriptural, it must have been written by a prophet.[21]

If Barton is correct, at least in the broad thrust of his argument, it can be seen that the whole question of the existence of a canon outside the Torah becomes anachronistic when applied to the Second Temple period.[22] Indeed, we may presume that "new writings which purported to come from the acknowledged prophets of old could be passed off as no less sacred than longer accepted books".[23] As a result, works now classed as belonging to the Apoc or Pseud would have been able to take their place as inspired texts alongside books that would later form the collections known as Nevi'im and Ketuvim in the Rabbinic period. In sum, therefore, we may conclude that

---

20 See also Mt 5:17; 7:12; 11:13; 16:16; 22:40; Ac 13:15; 24:14; 28:23.

21 For Daniel, see Mt 24:15 and *AJ* 9.267-269; for David as prophet, see Ac 2:30. As for Josephus, *CA* 1.37-39 states:

"It therefore naturally, or rather necessarily, follows (seeing that with us it is not open to everybody to write the records, and that there is no discrepancy in what is written; seeing that on the contrary prophets alone had this privilege, obtaining their knowledge of the most remote and ancient history through the inspiration which they owed to God, and committing to writing a clear account of the events of their own time just as they occurred) - it follows, I say, that we do not possess myriads of inconsistent books, conflicting with each other. Our books, those which are justly accredited, are but two and twenty, and contain the record of all time."

Schürer, II, p. 317, interprets these twenty-two books as those of the three-fold canon, while Barton is of the view that Josephus' list concords better with his own thesis.

22 Note that Ulrich, *op. cit.*, pp. 33-36, has come to a similar conclusion as to the open-ended nature of what constituted scripture in this period.

23 M.D. Goodman, 'Sacred Scripture and 'Defiling the Hand", *JTS* 41 (1990), p. 99.

during the second half of the Second Temple period a broad and open-ended class of 'prophets' contained a mixture of what were in fact, from a historical-critical viewpoint, both ancient and more recent works, all believed to be antique and venerable by their respective users in the last two centuries BCE and the first century CE.   Such a reconstruction goes some way towards explaining the considerable religious literary output of these centuries, as well as the pseudonymous nature of much of it.

Returning to Qumran and our own topic, the surprising fluidity of the text and the likely extensive nature of what counted as 'scripture' present two potential problems The first is that an almost infinite number of sources could in theory be related to our examination of CD 1-8 and 19-20. Even so, if we assume it would be unnecessarily cautious to prohibit our inquiry on the grounds of the profusion of prospective sources, it seems reasonable to start with the contents of the later three-fold canon.   In justification of this, a statement by Barton is relevant:

> "By New Testament times the scrolls of the 'Deuteronomic History' and of the three great prophets and the twelve were, we may suppose, widely known, and all synagogues would aspire to possess copies. Later books, such as Chronicles or Daniel, were becoming known but were not yet common property".[24]

Accordingly, we can envisage a broad situation in which most of the contents of the later Hebrew Bible were widely disseminated in the late Second Temple period in view of their genuine antiquity.   1,2 Chr and Dn may have been among the exceptions here, although those who had access to these books, as well as to works such as 1 En or Jub, probably viewed them as having as much authority as Is or Pss.   Nevertheless, it makes sense to remember that, in general, the greater the age of a text, the greater its geographical spread and the penetration of its influence. This means that a work like CD, itself stemming from perhaps as early as 100 BCE, will almost inevitably have succumbed in the main to influence from those scriptural texts which were genuinely ancient in origin, from the modern scholar's viewpoint, among which the majority of books entering the later collections of Prophets and Writings are to be counted.[25] Hence, whilst a familiarity with the major works from the Apoc and Pseud would enable the noting of possible allusions to, or quotations from, these texts, this question will only be considered again briefly in our concluding chapter.

---

24   Barton, *op. cit.*, p. 79.

25   CD was probably written before the start of Roman rule in Palestine; for its date of composition in relation to other sectarian DSS, see initially Knibb, pp. 13-15; Schürer, III.1, p. 395f; *DSSE*, p. 95.

A potential second difficulty concerns the location of citations and allusions within CD 1-8 and 19-20, inasmuch as the fluid state of the biblical text in Second Temple times could hinder the precise delineation of where they begin and end. Fortunately, this will not be a problem in practice, even if the limits of a given quotation or allusion are not always clear.[26] Indeed, it will suit our purposes to restrict ourselves for the most part to the MT only, when citing biblical passages that have influenced the Admonition.

2.2 The Use of Scripture at Qumran

The Caves around Khirbet Qumran have become famous chiefly on account of the non-biblical texts they yielded, especially those previously unknown to scholarship. Such works can be described as of two types: those which were probably widely known throughout Palestine and had an impact on the sect in its formative years; others originating among the sect at Qumran, or a parent-group, and expressive of a distinctive identity and ideology. Whilst it is clear to which of these two categories most of the material belongs, scholars disagree about a number of works, depending partly on which particular theory of Qumran origins is advocated.[27] Counted among those of disputed provenance are Jub, 11QT and, to a lesser extent, CD.

In a broad sense, both types of material relate to the scriptures, as we might expect any writing from the mid- to late Second Temple period to do, but a further, unrelated division can be made. On the one hand, there are texts whose starting point is a portion or portions of the bible, while others begin with a theme or topic for consideration, as part of which the scriptures are used secondarily. The aim of the former is to harmonize, elucidate, modernize, or otherwise comment on the biblical material, whether a complete book, several books, or parts of a book(s). The latter are theological and/or legal treatises which, in order to bolster their argument, are related in various ways by the authors to the scriptures. It will be helpful to comment briefly on each of these types of relationship to the bible, especially the latter, since it is in that category that CD is included.

---

26   As is well known, the sectarians used varieties in the MS tradition to their own advantage. See, e.g., 1QpHab 11:8b-15, with its pun on הערל and הרעל.

27   For the impact of the DSS on our understanding of the Apoc and Pseud generally, see Schürer, III.1, pp. 177-341.

As will be clear already, a number of different types of literature fit into the first category. Vermes has usefully classified these in the following way:[28]

(i)   Implicit exegesis of an editorial kind;
(ii)   Exegesis of individual books;
(iii)   Thematic exegesis.

The first is well exemplified in 11QT, and follows the pattern of the sort of internal editorial redaction detectable in the final form of the scriptures themselves.[29]   The third type, bringing together a number of texts from different parts of the bible, includes 4QTest (4Q175) and 4QFlor (4Q174); it is also found in the NT or, in a more developed form, in later Rabbinic Midrash.[30] As for the second category, it covers both what may be called 'rewritten bible' and Qumran 'Pesher' exegesis. The former, as in Jub and 1QapGen, bears a strong resemblance to the later Targums and need not detain us.[31] The latter, however, appears to be unique to the DSS, and this has meant that the so-called Pesharim have attracted much attention in the scholarly world, since, it is thought, therein must surely lie the heart of Qumran exegesis.[32] Because much work has already been done, we may leave to one side a descriptive analysis of the Pesharim. Nevertheless, since they are central to theories about the Qumran sect and its use of scripture, it is necessary to mention two main problems.

The first relates to the genre of the Pesharim and how this is best defined. The difficulty centres on the fact that, whereas the Pesharim proper (i.e., 1QpHab, 1QpMic, 4QpHos, 4QpNah, 4QpPs) utilize a certain combination of vocabulary and style, there are portions in other documents which follow the latter but not the former. Thus, throughout 1QpHab, citations from Hab

---

[28]   G. Vermes, 'Bible Interpretation at Qumran', *Eretz-Israel* 20 (1989), pp. 184-191.

[29]   Vermes, *op. cit.*, p. 185f, lists four major ways in which this is accomplished: grouping and collating parallel texts; harmonizing expansions; clarifying additions; recasting and supplementation. For similar editorial work in the Hebrew Bible, see M. Fishbane, *Biblical Interpretation in Ancient Israel*, Oxford (1985).

[30]   For 4QTest and 4QFlor, see Schürer, III.1, pp. 445-447, in the first instance.

[31]   For Jub and 1QapGen, see Schürer, III.1, pp. 308-317 and 318-325; for the Targums, see initially J. Mulder, *Mikra*, Assen-Philadelphia (1988), pp. 217-253.

[32]   Thus, e.g., see W.H. Brownlee, 'Biblical Interpretation among the Sectaries of the Dead Sea Scrolls', *BA* 14 (1951), pp. 54-76; D. Dimant, 'Qumran Sectarian Literature: Biblical Interpretation', in M.E. Stone (ed.), *Jewish Writings of the Second Temple Period*, Assen-Philadelphia (1984), II, pp. 503-508; M.P. Horgan, *Pesharim: Qumran Interpretation of Biblical Books*, Washington (1979). For individual Pesharim, consult Schürer, III.1, pp. 425-439.

and their interpretation are separated by phrases like פשר הדבר על or simply פשרו. On the other hand, although CD 4:14f uses the word פשרו, there are several portions in that work and in other documents which do not employ this terminology but, as far as their overall style is concerned, are what might be termed 'pesher-like'.[33] The crux of the matter, therefore, is that the main characteristic of a group of writings appears, on further analysis, to be purely formal and of less concrete importance than might otherwise be thought. This has led Brooke to the conclusion that Pesher is merely a sub-genre within Midrash.[34]

A second problem concerns how best to view what precisely is going on in the text of, say, 1QpHab, CD 4:14ff or CD 7:11-21. Are these and other passages best described as containing interpretation comparable to the application of the מדות by the later rabbis, or as revelation after the pattern of the dream-visions in Dn?[35] Although the issue pertains primarily to understanding the Pesharim, especially 1QpHab, it also relates to texts with pesher-like sections, such as CD, as well as Qumran bible exegesis in general. Unfortunately, length forbids a detailed discussion of these two problems here but, since they belong to a wider set of historical and literary complications, we shall come back to them briefly in the next chapter.

We may now turn to the second class of material, namely, those works whose starting point does not appear to be the bible itself, but in which the scriptures are brought in secondarily to aid argumentation. As far as grasping the use of the bible in this type of literature is concerned, most scholarly work has concentrated on scriptural quotations in 1QS, 1QM, and CD, as well as the interpretation of them by the authors of these documents.[36] This has primarily involved CD, which contains most of these citations; it has then

---

[33] See, in particular, CD 4:2-4; 6:3-11; 7:14-21; 8:9-12 and the units that make up 4QFlor.

[34] See G.J. Brooke, 'Qumran Pesher: Towards the Redefinition of a Genre', *RQ* 10 (1981), pp. 483-503. On the other hand, Vermes, *op. cit.*, p. 190, continues to describe Qumran Pesher as a "genre" in its own right.

[35] G.J. Brooke, *Exegesis at Qumran: 4QFlorilegium in its Jewish Context*, Sheffield (1985), pp. 36-44, lists scholars supporting either side of the argument or a mid-way position.

[36] See J. Fitzmyer, 'The Use of Explicit Old Testament Quotations in Qumran Literature and in the New Testament', in *Essays on the Semitic Background of the New Testament*, London (1971), pp. 3-89; O.J.R. Schwarz, *Der erste Teil der Damaskusschrift und das alte Testament*, Diest (1965); J. de Waard, *A Comparative Study of the Old Testament Text in the Dead Sea Scrolls and in the New Testament*, Leiden (1965).

often been related to the limits of the canon and the state of the text of the bible during the Second Temple period.[37]

In another helpful article, Vermes has collated the evidence for citations from the bible in this category of Qumran material; he has also commented on the literary structure of the units containing these quotations and the exegetical purpose behind them.[38]   He lists a total of fifty-two citations in some thirty-four units of material in 1QS, 1QM, CD and the very fragmentary 4Q509/275, describing the literary structure of the units variously as bipartite, tripartite or quadripartite.[39]   In other words, each unit consists of up to four of the following component parts:

(i)   doctrinal statement, e.g., 1QS 8:12b-13;
(ii)   introductory formula, e.g., 1QS 8:14a;
(iii)   citation, e.g., 1QS 8:14b;
(iv)   interpretation, e.g., 1QS 8:15-16a.

The example given here, 1QS 8:12b-16a with each of (i)-(iv), is one which Vermes regards as "the regular form of the Qumran biblical reasoning, the final element being an explanation linking the proof-text to the statement which is to be established".[40]   There are, however, other examples which contain only two or three of (i)-(iv), including the repetition of one of them, while the most complex case is to be found in CD 7:9-21.[41]   The citations isolated by Vermes are as follows:

Gn 1:27	CD 4:21	Is 7:17	CD 7:11f
Gn 7:9	CD 5:1	Is 10:12	4Q509/275
Ex 23:7	1QS 5:15	Is 24:17	CD 4:14
Lv 18:13	CD 5:8f	Is 27:11	CD 5:16

---

[37]   Thus, Fitzmyer, *op. cit.*, pp. 3-89, describes the quotations in CD, 1QS and 1QM, notes the open-ended nature of the canon and, in detailing their relation to the MT, the fluid state of the biblical text at this time; he maintains that citations are used to bolster an assertion, act as a point of departure or as an illustration of an argument, as well as to serve as proof texts. Fitzmyer then specifies each of the 42 quotations in 1QS, 1QM and CD, dividing them into four classes.

[38]   G. Vermes, 'Biblical Proof-Texts in Qumran Literature', *JSS* 34 (1989), pp. 493-508.

[39]   There are only 3 and 5 citations in 1QS and 1QM, respectively, over against CD's 43; 4Q509/275 contains only one. Fitzmyer, *op. cit.*, p. 6f, notes only 30 quotations in CD, but he, unlike Vermes, does not include cases of 'virtual citation'; these are deliberate references to the bible without any introductory quotation formula and will be described below.

[40]   Vermes, *op. cit.*, p. 497.

[41]   For the latter, see Vermes, *op. cit.*, p. 500f.

Lv 19:17	CD 9:8	Is 31:8	1QM 11:11f
Lv 19:18	CD 9:2	Is 40:3	1QS 8:14
Lv 23:38	CD 11:18	Is 50:11	CD 5:13
Nu 10:9	1QM 10:2-4	Is 54:16	CD 6:8
Nu 21:18	CD 6:3-4	Is 59:5	CD 5:13f
Nu 24:17	CD 7:19f	Ez 9:4	CD 19:12
Nu 24:17-19	1QM 11:6f	Ez 13:10	CD 8:12 (19:24f)
Nu 30:9	CD 16:10	Ez 44:15	CD 3:21-4:2
Nu 30:17	CD 7:8f (19:5)	Hos 3:4	CD 20:16
Dt 5:12	CD 10:16f	Hos 4:16	CD 1:13f
Dt 7:8	CD 8:15 (19:28)	Hos 5:10	CD 8:2f (19:15f)
Dt 7:9	CD 7:6 (19:1f)	Hos 7:11	CD 4:10-12
Dt 7:21f	1QM 10:1f	Am 5:26f	CD 7:14f
Dt 9:5	CD 8:15 (19:28)	Am 9:11	CD 7:16
Dt 9:23	CD 3:7	Mic 2:6	CD 4:20
Dt 17:17	CD 5:2	Mic 2:11	CD 8:13 (19:24f)
Dt 20:2-5	1QM 10:2-4	Mic 7:2	CD 16:16
Dt 23:24	CD 16:6f	Mic 7:11	CD 4:12
Dt 32:28	CD 5:13f	Nah 1:2	CD 9:5
Dt 32:33	CD 8:9f (19:22)	Zec 13:7	CD 19:7-9
1 Sa 25:26	CD 9:9	Mal 1:10	CD 6:13
Is 2:22	1QS 5:17	Pr 15:8	CD 11:20f

As is clear from the above table, it is CD that contains most of the citations in the second type of exegetical material among the DSS, although, when recently released texts have been analysed thoroughly, the balance of this domination will probably shift.[42]   In CD also is the greatest variety in combination of components (i)-(iv), manifested in "every shade in the spectrum from the pale simplicity of an implicit biblical inference to the variegated intricacies of a multi-level exegetical construct".[43]   Again relying chiefly on CD, with its virtual monopoly on the evidence, Vermes describes the overall units as being of four types.   The first, "eschatological actualisation", is always bipartite and limited to 1QM 10-11, in which the rules for war from the Pentateuch are simply reapplied to the final battle. "Direct proof", the second category, has three of the component parts, usually (i)-(iii), since further explication is not necessary; this is because use

---

[42]   Thus, we can note, e.g., that 4Q521 has very strong allusion to, or even what might be classed as 'virtual citation' of, Ps 146:7-8 and Is 61:1. See EW, pp. 19-23, and *DSSE*, p. 244f, for representations of this work.

[43]   Vermes, *op. cit.*, p. 497.

of the biblical material is relatively straightforward or, on the contrary, because it is given a significance altogether different from that in its biblical context and which cannot be 'proved'. However, "reinforced proof", Vermes' third type, usually contains the fourth component in order to convey more clearly the sect's own special inference from the scriptural passage. Finally, there are units which seek to give "proof of historical fulfilment", where a passage is singled out and given a peculiar 'pesher-like' treatment.[44]

In conclusion, Vermes compares the variety in Qumran exegesis to the fluidity of the text of the bible and of the limits of the canon for those at Qumran. In so doing, he reiterates our points above and adds a further comment:

> "...exegetical elasticity matches the textual elasticity of the Qumran Bible. It still requires an explanation. I believe this should be sought in the paramount doctrinal authority of the Priests, the Sons of Zadok, the guardians of the Covenant".[45]

We shall return to this observation later.

In the meantime, our consideration of the bible and the DSS has thus far underlined the centrality of scripture for the group(s) behind the sectarian documents, notwithstanding certain ambiguities concerning the state of the biblical text, what exactly constitutes 'scripture', and the precise boundaries between sectarian and non-sectarian literature. More specifically, we have noted the numerous citations present in CD 1-8 and 19-20, and this forms a useful backcloth to our own study, since we have already remarked on the presence of its many allusions, which may profit from further attention.[46] In particular, it will be of interest to engage in a descriptive analysis of the latter in order to judge how they relate to the document's quotations.

Let us now turn to the Admonition in greater detail.

---

[44]   Respective examples of each category include: 1QM 10:6; CD 7:6-9; 1QS 5:16-18; CD 8:8-12. For these, see Vermes, *op. cit.*, pp. 496, 502-505. Cf. Fitzmyer, *op. cit.*, pp. 16-52, who suggests four different classes of bible usage: texts employed in a literal/historical manner; those which are modernized; accommodated texts; and passages interpreted eschatologically. The first, according to Fitzmyer, uses a text as intended by the biblical writer; the second does so in an extended way; the third removes a passage from its context and adapts it to a new one; and the fourth reapplies a biblical threat or promise to the eschaton.

[45]   Vermes, *op. cit.*, p. 508.

[46]   Vermes, *op. cit.*, p. 502, also points to the presence of allusions but otherwise leaves them without comment.

2.3 Schwarz on Scripture in the Damascus Document

A number of years ago, Schwarz worked through CD 1-8 and 19-20, noting references to scripture in terms of both quotations and allusions.[47] In so doing, he reflected that CD 1-8 is more than an 'Admonition', since it seeks to impart instruction. This instruction consists of information about God's dealings with the righteous and the wicked throughout the history of Israel, and includes a "Vogelschau" of the history of the sect from its foundation to the eschaton. Unfortunately, it is not possible to distil a chronological narrative from this information, since the author goes around in circles - there is a "Gedankenkreis" to which CD keeps returning on the formation and growth of the group, and another cycle of ideas antithetically mixed in between on Belial and the wicked.[48]

Chief among Schwarz's observations was that three types of material, or what he calls three genres, can be found within the document. The first, "Die Erzählenden Texte", describes events in ancient Israel's history, as well as parallels regarding the sect at later times; both are expressed in terms of two high points in the biblical narrative, namely, the exodus and the exile.[49] After a certain point in the story, Schwarz notes, the positive language applied to the whole of Israel in the bible is taken over and used only of the sect. The second type of material in CD, "Die Exegetischen Texte", is two-fold and covers all examples of "Schriftaktualisierung".[50] This includes both "Schriftbezug" and "Damaskuspescher". In the former, a biblical text is applied ("bezogen") at the climax to a particular situation being described; the latter, invariably following on from an example of such "Schriftbezug", involves the atomistic interpretation of such a text (or of a another passage brought in to help) after the fashion of the Pesharim. The third category of material in CD is "Die Gesetzlichen Texte", likewise divisible into two forms.[51] The first reflects the idiom of biblical legislation but the second,

---

[47] O.J.R. Schwarz, *Der erste Teil der Damaskusschrift und das alte Testament*, Diest (1965). In the same year J. de Waard, *A Comparative Study of the Old Testament Text in the Dead Sea Scrolls and in the New Testament*, Leiden (1965) was published.

[48] See Schwarz, p. 70.

[49] Schwarz, p. 74ff.

[50] See Schwarz, p. 89ff.

[51] Schwarz, p. 136ff.

while of a legal character, is unrelated to the scriptures. We can summarize
Schwarz's categorization of CD 1-8 and 19-20 thus:[52]

A	1:1-13a	C1	6:11c-7:6a
B1	1:13b-2:1a	C1	7:6b-9a
A	2:2a-13d	B1	7:9b-14a
A	2:14a-3:20d	B2	7:14b-21a
B1	3:20e-4:2b	B1	7:21b-8:1a
B2	4:2c-4c	B1	8:1b-2c
A	4:4d-12b	C1	8:2d-9a
B1	4:12c-14d	B1	8:9b-10a
B2	4:14e-19a	B2	8:10b-12a
C1	4:19b-5:13a	C1	8:12b-13d
B1	5:13b-6:4a	B1	8:14a-18a
B2	6:4c-11b	C1	8:18b-19e

Of course, this summary hardly does justice to Schwarz's full and, in many
ways, helpful descriptive analysis.[53] However, it does bring out his main
point, which is that the whole of the Admonition can be broken up into the
following three categories:

A or C1 or C2	the description of a situation in historical or legal terms;
B1	*Schriftbezug*, adding force to A, C1 or C2;
B2	an optional further pesher(-like) section, always following an example of B1.

A concrete instance of this can be seen in the following:

A	CD 3:19-20d	(Positive) situation described;
B1	CD 3:21f	Quotation of Ez 44:15;
B2	CD 4:2f	Pesher-like interpretation.

Schwarz's purpose in conducting his analysis, as it appears from this
outline, was to consider how the citations, along with their sometimes-
present interpretations, fit into the rest of CD's material engaged in neither
quotation nor interpretation and classified by him as A, C1 and C2. His

---

52   Schwarz's three types of material within CD 1-8 and 19-20 are represented here by
      A, B1 and B2, and C1 (and C2), respectively.

53   The above arrangement means that certain overlaps have been omitted, as also
      complications in respect of Mss A and B, into which Schwarz enters in some detail;
      we have further left out C2 material which, according to Schwarz, exclusively
      belongs to Ms B. These simplifying omissions do not, however, affect the points
      outlined here.

dividing up of the document is comparable to Vermes' isolation of units formed around explicit citations, outlined above, and his attempt to understand their structure and purpose.

There are, however, two issues that ought to be raised in relation to the above and to our own task. Firstly, it is not clear to what exactly Schwarz's divisions within the Admonition correspond. If they are intended to represent sources and redactional work, then his classifications are unsatisfactory, not least because, although Schwarz poses the question of CD's characterization as a unified or disparate work, he does not address it adequately. Alternatively, it might be said that Schwarz has simply described the different kinds of material present within the document, and to a large extent this is true. Nonetheless, Schwarz's sections at times go against what is arguably the natural flow of the text. This can be seen, for instance, in CD 5, where the best division within the shape of the passage as it now stands is between 5:15a and 5:15b, not 5:13a and 5:13b. Similarly, although Schwarz maintains that 7:6-9 is a later interpolation, he does not address the issue of how, if at all, CD copes with these lines in their present position. In other words, whilst it is important and helpful to notice changes in style, and Schwarz has indeed correctly noted most of these, his divisions do not always correspond to the unfolding of the text in terms of its inner shape and 'paragraphing', as we shall see in subsequent chapters.

A second question raised by the work of Schwarz concerns the numerous allusions to scripture found throughout CD 1-8 and 19-20 (in his A and C1 and C2 portions), to which he initially drew attention. At times, he suggests that they are not of great importance. On the contrary, however, it is to be suspected that we would do well to relate the quotations to this mass of biblical allusion, since, as proposed, enough interconnection exists to suggest that this will prove enlightening.

2.4 The Damascus Document and Scripture

We have already remarked that scholars have pointed to the Admonition's general and allusive debt to the language of the scriptures, as well as to its explicit citations.[54] But there has been a tendency to evaluate both in differing ways. On the one hand, some see fit simply to note the document's allusions and quotations as a clever, but superficial, web of scriptural

---

[54] See, e.g., Schürer, III.1, p. 392.

borrowings which can otherwise be passed over.   For example, Rabin comments as follows:

> "I am convinced that the Admonition...is all of it a mosaic of quotations, both from O.T. and other, now lost, writings, a clever presentation of *testimonia*, not a history of the sect".[55]

This assertion implies, in particular, that those quotations and allusions which find themselves in CD's historical sections are of little help in evaluating the document's accounts of the origins of the sect; they should, rather, make us wary of taking its narrative portions at face value. Thus, Knibb says of CD 2:14-4:6a that "this passage...provides no precise information about the group to which it refers", although its employment of the bible may contribute to our understanding of the contemporary religious identity of the sect itself.[56]

At the same time, others have suggested that there may be more to CD's employment of scripture than some scholars allow.   We noted Davies' statement above and, indeed, his detailed study frequently refers to scriptural contexts drawn upon by the author as a means of throwing light upon the finished form of the Admonition, including its apparent claim to exilic origins for the group it commends.[57]

Both viewpoints are based on valid observations about the text.   The group behind the document must have had an origin and early history, which, being a religious community, we might expect it to have expressed in terms based on biblical phraseology. On the other hand, ancient Jewish tradition is often inaccurate when it comes to recounting the history of the Persian period, due largely to a predominant interest in the theological evaluation of events as much as the events themselves.[58]   While many have noted the mass of biblical allusion and parallel in the Admonition, therefore, no one has attempted a systematic evaluation of it. Nonetheless, this is understandable,

---

[55] Note that C. Rabin, *The Zadokite Documents*, Oxford (1958), p. ix, appears to use the term 'quotation' in a sense broad enough to include many of what we shall designate allusions; see below, note 65.

[56] M. Knibb, 'Exile in the Damascus Document', *JSOT* 25 (1983), p. 110.

[57] E.g., see Davies, p. 66, regarding the probable influence of Lv 26:45; Jer 25:31 and Ez 20:18ff, 22 in the context around CD 1:4, or again p. 188f, referring to Hos 3:4; Is 59:20 and Mal 3:16-18 as helpful in appreciating the various facets of CD 20:13b-22a.

[58] See Schürer, III.1, pp. 249 and 513ff, for a consideration of some Second Temple historians; see also A. Laato, 'The Seventy Yearweeks in the Book of Daniel', *ZAW* 102 (1990), pp. 212-225.

for, of the three types of scriptural usage found in the work (quotation, allusion and biblical imitation), none is problem-free.

The first of these is explicit citation, introduced with formulae such as אשר היה כתוב or אשר אמר. As will already be clear, there are a large number of these in CD 1-8 and 19-20. While this employment of the bible might seem the most transparent, it has its own complications. In particular, it can be difficult for the modern person to see a connection between the biblical text cited and the argument being expounded in CD itself. Although 'techniques' of exegesis, generally accepted as valid among Jewry, may sometimes form a bridge between the text and the resultant interpretation, there are obscurities regarding the function of such techniques.[59]

Allusions to the scriptures, of which CD 1-8 and 19-20 is full, are more difficult to define and discuss. This problem is mainly due to the fact that the very nature of the allusions means that the author does not inform us of what he is doing, nor why and to what effect, and we are left to our own devices. Not only must the scholar be wary of the subjectivity entailed in finding the allusions in the first place, but he or she has then to extrapolate from them what led to their incorporation. Nevertheless, given that the specific biblical contexts which supply CD's citations also seem to provide most of its allusions, it is reasonable to suppose that a distinction between quotation and allusion is largely relative and essentially formal. Both are part of one overall phenomenon, as implicitly acknowledged by the inclusion of CD's instances of 'virtual citation' in Vermes' above-mentioned discussion of scriptural quotation in Qumran texts.[60] This conclusion is further supported by the fluidity evident in the fact that, while CD 19:15f cites Hos 5:10, the parallel passage in CD 8:3 merely alludes to it.[61]

The third type of scriptural usage involves the employment of a general style of vocabulary and phraseology which sounds 'biblical'. This can be attributed to a habit, perhaps unconscious, on the part of the author of putting things in a way which lends credibility to them. The need to speak convincingly through the adoption of a certain manner of expression

---

[59] G.J. Brooke, *Exegesis at Qumran: 4QFlorilegium in its Jewish Context*, Sheffield (1985), argues that equivalents to the rabbinic מדות largely control exegesis in the sectarian DSS.

[60] Thus, Vermes, *op. cit.*, p. 493f, makes reference to Mic 7:11 in CD 4:12, as also to Is 50:11 and 59:5 in CD 5:13f.

[61] See S.A. White, 'A Comparison of the 'A' and 'B' Manuscripts of the Damascus Document', *RQ* 12 (1987), pp. 537-553. Note too that, as predicted by Vermes, *op. cit.*, p. 498, note 12, the equivalent in 4QD[b] of the biblical reference in CD 6:3f is preceded by אשר אמר מושה.

obviously covers all three categories in a broad sense. Nevertheless, in as far as the third is not connected to the specific meaning or ideology of CD nor, apparently, to any deliberate appeal to a set body of scriptural texts, it is of least interest in the present study. Regarding some instances of this third mode of scriptural dependence, however, we cannot always be sure that some device connecting a word, phrase or idea - which would render them suitable for inclusion in the second category - in one passage with that in another has not eluded us.

Unfortunately, there is no way around the uncertainties involved in undertaking an examination of the use of the scriptures in CD 1-8 or 19-20, and the limitations must be continually kept before us. Indeed, where allusions are either possible only, or of limited significance if more certainly present, or beyond our ability to evaluate, they are best left to one side to avoid unnecessary proliferation.[62]

Before going any further, it is in order to illustrate briefly these different types of scriptural usage, as well as the difficulties in being too clear-cut about them. Hos 4:16 is cited in CD 1:13f, and this is the first explicit quotation in the document:

היא העת אשר היה כתוב עליה כפרה סוריה כן סרר ישראל.

The inclusion of the introductory formula is noteworthy here. The biblical text itself reads:

כי כפרה סררה סרר ישראל עתה ירעם ה׳ ככבש במרחב:

From the perspective of our analysis of scripture in the Admonition, the chief point to notice is that the general context of Hos 3f informs the language adopted by our author on a wide front; appeal to Hos 4:16 in CD 1:13f is only a part of this. Indeed, other allusions to Hos in CD are indicative of an interconnected framework of language and ideas in the mind of our writer.[63] More generally, as already hinted, some instances of what appear at first sight to constitute allusive references to the scriptures are better classed as quotations, even though they lack an introductory formula. This is because such cases utilize phrases from the bible in a deliberately intended way, an example of which can be found in CD 5:15b-17a, which reads:

כי אם למילפנים פקד אל את מעשיהם ויחר אפו בעלילותיהם כי לא עם בינות הוא הם
גוי אבד עצות מאשר אין בהם בינה.

---

62   In subsequent chapters, such cases will be pointed out in notes but otherwise left without comment.

63   Notice too that the author does not consider it important that two different Hebrew roots are involved in CD 1:13f, namely, סור and סרר.

The allusions to Is 27:11 and Dt 32:28 here are so lengthy and strong that we may suspect the writer intended them to signal overt employment of the bible and expected that most of his readers or hearers would recognize them. This view is corroborated by surrounding references to scripture in CD 5:8, 5:13,14, as well as 6:3f, and explains Davies' utilization of inverted commas in his translation:

> "For in earlier times God punished their deeds and His anger was aroused against their doings, for 'it is not a people of understanding'; 'they are a nation devoid of counsel, because there is no understanding in them'".[64]

These instances of 'virtual citation' confirm our contention that the distinction between quotation and allusion has become blurred and, as noted before, this tends to favour our proposed course of study.

As for the allusive type of reference, a clear example is mention of the חרב נקמת נקם ברית in CD 1:17f, which reflects the language of Lv 26:25, with curses following on disobedience mentioned in both contexts. The biblical verse reads:

והבאתי עליכם חרב נקמת נקם ברית ונאספתם אל עריכם ושלחתי דבר בתוככם ונתתם
ביד אויב:

We can be sure that allusion to Lv 26 informs CD at this point, because that scriptural passage reappears as the source of numerous other phrases in CD, as well as of a more general story-line important for our author. Of course, such examples only fulfil their role as allusions if the reader or hearer is familiar with the biblical texts concerned. At the same time, and whilst they are meaningfully present in the text, they do not exclude those who cannot appreciate them from being able (or being permitted) to consult CD.

The third category of usage can be illustrated in the phrase תוהו לא דרך in CD 1:15, which is precisely the same as that found in Ps 107:40 and Job 24:24. This example is not very enlightening, and does not contribute significantly to the meaning of CD nor connect to other allusions or citations. There are instances, however, where it is more difficult to judge to what extent biblical phraseology has been incorporated with intent or as part of some wider exegetical schema. For example, it seems at first sight that Jer 27:6 has simply been extracted and used in CD 1:6 with little by way of forethought. The biblical text reads:

ועתה אנכי נתתי את כל הארצות האלה ביד נבוכדנאצר מלך בבל עבדי וגם את חית
השדה נתתי לו לעבדו:

But the repetition of the phrase in CD seems so exact and specific that more than mere linguistic imitation is to be suspected, since the theme of the exile

---

64   Davies, p. 245.

under Nebuchadnezzar is a major one for CD in one way or another. In this sort of example, the surrounding biblical context of an apparently not so important scriptural allusion comes to our aid. Thus, the use of Jer 27:6 in CD 1:5 can be better understood, when we view more closely the surrounding chapters - Jer 24-28. Unfortunately, numerous other cases will be encountered where dependence on the bible is possible, even probable, but of unclear significance, if genuinely present, with regard to its status as allusion or mere imitation. Sometimes, we have opted for incorporation in our analysis when it seems appropriate; at other times, we have not done so when the balance of probability seems to weigh against inclusion. There is no escaping the danger of erroneous judgement that such a methodology entails but the soundness of our basic theory will not be seriously affected thereby.

The lack of precision in being able to define the respective limits of quotation, allusion, and imitation should not entice us to multiply our classifications further. Rabin, for example, lists three types of citation and, whilst this is not invalid, it is purely descriptive and not necessary for our own work.[65] In fact, to be satisfactory, this sort of precision demands almost as many categories as instances of dependence on the bible. However, such profusion is unnecessary if, as is to be suggested, the Admonition's use of scripture can be viewed as at base a homogeneous whole. The numerous modes in which it finds expression are formal, and an over-detailed categorization of them does not help in understanding the overall significance of bible usage in the document. Rather, it will prove more fruitful to attempt the detection of an underlying and controlling use of biblical texts, surfacing sometimes in citation and at other times in less immediately obvious, and admittedly less quantifiable, allusion.

---

[65]   Rabin, p. xiii, suggests "literal quotation", "quotation with...adaptation", and "telescoped quotation" constitute three classes of citation in CD, while "allusion or reminiscence" cover other examples of dependence on the bible.

3 The Damascus Document and the Historical-Critical Method

3.1 Understanding Ancient Texts

In order to acknowledge their existence and explain our reluctance to seek solutions to certain difficulties in the Admonition, we must deal with two related methodological questions before moving on specifically to the employment of scripture in CD 1-8 and 19-20. First of all, we shall look at the usefulness of traditional methods of biblical criticism for understanding ancient texts over against a more holistic or 'literary' methodology. Secondly, in association with the opening Address which is present in 4QD but absent from CD, we shall view briefly the question of the relationship between different editions of the work. Regarding the former, however, it is worth describing both approaches in more detail, before entering into any consideration of how the issues raised relate to CD in particular, to avoid oversimplification.

The nineteenth and twentieth centuries saw the rise to prominence of critical methods of study and their application to the biblical records.[1] Scriptural problems, often long known to Synagogue or Church, were tackled in a new way, through scientific analysis centring on the idea of the development through time of texts and the communities that produced them. The first manifestations of this were source criticism and form criticism and, essentially, these appealed to previous stages within the development of a text, along with concomitant *Sitze im Leben* where relevant. Although a final editor or 'redactor' was deemed responsible for each scriptural book, his contribution to the whole was usually thought to be minimal. Such a negative conclusion seemed unavoidable because of the presence of difficulties in the finished form of many biblical books, which, according to scholars, lacked consistency and could not be read as though they made sense. Hence, it was felt necessary to appeal to earlier, more 'original', versions through source- and form-critical analysis.

---

[1] See J. Barton, *Reading the Old Testament*, London (1985), pp. 20-60, for an overview.

Research into the final form of biblical books became a discipline in its own right with the advent of redaction criticism, which attributed greater significance to the end-result of the editorial process and the author deemed responsible for it. Regardless of the sources that may have been incorporated into a work, scholars began to appreciate that the final redactor must have contributed substantially to his composition and was seldom likely to have been a mere compiler of other people's work. This realization, however, highlights the ultimate paradox of the critical method. On the one hand, it is clear that, where parallel passages exist, we can observe the use of sources, as evidenced supremely in 1,2 Sa and 1,2 Ki over against 1,2 Chr (a comparison of which provides us with a wealth of data), and in the interrelation of the Synoptic Gospels. As a result, it is reasonable to ask how the author of 1,2 Chr utilized his sources, and, moreover, it may justifiably be supposed that much ancient Jewish and Christian literature, even when parallel works are no longer extant, also made use of source material. Yet, on the other hand, it is difficult in cases of the latter to posit the grounds on which such sources can legitimately be isolated and analysed. With regard to the Pentateuch, Barton expresses this dilemma well:

> "...we cannot argue *both* that it is so full of inconsistencies that it must be highly composite *and* that it is so consistent and well-integrated that the redactor must have had a masterly touch with his source materials".[2]

In other words, to maintain solely on internal grounds that a particular biblical book is made up of sources, as evidenced by the supposed historical or theological tensions left within its final form, is incompatible with a claim that the final product is also the relatively unified, homogeneous result of conscious literary activity by an editor.

Partly due to such methodological inconsistencies in the application of critical methods of study, a second *modus operandi* has come to the fore more recently. This has involved the borrowing of ideas from literary theory, sometimes in conjunction with structuralist and post-structuralist linguistic models. The aim has been to view scriptural texts holistically and to avoid treating them as means to other ends - usually earlier and allegedly 'purer', albeit non-extant, forms of a given text. In some ways, this relates to redaction criticism, but the focus tends to be placed more on the text itself and/or the reader, rather than the original writer and his setting.[3] Thus, some would argue that a biblical work can be viewed as an artefact in its own right,

---

2 Barton, *op. cit.*, p. 58.

3 See Barton, *op. cit.*, pp. 77-197, for various theories stressing the text itself, the reader, or both. More generally, see also T. Eagleton, *Literary Theory: an Introduction*, Oxford (1983).

comparable to a painting or piece of music, with which the reader engages; authorial intention or hypothetically reconstructed previous forms of the composition are of little relevance for understanding that artefact on its own terms.

Undoubtedly, both means of inquiry have contributed to our understanding of biblical and other ancient texts. Consequently, few scholars would seriously doubt that the Torah, for example, consists of diverse sources of varying ages - whether written, oral or a mixture of both - finally brought together in the late exilic or early post-exilic period. On the other hand, no one general theory about the formation of the Pentateuch would command universal assent today, and this lack of unanimity can largely be explained as a consequence of a decreasing confidence in the ability of critical methods to supply conclusive answers to the problems that led to their employment in the first place.[4] Hence, while still widely in use, such methods are applied somewhat more cautiously than even a few decades ago.[5] At the same time, no doubt under the influence of more thoroughgoing applications of literary theory, viewing biblical books as literature is an approach with growing general support.[6] Difficulties remain, however, suggesting this method too cannot be viewed as constituting the definitive approach. In particular, it is not obvious that criteria adopted for describing and analysing Western Classical literature are always well-suited to ancient biblical or Second Temple texts.

3.2 Poetry in the Damascus Document

The above discussion relates first and foremost to the bible, but source, form and redaction criticism have also been applied to other ancient texts,

---

[4] For a recent study of the Torah, see J. Blenkinsopp, *The Pentateuch*, London (1993).

[5] Such circumspection, as well as a willingness to acknowledge approaches to the biblical text other than the historical-critical one, is exemplified in R.J. Coggins, *Introducing the Old Testament*, Oxford (1990), providing an overview of biblical studies for students newly approaching the subject.

[6] This can be seen in the evident popularity of a volume like J.B. Graber, C.B. Wheeler, *The Bible as Literature*, New York-Oxford (1990). More specifically, see D.J.A. Clines, *The Theme of the Pentateuch*, Sheffield (1978) or P.D. Miscall, *Isaiah*, Sheffield (1993) for alternative, 'holistic' studies of specific biblical books.

including the DSS.[7]   As far as CD is concerned, the employment of such methods is relevant in one major respect, namely, whether the Admonition is to be characterized as essentially a unified piece or the by-product of a complicated editorial process of redaction. In favour of the latter is the fact that one of the chief difficulties in understanding CD 1-8 and 19-20 is how to harmonize its apparently contradictory accounts of the origins of the sect it commends. These and other factors have led some to formulate complex redactional theories about the growth of the work during several phases of the sect, or parent-group, behind its compilation.[8]   Hence, using internal consistency as his main criterion, Davies encloses within brackets words and phrases considered awkward and secondary in his English translation of the Admonition.[9]   On the other hand, Knibb, although he considers possible developments of the text through time in the subsequent commentary, presents the text of CD 1-8 and 19-20 at the head of his comment in unabridged form.[10]   Indeed, and as we shall argue later, the Admonition counters its signs of apparent inconsistency by other aspects suggesting a carefully constructed text, not least in terms of patterns in its use of scripture which are detectable throughout.

Nevertheless, studies continue to take it for granted that a chief characteristic of the Admonition is the fact that it is made up of various literary layers with competing historical referents and theological standpoints. Such an assumption can create as many problems as it solves, however, as in the case of an examination of CD 1-8 and 19-20 by Boyce. He has sought to isolate original poems within the Admonition, just as a number of scholars before him have posited a poetic *Vorlage* behind part or all of this material.[11]

---

[7]   See, e.g., P.R. Davies, *1QM, the War Scroll from Qumran. Its Structure and History*, Rome (1976); J. Murphy-O'Connor, 'La genèse littéraire de la *Règle de la Communauté*', *RB* 76 (1969), pp. 528-549.

[8]   See the relevant series of articles by J. Murphy-O'Connor listed above, p. 6, note 16, and, of course, Davies, especially pp. 173-201.

[9]   See Davies, pp. 233-267.

[10]   This excludes minor changes to erroneous readings caused by copyists' errors. See, e.g., CD 5:15, where most commentators, including Knibb in his translation, omit the second accidental occurrence of אם. Note further Schürer, III.1, p. 393ff, for a brief consideration of the unitary nature of the Admonition.

[11]   See M. Boyce, *The Poetry of the Damascus Document*, Edinburgh (PhD, 1988); this takes up a suggestion by R.A. Soloff, 'Towards Uncovering Original Texts in the Zadokite Documents', *NTS* 5 (1958-9), pp. 62-67, and is summarized by Boyce in 'The Poetry of the *Damascus Document* and its Bearing on the Origin of the Qumran Sect', *RQ* 14 (1990), pp. 615-628. For other proposals concerning poetry

Boyce surmises that there are three poems beginning CD (1:1-2:1; 2:2-13; 2:14-3:20), and that secondary material has been added to these, disrupting the metre. A fourth poetic section exists in CD 5:11-6:3, with further metrical fragments in 8:4-9/19:16-21 and 20:27-34. Also, a poetic, credal psalm underlies twelve precepts found in 6:11-7:4. These poetic sections belong to the earliest form of CD, used by the first sectarians in association with an annual Renewal of the Covenant ceremony.[12] A redactor saw fit to add two law codes (now in CD 9-16), creating a manual for those sectaries who lived in מחנות away from Qumran.[13] The same person was responsible for 19:33-20:27, as well as chronological additions and references to the death of the Teacher. Midrashic passages in CD belong to yet a different, probably later, source, more developed theologically and strikingly similar to 4QFlor (4Q174). These are found in CD 1:12b-14a (on Hos 4:16's פרה סררה); 3:20-4:6 (a midrash on Ez 44:15); 4:12-5:11 (on the three Nets of Belial); 6:3-11 (the Well Midrash); 7:14-21 (the Am-Nu Midrash); 19:7-13 (the Zec-Ez Midrash); 8:9-12/19:21-24 (the Dt 32:33 Midrash). For our own purposes, it will be of interest to set out Boyce's reconstruction of the Poem in CD 1:1-2:1 as follows:[14]

a^1	1+3	2+6	ועתה שמעו כל יודעי צדק
a^2	3	6	[2] ובינו במעשי אל
b^1	1+3	1+6	כי ריב לו עם כל בשר
b^2	3	9	[3] ומשפט יעשה בכל מנאציו
a^1	1+3	1+6	כי במועלם אשר עזבוהו
b^1	3	8<5>	[4] הסתיר פניו מישראל <וממקדשו>
c^1	2	5	ויתן לחרב

---

12   within CD 1-8, see Charles, II, p. 799-823; Davies, p. 61ff; G. Jeremias, *Der Lehrer der Gerechtigkeit*, Göttingen (1963), pp. 151-152; Knibb, pp. 17-18.

For the latter, in the context of the religious life and ideas of the Qumran community, see *DSSE*, pp. 41-64.

13   See CD 7:6ff (=19:2ff). According to Boyce, the reason for the redaction was the civil war of 98-94 BCE under Alexander Jannaeus, mentioned in *AJ* 13.375-376, which encouraged an increase in the numbers of the sect.

14   The arrangement follows M. Boyce, 'The Poetry of the *Damascus Document* and its Bearing on the Origin of the Qumran Sect', *RQ* 14 (1989), p. 617f, dividing this 'First Poem' into four stanzas of 8, 10, 8 and 10 cola each (1:3-8a; 1:8b-11a; 1:11b-18a; 1:18b-21a), with an introduction and conclusion (1:1-2; 1:21b-2:1). Left-hand columns represent parallelistic arrangement, stress count, and syllable count, respectively. Numbers in square brackets on the right indicate lines within CD 1:1-2:1, while text in pointed brackets (<...>) marks out what is secondary disruption of the Poem, according to Boyce.

a^2	3	7	ובזכרו ברית ראשנים
b^2	3	7	השאיר שארית [5] לישראל
c^2	3	5	ולא נתנם לכלה
			ובקץ חרון <שנים שלוש מאות [6] ותשעים לתיתו אותם
a^1	3	5	ביד נבוכדנאצר מלך בבל> [7] פקדם
$a^2(c^1)$	3	9<4>	ויצמח מישראל <ומאהרון> שורש
$b^1(c^2)$	3	8	מטעת לירוש [8] את ארצו
$b^2(c^3)$	3	7	ולדשן בטוב אדמתו
a^1	2	7	ויבינו בעונם
a^2	3	7<2>	וידעו כי [9] <אנשים> אשימים הם
b^1	2	6	ויהיו כעורים
b^2	2	4<4>	וכי מגששים דרך [10] <שנים עשרים>
a^1	3	8	ויבן אל אל מעשיהם
b^1	3	7	כי בלב שלם דרשוהו [11]
a^2x^1	3	8	ויקם להם מורה צדק
b^2y^1	3	6	להדריכם בדרך לבו
a^1	3	8	ויודע [12] לדורות אחרונים
a^2	4	7<4>	את אשר עשה בדור אחרון <בעדת בוגדים [13]
			הם סרי דרך היא העת אשר היה כתוב עליה
			כפרה סוריה [14] כן סרר ישראל>
b^1x^2	3	8	בעמוד איש הלצון
b^2y^2	4	10	אשר הטיף לישראל [15] מימי כזב
a^1	3	7	ויתעם בתוהו לא דרך
b^1	3	6	להשח גבהות עולם
a^2	3	6	ולסור [16] מנתיבות צדק
b^2	3	6<6>	ולסיע גבול <אשר גבלו ראשנים ב>נחלתם
a^1	4	11	למען [17] הדבק בהם את אלות בריתו
a^2	4	9	להסגירם לחרב נקמת נקם [18] ברית
			בעבור אשר
a^1+a^2	2+2	5+8	דרשו בחלקות ויבחרו במהתלות
a^1+a^2	2+2	6+8	ויצפו [19] לפרצות ויבחרו בטוב הצאור
a^1+a^2	2+2	6+6	ויצדיקו רשע וירשיעו צדיק [20]
a^1+a^2	2+2	5+5	ויעבירו ברית ויפירו חוק
a^1	3	8	ויגודו על נפש צדיק
a^2	4	10	ובכל הולכי [21] תמים תעבה נפשם
b^1	2	5	וירדפום לחרב
b^2	3	6	ויסיסו לריב עם

a[1]	3	8	ויחר אף [1] אל בעדתם
b[1]	3	6	להשם את כל המונם
b[2]	3	8	ומעשיהם לנדה לפניו

As can be seen, this 'First Poem' is created by bracketing seven words or phrases which spoil an original arrangement.[15]   Although Boyce is not the first to posit a poetic original behind CD 1:1-2:1, he has extended the principle to the rest of the document, making out a case which, at first sight, seems convincing.   Nevertheless, it is important to ask on what grounds his argument can be sustained, for, upon examination of Boyce's layout, it appears that many texts could be arranged so as to conform to a poetic structure by excluding a selection of words or phrases.   Boyce could in theory be correct in his hypothesis but there is no evidence to support it, even with the release of 4QD in recent years.[16]   Whilst we may empathize with his procedure, particularly in view of the historical difficulties outlined previously, his approach entails an appeal to a reconstruction of a series of earlier versions of CD 1:1-2:1 and the remainder of the Admonition,

---

15   The reasons for designating them later additions are: better parallelism is achieved by removing וממקדשו (CD 1:3); "390...king of Babylon" (1:5-7) breaks the metre and is a fictitious gloss, based on Ez 4, to show that the exile was still continuing; מאהרן (1:7) spoils the metre and is a gloss; removing "20 years" (1:10), after the example of "390...", renders אנשים אשימים (1:9) too long, so that אנשים should be omitted; the whole of בעדת בוגדים...כן סרר ישראל (1:12-14) is secondary, like all CD's midrashic material, breaking the metre; אשר גבלו ראשנים בנחלתם (1:16) should be emended as above in view of Jos 16:5 and 19:10,41.

16   Further, what exactly may have constituted poetry in Second Temple Hebrew is problematic; the following words on so-called poetry in the Hebrew Bible by J.A. Soggin, *Introduction to the Old Testament*, London (1989), p. 71f, are relevant:

"Discussion of the nature and especially of the metre of Hebrew poetry, as of western Semitic poetry in general, is not only far from being exhausted but has yet to be correctly framed, even accepting...that such a discussion is possible at all. Apart from a very few instances...biblical criticism has yet to discover the key to Hebrew metre, always granted that such a thing existed. There are many reasons for this phenomenon. First of all, the revision of texts over the centuries and then the difficulty, and often the impossibility, of distinguishing the authentic parts from the additions, make it impossible to determine individual verses exactly.   Secondly, the vocalisation is that traditionally fixed by the Massoretes and necessarily presents a later stage; we cannot know the original vocalisation and accentuation of the texts, the poetic license allowed, and so on. There are even sound reasons for supposing that as early as the Hellenistic period Hebrew metre was no longer known: otherwise certain additions would be inexplicable".

presumably because it seems impossible to grasp the text's significance by reading it in its finished form. This *modus operandi* is less than satisfactory, however, inasmuch as the writer responsible for producing the final edition of CD 1:1-2:1 must have assumed he was engaging in a meaningful task. We may also note an unrelated but relevant comment by Thiering, describing Qumran poetry:

> "It may...be remarked that the attempt to treat the phrase ["390 years...king of Babylon" in CD 1:5b-6] as secondary on metrical grounds can scarcely succeed, since the poetry of Qumran, as evidenced in the Hodayot, is characterised by marked irregularity of metre, with a tendency for the parallelistic structure to break down into prose".[17]

Indeed, as far as CD as we now have it is concerned, Murphy-O'Connor's designation, "rhythmic prose", is certainly nearer the mark.[18]

To summarize our observations so far, it can be seen that problems over how to 'read' the Admonition, as well as related theories as to the possible redactional history of the work, connect to a wider situation that pertains to the reading of many ancient texts. We may sympathize with those who posit sources or redactional activity and hypothesize about earlier forms; we may also be in accord with attempts to read a particular work on its own terms in what is often the only extant edition. That the former sets to one side the finished product, as in Boyce's analysis, suggests it is not in fact understood. As with much work on biblical books, some studies of material pertaining to the Second Temple period have too often assumed that the hypothetical tracing of sources and the identification of earlier *Sitze im Leben* explain the current state and meaning of a text. In reality, this is not the case. On the other hand, if leaving a text intact creates such a high degree of tension that the modern reader cannot follow it, then neither is it understood on that wise.

Even where the detection of prior sources is possible, however, it is necessary to make a distinction between them, as viewed in their independent state before incorporation, and the end-result of the redactional process, which must be regarded in its own right separately. In other words, a text is more than the sum of its sources. Furthermore, and pre-empting our examination of scripture in CD 1:1-2:1, it can be argued that וממקדשו and שנים...מלך בבל in CD 1:3 and 1:5b-6, respectively, are integral to the final

---

17   B. Thiering, 'The Date of Composition of the Temple Scroll', in G.J. Brooke (ed.), *Temple Scroll Studies*, Sheffield (1989), p. 106.

18   J. Murphy-O'Connor, 'An Essene Missionary Document? CD II,14-VI,1', *RB* 77 (1970), p. 203. Boyce's own description of the poetry in CD 2:14-3:20 as less refined than that in 1:1-2:1 and 2:2-13 and, therefore, better designated "poetical narrative", would also point in this direction.

form of the Admonition, at least at the level of its dependence on the scriptures. There is a nexus of biblical texts appearing throughout the document in the form of quotation and/or allusion to which the wording at these points relates, and, therefore, no ostensible grounds exist on which to characterize them as alien interpolations.[19]

3.3 An Address to the Sons of Light

As noted earlier, 4QD has revealed an opening address which, while missing from CD, appears to have preceded the Qumran version of the document. Unfortunately, the remains of this introductory address are fragmentary, and the following is a simplified preliminary representation based on 4QD[a] 1:1-24; 2 i:1-6, with lacunae supplied as appropriate in light of overlaps with 4QD[b] 1:2-6 and 4QD[c] 1:2-8:[20]

1	]	בן[ני אור להנזר מדר]כי	[
	]	]עד תום [7]מועד פקודה ב[אחרית]	
	[הימים	וירן]א אל את כול מעשיה להבי כל[ה]	
	בת[ן	ובקץ חרבן הארץ עמדו כו]ל מסיגי גבול וכלה יעשה [במה]	
5	רשע ה[ן	] לו אודיעה לכם [	[
	הנורא]	]פלאו [x]אספררה לכ[ם	[
	מאנוש]	ש]מים אשר חי כ[ו][ל]ן	[
	בעמק[ת]		[

---

19   Boyce maintains that a distinction in bible usage accompanies and thereby corroborates his isolation of sources: CD's poetry uses scripture allusively, with a few quotations introduced in a short, unspecifying manner; the midrashic parts are more deliberately dependent on the bible, quote it more frequently and explicitly interpret such citations; the prosaic redactional additions tend to employ sectarian language. However, our subsequent analysis of the use of scripture in the Admonition will show a common dependency underlying all portions of the document.

20   See WA, pp. 1, 3-4, 28, for the relevant portions of 4QD[a,b,c]. Note, however, that WA's distinctions between certain, probable and possible readings have not been shown. Note, further, that 4QD[b] 1:7-8 contains two additional lines, following the equivalent of 4QD[a] 1:24, not present in the remains of the latter or 4QD[c]:

7	[	]ובפיותכה
8	[	]ד כול בשר ובר[יאה

Similarly, an additional line is present in 4QD[c] 1:1, preceding the equivalent of 4QD[a] 2 i:1, and reads:

1	[	דורות]אחרונות הלוא כן תבואינה]	[

[חתם]

10

[

[

ולוא שמעו]   במצו|ות

[בתרומ|ת 15

[לקול מושה]

לעשות]   רכיל בחוק|ין] ומברית אל|

[קטנה וגדולה ל]

[הודיענו נא א|ת דרכיכה

[שיחתך אם] 20

[עמדתה והתבונן]

ואנוכי עפר]   א   ישיבו א|ת

לא]   ואפר ומיאש ק]

[התבונן|נתה

[ע|ד] אשר   תחלתו ואיזה סופו] 1

כי אין ל|להת|ק|ד|ם ולהתאחר ממועדיהם]   יבוא במה כי]

הלוא חקוק קץ חרון לעם לא ידעהו]   ]

רצון לדור|שי מצוותו ולה|ללכים בתמים דרך   ]

ודורשיה בנסתרות וא|וזנם פתחו וישמעו עמוקות ויבינו] 5

בכול נהיות עד מה יבוא במה]   ועתה שמעו כול יודעי]

Clearly, there are numerous turns of phrase which link this passage to the language of Qumran in general and to the remainder of the Admonition in particular. As well as the call to attention, ...ועתה שמעו, common to both 4QD^a 2 i:6 and CD 1:1, mention of the ב]ני אור [in 4QD^a 1:1, for example, is reminiscent of the repetition of this designation in 1QS and 1QM, while מסיגי גבול and קץ חרון לעם in 4QD^a 1:4 and 2 i:3, respectively, remind us of CD 5:20 and 1:5. Beyond this, however, the text is too fragmentary to consider accurately its possible use of the bible by way of either quotation or allusion. Nevertheless, and as we will have occasion to remark again below, we can simply note that reference to the מסיגי גבול does connect this Address to the Admonition's consistent tendency to draw upon Hos elsewhere, including the specific designation מסיגי גבול which derives from Hos 5:10.

More generally, the presence of this opening Address at Qumran raises a second important methodological issue concerning the nature of the relationship between the various witnesses to this work - both those found at Qumran (4QD^{a-h}) and that represented by the Cairo Genizah material as attested in Mss A and B. As with a number of other sectarian DSS, especially 1QS/4QS and 1QM/4QM, it appears that divergent editions of these texts existed side by side at Qumran. This state of affairs is comparable to that pertaining to biblical books, as described previously, and raises a similar two-fold question: how did the sectaries respond to this diversity, and at what point do differénces between MSS of a particular text become so numerous or otherwise significant as to require us to designate the witnesses as deliberately divergent editions or even distinct compositions? This difficulty relates to much Second Temple literature but an answer to it remains, as yet, elusive.[21] In reality, it does not pose a serious threat to our study, however, because the fragmentary state of the opening Address in 4QD precludes its inclusion within our analysis and allows us to leave open the question as to whether it should properly be included, alongside the text of the Admonition as evidenced from the Cairo Genizah MSS, in our study.

On the other hand, the same issue will reappear in a milder form in subsequent chapters, when we note alternative readings in 4QD for words or phrases in CD 1-8 or 19-20. On occasion it is clear that the former has preserved a text that is purer than that contained in CD, as in the case of the simple כי found in 4QD[a] for כי אם in CD 5:15b. Where competing but equally plausible readings are preserved in 4QD and CD, however, it is often far from certain how they are to be judged in relation to each other. This can be illustrated by comparing אנשים אשימים הם in CD 1:9 with the shorter אשמים המה in 4QD[a]. Although, even before the release of the 4QD material, some scholars, as we have seen, proposed that אנשים in CD 1:9 should be regarded as secondary, it is by no means clear that the 4QD[a] reading supports such an emendation to the text of CD.

3.4 Literature and Culture

This chapter has sought to demonstrate the problems scholars can experience in attempting to understand some ancient texts, even allowing for the contribution to be made by source, form, and redaction criticism, as well as literary theory. Of course, this is neither universally nor uniformly the case but may be related to what Barton calls 'literary competence', an idea well-illustrated by the same author in the following contemporary example:

---

21   Numerous examples from the bible and other Second Temple works could be cited here by way of illustration, including Jer (in MT and LXX), Dn (in LXX and Theod), 1 En (in Aramaic and Ethiopic), Ps 151 (in LXX and 11QPs[a]), and Ac (in א and B over against D).

"Dear Sir,
Account No 23579D
Since this account continues to show a debit of £559.67, I have no alternative
but to inform you that unless it is cleared within seven days from the above date
we shall be obliged to take steps to recover the sum in question.
Yours faithfully,
A. Clerk".[22]

The skills required to grasp the significance of this letter are considerable and
at a level above mere vocabulary and grammar. The point of its inclusion
here is simply to show the extent to which texts are embedded within the
culture which produced them.[23]   We may suppose that analogous skills were
required for a successful reading of many ancient texts, including the
Admonition within its Second Temple context.   Such competence would
presumably allow CD 1-8 and 19-20 to be read with its historical tensions,
which, as with many other works from this period, appear unacceptably high
to the modern reader.   In other words, it is possible to view the difficulties
scholars have experienced in trying to understand the Admonition in cultural
terms, as though all the pieces necessary to complete the *Weltanschauung*
required by the document are only partially accessible, leaving us with an
incomplete two-dimensional picture, as it were.[24]   If what constitutes
historical or theological consistency fluctuates over time, then a considerable
cultural gap between the *Weltanschauung* informing a text like CD and that
of modern people is manifest in the fact that recourse to the theories
mentioned above are felt necessary in the first place - yet are not fully
satisfactory.   Thus, the invocation of source or form criticism might
sometimes be deemed to constitute a flight from the finished form of texts
which cannot be fitted into any experienced modern category, while a holistic

---

22   See Barton, *op. cit.*, pp. 8-19.

23   Indeed, as Barton, *op. cit.*, p. 13, points out, "...it must be something more than
merely linguistic competence that leads me to go and consult my bank manager
when I receive a letter like this...Suppose I were a Martian who had learned the
English language but had no knowledge of English life, customs or social
conventions. My linguistic competence would then enable me to understand the
'meaning' of the text...but I would have no idea at all how to interpret it...For
example, it could easily be some kind of lyric poem, shown...by the short paired
opening and closing lines, which have an aesthetically pleasing effect..."!

24   This is comparable to, although on a different level from, the "key" envisaged by G.
Vermes, 'Bible Interpretation at Qumran', *Eretz-Israel* 20 (1989), p. 189: "The
meaning of this exposition [in 1QpHab 8:1-3] was patent to the initiates who
possessed the key to the cryptograms "House of Judah"...". See the discussion in J.
Barr, 'Cultural Relativism and the New Radicalism', in *The Bible in the Modern
World*, London (1973), pp. 35-52.

reading must guard against imposing literary expectations from a later period onto the products of an earlier one.[25]

In view of all these factors, we shall remain sceptical, or at least agnostic, about previous forms of CD 1-8, 19-20. Instead, because it is arguable that we do not have sufficient data to hypothesize with any degree of certainty about sources or redaction, we shall take the Admonition as it now stands as a given, since it is also arguable that it has a largely discernible literary structure which is relatively objectively fixed in the text. Where obstacles prevent its detection, it will be assumed that limitations on our part are the primary cause.[26] Further, it ought to be made clear that, when we refer to the 'writer' or 'author' of CD, we are doing so for the sake of convenience but do not take for granted any particular group(s), individual(s), or redactional history behind the document, except an association with Qumran, where copies of an edition(s) of our document have been found. Similarly, in speaking about the 'mind' of such an 'author', it may well be better to view the point of reference as the collective consciousness of a group. Alternatively, it is arguable that, with qualifications, meaning inheres in the text itself as a literary artefact, in which case 'mind' should be viewed somewhat metaphorically.

Finally, it is fitting to return to two related issues concerning the Pesharim and other works with pesher-like sections.[27] Both pertain to scholarly attempts to gain insight into the texts concerned, restricted by the cultural distance that falls between the modern world and those same texts. The first has to do with genre. Since the production and use of literature occurs within a cultural and religious milieu, genre is bound up with that milieu and genre-recognition is largely an automatic reflex.[28] Consequently, scholarly differences as to the generic category of the Pesharim or the Admonition are primarily contemporary academic debates prompted by an inability to categorize these texts. Indeed, it seems reasonable to suggest that the genre-question is one of a number of problems that arise when expectations divergent from those of the author or community responsible for it are placed

---

[25] Alternatively, a historical understanding is abandoned and ancient texts become literature for use in the here and now. However, although many assume this might be a fruitful way of approaching the bible, few today would wish to read CD 1-8 or 19-20 for edification!

[26] This is except for mistakes which inevitably occur when a text is transmitted in MS form, as exemplified above, note 10. In such cases, 4QD, or even 5QD and 6QD, can be of help in supplementing or correcting CD 1-8 or 19-20.

[27] See above, p. 20f.

[28] This certainly applies to the contemporary example from Barton cited above.

upon our document by its modern readers. Hence, in trying to relate the Pesharim to works such as CD containing pesher-like sections, the suggestion that Pesher should be viewed as a sub-genre within Midrash does not clarify the situation. Moreover, Schwarz's description of three genres for the material within CD 1-8 and 19-20, rather than a single one for the whole document, does not concern genre proper but reflects the confusion caused by a variation in style within one text for which no overall generic classification can be posited. Indeed, of the classes available to the modern reader, it is difficult to suggest one than can incorporate all of the Admonition. Presumably, this was not a great difficulty for its Second Temple readers and, if we are correct, this puts into perspective discussions of genre in scholarly literature.[29]

The second problem concerns exegesis. As noted earlier, scholars have concentrated on attempting to clarify the inner exegetical workings of the sectarian DSS, in particular whether the contents of the Pesharim are best viewed as analogous to the revelatory dream-visions of Dn or to later rabbinic Midrash. Brooke has argued convincingly that interpretative techniques determine the outcome of exegesis throughout the DSS, and that these, akin to the rabbinic מדות, were widespread in Second Temple times.[30] They were necessarily used, if an author wished to carry authority in the eyes of his readers, for without some such standard, he could not convince his contemporaries as to the validity of his interpretations. This makes sense and Brooke furnishes us with ample demonstration of גזרה שוה and נוטריקון in the DSS.[31] That similar connections were made by the writer of CD 1-8 and 19-20 will be apparent in subsequent chapters, although their discovery will not be our main task. However, caution is required inasmuch as the rabbis' מדות and, presumably, their Qumran equivalents were primarily literary devices around which to organize texts; on their own, they elucidate little in terms of why one particular combination of words or passages in the bible should have been chosen in preference to another.

Therefore, a more generalized observation may be pertinent. Because its narratives are often brief or contradictory and its legislation evinces gaps and tensions, interpretation of the bible can be seen essentially as a necessary response to the biblical corpus itself, which requires what may be called

---

29   While appeal to myth or legend may enable the modern person to read the text meaningfully, it cannot relate to Second Temple readings of the document.

30   G.J. Brooke, *Exegesis at Qumran: 4QFlorilegium in its Jewish Context*, Sheffield (1985), especially pp. 1-79.

31   For examples, see Brooke, *op. cit.*, pp. 302-311.

aggadic and halakhic elaboration, although there is no set form such speculation should take.[32]   In other words, although the Law and other scriptures were counted as authoritative by religious groups in the Second Temple and Rabbinic periods, their open-ended and polyvalent nature necessitated exegesis. Thus, on the one hand, the most pious individual or community would not have been able to avoid supplementing or harmonizing the texts in order to appropriate them; on the other, there was no one predetermined way in which this should inevitably take place. As a result, the interpretations of gaps or tensions in biblical law or narrative by various groups in Second Temple times and beyond were by no means uniform, notwithstanding the undoubted use of exegetical 'techniques' to bolster their persuasiveness. In fact, the resultant diversity is to be explained largely by the random and imaginative nature of the interpretative exercise itself, although circumstantial factors will also have been important (e.g., interpretations would have had to have been consonant with earlier elaborations and, probably, different from opponents' views).

Indeed, the arbitrariness evident in the interpretation of scripture strikes the modern reader foremost and is manifest not least in the fact that the same biblical verse can be interpreted differently in alternative sectarian documents.[33]   The situation is rather like that pertaining to scriptural citations in the Admonition and other DSS; the way they are employed seems decidedly unconvincing to the twentieth-century person standing outside both the wider cultural milieu and the particular mythology of the sect. Nevertheless, as far as the Second Temple readers of CD 1-8 and 19-20 were concerned, it may be necessary to conclude that the presence of a web of scriptural citation and allusion, however superficial it may now seem, was of much greater significance to the document's contemporaries than we might naturally assume ourselves.

In any case, as has been suggested already, the citations may well be part of a wider phenomenon, examination of which should prove profitable. Even if we are unable to enter fully into the psyche of the writer of the Admonition or his community, we shall be able to inquire into the use of scripture in CD 1-8 and 19-20 as it now stands. Given that both the quotations and stronger

---

32   For an outline of the nature of both halakhah and aggadah, see Schürer, II, pp. 337-355.

33   See, e.g., Am 9:11 as employed in both 4QFlor 1:10-13 and CD 7:13b-8:1a. In the former, Am 9:11 appears to have been linked, via גזרה שוה, to 2 Sa 7:12 by analogous employment of the root קום; see Brooke, *op. cit.*, p. 138f. Regarding the latter, the writer of CD may have brought Am 9:11 into his discussion in view of a linguistic connection between Am 9:13 and Lv 26:5; see below, p. 184, note 18.

allusions can safely be said to inhere within the text, it will be possible to outline a structure of biblical citation and allusion, relatively independent of the cultural limitations placed upon us by the intervening centuries.

4   Scripture in the Historical Sections of the Damascus Document

4.1 The Historical Sections

At this point, it is appropriate to move on to the text of the Admonition itself. In this chapter, we shall consider those portions which may be classed as 'historical', namely, CD 1:1-2:1, 2:14-4:12a and 5:15b-6:11a.[1] These three passages describe the origins of the movement or specific group behind our document, and we can be confident in isolating them, although it has to be admitted that the precise boundaries of 2:14-4:12a and, especially, 5:15b-6:11a are not entirely unambiguous. Nonetheless, 1:1-2:1 clearly constitutes a block of material that can be dealt with, whatever its literary or redactional origin, according to the rubrics in 1:1 and 2:2 (the latter of which constitutes the beginning of the next section). Similarly, 2:14 marks the start of another portion, whose end, however, is less obvious, although it seems reasonable to view 4:12a as a suitable conclusion. While 5:15a/15b and 6:11a/11b are also less clear-cut than 1:1, 2:2 and 2:14, we may view them comparably, as will be argued below.[2]

However, it is not to be maintained that these divisions necessarily mark the beginnings and endings of sources used by the final redactor, although some or all of them may do so. Rather, it is reasonable simply to differentiate

---

[1]   The three introductory formulae in the Admonition, at 1:1f, 2:2f and 2:14ff, are variously interpreted by scholars, in conjunction with other points, to identify the addressees in CD 1-8. Unfortunately, it is not safe to argue directly from the formulae themselves in this connection, because they could, in fact, be addressed to almost anyone who happened to be listening or reading. Cf. J. Murphy-O'Connor, 'An Essene Missionary Document? CD II,14-VI,1', *RB* 77 (1970), p. 204, who maintains that, while 2:14f is addressed as a tract to outsiders, the language of 1:1f and 2:2f refers to members of the community.

[2]   See P.R. Davies, *Behind the Essenes: History and Ideology in the Dead Sea Scrolls*, Atlanta (1987), pp. 107-134, for a comparison of CD's historical sections with similar so-called *Heilsgeschichten* in Jub and 1 En. For other detailed studies of CD 1:1-2:1; 2:14-4:12a; and 5:15b-6:11a, some of which will be brought into our subsequent discussion, see the useful bibliographical data in Broshi, pp. 65-72.

sections of CD 1-8 and 19-20 according to the contours of the text, along with changes in subject-matter and style. On such grounds, the historical passages stand out and can be taken together for the purposes of our analysis.[3]

Nevertheless, in setting aside and describing CD 1:1-2:1, 2:14-4:12a, and 5:15b-6:11a as 'historical', this is a term which must be immediately qualified, because it is not to be suggested that these portions of the Admonition are modern historiography. They do, however, share a common style, exercise a similar role, and might well be described as 'history-like'. In other words, they appear to be flowing narratives, with events presented as subsequent to or consequent upon preceding ones, although not historical in a scientific sense.[4] This means that the reader is presented with a string of persons and happenings, beginning no later than the exile and arranged consecutively, often expressed in terms of cause and effect, albeit with the interjection of moral or spiritual evaluations by the author.[5] Whilst it is difficult to pin down this historical style to specific characteristics, there is a certain tone to these parts of CD, whose mood is different from that in, say, 4:12ff or 8:3ff. In fact, the historical sections give the impression of being rather matter of fact, objectively narrated in the third person, and descriptive of a stream of events culminating in one of particular import. The latter has to do with the founding or development of the sect, and is accompanied by a shift in focus from the wider to the sectarian Israel.

Indeed, it is noticeable that the style alters at the climax of the narratives, so that the reader may find CD 1:13ff, 4:1ff and 6:3ff more akin to the contents of 4:12ff or 7:9ff. At these high points we find an increased personal interest in what is being narrated, as well as a greater use of religious epithets. In addition, there is a more obviously deliberate employment of scripture, including the utilization of specific citations. There is a lot of biblical language underlying the rest of the historical sections, however, although much of it takes the form of allusion rather than quotation proper.

---

3   For Murphy-O'Connor's source divisions, aligned with consecutive stages in the history of the sect, see the bibliographical details on p. 6, note 16, above. Davies, pp. 56-104, describes CD 1:1-4:12a as the Admonition's historical section; 4:12b-7:9a he designates a portion on law. This is not in contradiction to our divisions, however, because, as indicated in the previous note, Davies himself isolates the same passages in another study.

4   In this regard, they are not unlike 1, 2 Sam or 1,2 Ki or, nearer our period, Est, Bar, and 1, 2 Mac.

5   A positive example of such evaluation can be found in CD 2:2, regarding Abraham; a negative one is present in 2:17-18 on the moral state of the Watchers.

In any case, it is clear that adopting the designation 'historical' for these three parts of the Admonition, with the necessary caveats, does not imply that other portions of the work contain no similar material. But where this is the case, such units tend to be shorter, or they belong to sections where material of a different character predominates, or else they focus more clearly on what appear to be contemporary referents within a narrower time-scale.[6] See, for example, CD 2:2-13 and 8:3-19, both of which will be examined in the next chapter.

These observations help us to begin to appreciate the contours of the text of the Admonition, although our divisions are not necessarily definitive, especially in the second half of CD 1-8. Rather, it should be stressed that we are searching for a sensible and practical demarcation in terms of the internal shape of the document; in a modern text we might speak of 'paragraph' breaks. Indeed, it has to be admitted that the boundaries of any suggested category are frequently vague, so that portions elsewhere within CD 1-8 or 19-20 could be included in this part of our study, especially 2:2-13. Conversely, various blocks within 1:1-2:1, 2:14-4:12a, or 5:15b-6:11a might be omitted and dealt with separately, particularly 4:1ff and 6:3ff, which are dependent, at least formally, on Ez 44:15 and Nu 21:18, respectively.[7] In their present contexts, however, these parts of the Admonition are integral to the description of a flow of events, distinctive of these historical sections, and are best included when dealing with their surroundings.

4.2 Scripture in CD 1:1-2:1

We shall begin our analysis of the use of scripture in the Admonition by examining CD 1:1-2:1, a passage neatly demarcated within CD 1-8, due to the similar formulae at 1:1f and 2:2f.[8] Although it is one of three portions dealing with the origins of the community, all similar in content and style, CD

---

6   This excludes the above-mentioned climaxes to the historical sections, which also have a more contemporary flavour to them.

7   We similarly had no choice but to accept a degree of ambiguity when discussing the three categories of bible usage in the Admonition; see above, pp. 27-32.

8   Much of the following discussion of CD 1:1-2:1 appeared in J.G. Campbell, 'Scripture in The Damascus Document 1:1-2:1', *JJS* 44 (1993), pp. 83-99. It is with the kind permission of the editor, Prof. G. Vermes, that it is reproduced here in a revised form.

1:1-2:1 tends to be used by scholars for reconstructions of the group's history, both because it begins the document and because it gives what appears to be information more easily paralleled in other sectarian DSS. In particular, this historical section alone mentions the מורה צדק, although a certain יורה הצדק features in CD 6:11; outside the Admonition, he appears seven times in 1QpHab, five times in 4QpPs, and once in 1QpMic.

In CD 1:1-2:1 appeal is made to the lessons of the past in order to make sense of the present, both of God's ריב with his enemies (1:2) and of his dealings with their pious counterparts (1:4f). From 1:13 a change of direction is noticeable in the text, inasmuch as an attempt is made to explicate further the group mentioned in 1:12, the עדת בוגדים. Another marker can be detected in 1:18a, in that, from בעבור אשר up to 2:1, there is a listing of the grave sins of the party under discussion, parallel to that in 1:13-18a, followed by God's judgement upon them.[9] Yet, despite the obvious history-like nature of CD 1:1-2:1, its interpretation is riddled with difficulties. In order to contrast this with our own thesis, it will be useful to set out the Hebrew text of the passage and then detail the main problems:[10]

ועתה שמעו כל יודעי צדק ובינו במעשי	1
אל כי ריב לו עם כל בשר ומשפט יעשה בכל מנאציו	
כי במועלם אשר עזבוהו הסתיר פניו מישראל וממקדשו	
ויתנם לחרב ובזכרו ברית ראשנים השאיר שארית	
לישראל ולא נתנם לכלה ובקץ חרון שנים שלוש מאות	5
ותשעים לתיתו אותם ביד נבוכדנאצר מלך בבל	
פקדם ויצמח מישראל ומאהרן שורש מטעת לירוש	
את ארצו ולדשן בטוב אדמתו ויבינו בעונם וידעו כי	
אנשים אשימים הם ויהיו כעורים וכימגששים דרך	
שנים עשרים ויבן אל אל מעשיהם כי בלב שלם דרשוהו	10
ויקם להם מורה צדק להדריכם בדרך לבו ויודע	
לדורות אחרונים את אשר עשה בדור אחרון בעדת בוגדים	
הם סרי דרך היא העת אשר היה כתוב עליה כפרה סוררה	
כן סרר ישראל בעמוד איש הלצון אשר הטיף לישראל	
מימי כזב ויתעם בתוהו לא דרך להשח גבהות עולם ולסור	15
מנתיבות צדק ולסיע גבול אשר גבלו ראשנים בנחלתם למען	

---

9   Davies, p. 70f, is not alone in suggesting that either 1:13-18a or 1:18b-21b may be an interpolation.

10   The Hebrew text of CD 1:1-2:1 and of the rest of the Admonition is based on Broshi, pp. 10-49. The intermittent medieval vocalization in Mss A and B has not been reproduced, however, nor have Broshi's sigla for unclear letters, except those placed within [...].

הדבק בהם את אלות בריתו להסגירם לחרב נקמת נקם

ברית בעבור אשר דרשו בחלקות ויבחרו במהתלות ויצפו

לפרצות ויבחרו בטוב הצואר ויצדיקו רשע וירשיעו צדיק

20   ויעבירו ברית ויפירו חוק ויגדו על נפש צדיק ובכל הולכי

תמים תעבה נפשם וירדפום לחרב ויסיסו לריב עם ויחר אף

1   אל בעדתם להשם את כל המונם ומעשיהם לנדה לפניו

A number of minor divergences in 4QD are worthy of note. 4QD^c reads שמעו לי for CD 1:1's שמעו (cf. CD 2:14, שמעו לי), while 4QD^a prefers the shorter אשמים המה for אנשים אשימים הם in CD 1:9. Similarly, 4QD^a contains the reading ולוא דרך for CD 1:15's לא דרך, as well as ו]להסיע for the apparently defective ולסיע of CD 1:16.[11]

CD 1:1f starts with an exhortation to understand the "dealings of God", against the background of his "dispute with all flesh" and the fact that he works "judgement against all who despise him". This is then connected to what happened to Israel when they committed מעל: God "hid his face" from them and their temple and handed them over to the sword to be punished at the hand of Shalmeneser and/or Nebuchadnezzar.[12]   Here the picture becomes obscure, for God is now described as acting positively in disallowing complete annihilation: "But when he remembered the covenant of the first ones, he left a remnant to Israel and did not give them to destruction". Except for the phrase ולא נתנם לכלה, which suggests a link with the preceding negative event, we are not told when this remembering took place.   That unexplained, there is another time-clause: "and in the age of wrath, 390 years after giving them into the hand of Nebuchadnezzar king of Babylon, פקדם and he made sprout from Israel and Aaron a root of planting to inherit his land and grow fat on the goodness of his soil".   Whatever group(s) this actually refers to, they "understood their iniquity and knew that they were guilty men; but they were like the blind and like those who grope for the way for twenty years".   Next, something rather more definite is recounted: "Then God considered their deeds, for they sought him with a whole heart, and he raised for them a מורה צדק to lead them in the way of his heart".   But we return to obscurity: "and he made known to the final generations what he did/had done to the final generation, the congregation of traitors".

There follows an attempt to define this latter group, aided by Hos 4:16. They are the "turners from the way...[as] it is written, 'Like a stubborn heifer, thus was Israel stubborn', when the איש הלצון arose and preached to Israel

---

11   See Broshi, pp. 11 and 13.

12   Cf. E. Wiesenberg, 'Chronological Data in the Zadokite Fragments', *VT* 5 (1955), pp. 284-308.

waters of deceit". This figure was also responsible for leading them astray into a trackless waste, "so as to bring down the eternal pride, to turn aside from the paths of righteousness, and to remove the boundary which the first ones had laid in their inheritance, so as to make the curses of his covenant cling to them, delivering them to the sword wreaking the vengeance of the covenant". This barrage of criticism is elaborated (after בעבור אשר in 1:18) by further accusations: "...they sought smooth things and chose illusions, and watched for breaches and chose the fair neck, and justified the wicked and condemned the righteous, and transgressed the covenant and broke the statute, and banded together against the soul of the righteous, and all who walked perfectly their soul abhorred, and they pursued them with the sword, and exulted[13] in the dispute of the people". The section comes to a close with a general negative statement: "And the anger of God was kindled against their congregation, ravaging all their multitude, and all their deeds were as impurity before him".

Even such a brief overview shows that the difficulties of CD 1:1-2:1 are interconnected: the manner in which one phrase is taken affects the way another is read. It is not surprising, therefore, that the theories developed to explain the section are many and varied. The main problems concern the origins of the group(s) recommended, the identifications of the שארית, the שורש מטעת, and the מורה צדק, as well as those with whom they are contrasted. Since 1:1-12 mixes both positive and negative elements, it is particularly problematic. Regarding the group's emergence, we find a description of the remnant's formation in 1:4f, after reference to the Babylonian devastation. The relation in time between the former and the latter is not spelled out in this part of the document, which proceeds to the growth of the שורש מטעת some 390 years after Nebuchadnezzar's invasion of Judaea. Again, any link between the formation of the "remnant" and the "root" is not explicated, although the appearance of the מורה צדק is clearly placed twenty years after the foundation of the "root".

CD 1:13-2:1 concerns only God's enemies, their activities and end, but it is difficult to relate these lines to what has just been narrated, and so we encounter a new set of problems. הם in 1:13 obviously refers to the עדת בוגדים and what follows is intended as a correct understanding of them, as revealed by the Teacher of Righteousness or God. After this, however, the exact relation to the events narrated in 1:1-12 is unclear. Does הם and what

---

13   Most understand ויסיסו as an equivalent to וישישו. Cf. Davies, p. 235, who translates it as "fomented <public strife>".

follows designate contemporaries of the מורה צדק or of an earlier generation? Even if the שארית and the שורש מטעת are equated and placed in the second century BCE, the negative description in 1:13ff might best refer to the exile, in view of 1:3f and since no other catastrophe has been mentioned. On the other hand, 1:13-2:1 contains some elements that almost certainly describe less ancient events, especially reference to the איש הלצון, who can hardly be a sixth century figure.

It is not our intention to engage in arguments for or against certain identifications of the cryptic data in CD 1:1-2:1, but the above outline shows that the problems of any reconstruction are substantial. While most agree that the Essenes were in Palestine from the second century BCE, it is still disputed whether those present at Qumran, from c. 130/100 BCE to 70 CE, were either: (i) the main branch (or a particularly strict group) of Essenes; or (ii) a schismatic group from a wider Essene movement. If the former is accepted, then the Essenes were of second century origin only; if the latter is maintained, then the Qumranites arose during the second half of the second century but the Essenes may be older - with or without exilic roots. As noted earlier, two theories regarding Qumran origins were prominent by the 1960s, with a third or intermediate position being outlined more recently.[14] In addition, whilst it is not our aim to argue for one or other of these hypotheses, it is well to recollect that one of the main determining factors is how scholars relate CD 1:1-2:1 to 2:14-4:12a and 5:15b-6:11a, as well as to 1QpHab and 4QpNah. If we consider use of the bible in 1:1-2:1, however, a different dimension comes to the fore. In view of this, the text of 1:1-2:1 is set out below (p. 56), with the allusions and one citation highlighted. Only allusions beyond reasonable doubt are included, or those which are confirmed by a citation from the same scriptural context elsewhere in CD 1-8 or 19-20.[15] It is difficult to appreciate the parallelism that exists between this historical section and the biblical passages specified without thoroughly perusing the Hebrew of the relevant scriptural contexts alongside CD 1:1-2:1; obviously, this must be left to the reader. Our aim will now be to justify the layout below in more detail, although it must be noted that some of the allusions highlighted are in part corroborated by similar analyses of other portions of CD 1-8 or 19-20 which will follow.

---

14   See above, pp. 4-6.

15   In the arrangement, underlined, *italicized* or **bold** text denotes dependence on the Torah, *Nevi'im* or **Ketuvim**, respectively; where appropriate, two or three of these are mixed. References on the right are placed on the line in which the citation or allusion begins.

ועתה שמעו כל יודעי צדק ובינו במעשי — *Is 51:1,7*

אל כי ריב לו עם כל בשר ומשפט יעשה בכל מנאציו — Nu 14:23 Dt 31:20 *Jer 25:31 Hos 4:1*

כי במעלם אשר עזבוהו הסתיר פניו מישראל וממקדשו — Lv 26:40 Dt 28:20 Dt 31:17 *Ez 20:27 Ez 39:23* **Dn 9:7**

ויתנם לחרב ובזכרו ברית ראשנים השאיר — Lv 26:42,45 *Mic 2:12* **Ps 106:45 Ezr 9:8**

5 שארית לישראל ולא נתנם לכלה ובקץ חרון — *Ez 4:5*

שלוש מאות ותשעים שנה לתתו אותם ביד נבוכדנאצר — *Jer 25:9 Jer 27:6*

מלך בבל פקדם ויצמח מישראל ומאהרן שורש מטעת לירוש — Is 60:21 **Ps 37:29 Ezr 9:12**

את ארצו ולדשן בטוב אדמתו ויבינו בעונם וידעו כי — *Is 59:12*

אנשים אשמים הם ויהיו כעורים וכימגששים דרך — Dt 28:29 *Is 59:10*

10 שנים עשרים ויבן אל אל מעשיהם כי בלב שלם דרשוהו — *Is 30:20 Hos 10:12*

ויקם להם מורה צדק להדריכם בדרך לבו — *Dt 29:21*

לדורות אחרונים את אשר עשה לדור אחרון בעדת בוגדים — Ex 32:8/Dt 9:12,16 *Is 30:11 Hos 4:16*

הם סרי דרך היא העת אשר היה כתוב עליה כפרה סוררה — *Is 28:14,22*

כן סרר ישראל כאשר עמד איש הלצון אשר הטיף לישראל — **Ps 107:40**

15 מימי כזב ויתעם בתוהו לא דרך להשח גבהות עולם ולסור — Dt 19:14/27:17 *Hos 5:10*

מנתיבות צדק ולסיע גבול אשר גבלו ראשנים בנחלתם למען — Dt 29:20 Lv 26:25 **Ps 78:62**

הדבק בהם את אלות בריתו להסגירם לחרב נקמת נקם — *Is 30:10*

ברית בעבור אשר דרשו בחלקות ויבחרו במהתלות ויצפו — *Hos 10:11*

לפרצות ויבחרו בטוב הצואר ויצדיקו רשע וירשיעו צדיק — *Is 24:5* **Ps 94:21**

20 ויעבירו ברית ויפרו חוק ויגודו על נפש צדיק וכל הולכי — Ex 32:10 Dt 29:26 **Ps 106:18,40**

1 תמים תעבה נפשם וירדפום לחרב **אל**

Quotation and Allusion in CD 1:1-2:1

4.2.1 Torah in CD 1:1-2:1

As can be seen, allusions to the Pentateuch in the first historical section centre on Ex 32/Dt 9, Lv 26, Nu 14, and Dt 27ff. All of these contexts have to do with events of major moment in Israel's past or 'prophesied' future and must be considered in more detail.

Ex 32 narrates the story of the golden calf. While Moses is on Mount Sinai, Aaron leads the people to make their ornaments into an idol. God informs Moses of this, saying סרו מהר מן הדרך (v 8) and wishing to be left to his anger (v 10, ויחר אפי בהם) so that he might destroy them. However, Moses pleads with God for his good name's sake and for the sake of the promise to the Patriarchs, and God relents. Moses then returns to the people and, at his behest, the sons of Levi carry out vengeance by the sword on those guilty of rebellion, who are to be blotted out of the Lord's book (v 33, ספרי). Turning to Nu 14, it deals with another incident of rebelliousness, namely, that generated by the spies returning from the reconnaissance of the land. Their complaints about the might of the Canaanites provoke in the people a desire to retreat to Egypt. God's response is to destroy those who do not trust in his power to remain faithful to his promises, but Moses' intercession once more saves them. After an appeal to his patience, God agrees to forgive, but of those who did rebel he says וכל מנאצי לא יראוה; this is from Nu 14:23, and CD 1:2 is clearly based upon it.

Both Lv 26 and Dt 28ff are similar in their content, describing the consequences of Israelite obedience or disobedience, once resident in the land of Canaan. Lv 26 threatens various punishments, which will take place in stages, should the covenant be broken (v 15, להפרכם את בריתי); if Israel refuses to be disciplined, the "sword wreaking the vengeance of the covenant" (v 25) will come, with the desolation of cities and land (v 33, ארצכם שממה ועריכם...חרבה) and dispersal of the Israelites. However, in exile, הנשארים will realize their sin (v 39) and confess to God, who will remember both covenant and land. Note especially verses 40-42:

והתודו את עונם ואת עון אבתם במעלם אשר מעלו בי ואף אשר הלכו עמי בקרי: [41]ואף
אני אלך עמם בקרי והבאתי אתם בארץ איביהם או אז יכנע לבבם הערל ואז ירצו את
עונם: [42]וזכרתי את בריתי יעקוב ואף את בריתי יצחק ואף את בריתי אברהם אזכר
והארץ אזכר:

This excerpt has influenced the shape of CD 1:1-2:1 in several obvious respects.

Dt 28 exhorts the Israelites to obedience. Should they stray, however, curses will befall them מפני רע מעלליך אשר עזבתני (v 20). They will be smitten with scourges from which they cannot be healed, wandering like a

blind man at midday (v 29), while God will take them and their offspring into
שבי (v 41). According to Dt 28:45, this will be because "you did not obey
the voice of the LORD your God to keep his commandments and his
statutes..." (RSV; cf. similar language at various points in CD 2:14-3:12).
Those who are left (v 62, ונשארתם) will become few in the land into which
they have been scattered. Dt 29 contains further exhortations to be faithful
and to avoid walking with a stubborn heart (v 18), so as not to incur כל אלות
הברית הכתובה בספר התורה הזה (v 20). In the day of such destruction, הדור
האחרון בניכם and all the nations shall ask, "Why has the LORD done thus to
this land? What caused this great display of anger?". The answer will be that
the people have forsaken the covenant, so that God exiled them in his wrath
(vv 24-28). Strikingly similar to what we find in CD 3:13f, the chapter ends
with the following enigmatic words:

הנסתרת לה׳ אלהינו והנגלת לנו ולבנינו עד עולם לעשות את כל דברי התורה הזאת:

Dt 30 continues with the theme of exilic repentance, stating that God will
reverse the captivity of his people (v 3) and bring them back אל הארץ אשר
ירשו אבתיך (v 5). In 31:16ff God warns Moses of future apostasy, telling him
to teach the people a song, which reiterates many warnings in Dt 29f and
includes phraseology we have already met.[16]

From this survey, it is clear that there are numerous links between CD 1:1-
2:1 and Ex 32/Dt 9, Lv 26, Nu 14 and Dt 28ff, suggesting that the former's
usage of scripture is more subtle and involved than has often been thought.
In Ex 32 the phrase סרו מהר מן הדרך immediately reminds us of CD 1:13,
with its epithet סרי דרך, as well as the citation from Hos 4:16; there are other
סור/סרר phrases used in the Admonition.[17] Indeed, it is of interest to note
that similar wording, סרו מהר מן הדרך and סרתם מן הדרך, is employed in Dt
9:12 and 16 in a summary of the Ex 32 events; significantly, Dt 9 is also the
source of other allusions and quotations elsewhere in CD 1-8 or 19-20.[18]
Similarly, ויחר אף אל in CD 1:21f, reminiscent of Ex 32:10, is almost a refrain
in CD's historical sections, especially in the longer narrative of 2:14-4:12a.
There is also a more general parallelism between Ex 32 and our text: the
overall story-line describes a special election, which is met with rebellion by
the chosen; this leads to anger on God's part, and a resultant purging to
enable a fresh start. It may well be that, for the author of our document, this

---

[16] Thus, note the following points of contact: v 16, ועזבני והפר את בריתי (cf. CD 1:3,
20); v 17, וחרה אפי בו...והסתרתי פני מהם (cf. CD 1:3, 21); v 18, ואנכי הסתר אסתיר
פני (cf. CD 1:3); v 20, ונאצוני והפר את בריתי (cf. CD 1:2, 20).

[17] See, e.g., CD 2:6, סרורי דרך, and cf. 8:4, לא סרו מדרך.

[18] See, e.g., CD 8:14ff/19:27ff, citing Dt 9:5.

was viewed as analogous to the history and status of the group(s) he commends and its relation to the rest of Israel. In fact, as in Ex 32:3, a special book with a list of names is mentioned in CD 4:4ff and 20:19. Moreover, that Ex 32 is connected to Dt 9, in both the Torah and the Admonition, as well as the fact that, as we shall see, Dt 9 in turn is related to other texts and passages by our author, is further evidence that bible usage here is more than superficial or haphazard. Turning to Nu 14, there are again parallels both of language and of thought.[19] In particular, and as in Ex 32, it contains a pattern of events like that in CD 1:1-2:1.

It is when we turn to Lv 26 and Dt 28-32, however, that we come across the most noticeable parallels with CD 1:1-2:1. Striking is the similarity not only in items of vocabulary but also in the order of events between the first historical section and both Lv 26:40-42 and Dt 28ff.[20] That a connection existed between these two biblical contexts in the eyes of the author of the Admonition is confirmed by CD 1:3, where במועלם אשר עזבוהו appears to combine words from Lv 26:40 and Dt 28:20. In any case, as in Ex 32 and Nu 14, the pattern in both involves disobedience, followed by God 'hiding his face' in the form of the exile, from which, unlike the incidents in Ex 32 and Nu 14, there is no immediate purge and consequent new start. Rather, the people are to be cast out of the land and suffer in exile. There, a number will turn back to God and eventually be restored to him and to the land.

Finally, it has to be remarked that the wording of CD 1:16, גבול אשר גבלו ראשנים בנחלתם, strongly resembles Dt 19:14, לא תסיג גבול רעך אשר גבלו ראשנים בנחלתך. Although we will not encounter any other links with this scriptural context, it has been included in the highlighted text above, both because of the strength of the linguistic overlap and because we may hypothesize that our writer picked up on the verbal link with the curse in Dt 27:17, ארור מסיג גבול רעהו ואמר כל העם אמן, which precedes material (i.e., Dt 28ff) that is undoubtedly very influential in the Admonition.

---

[19]   As already observed, we find נאץ employed in CD 1:2 and Nu 14:23. Further connections between this biblical context and other sections of the Admonition exist: the 40-year desert wanderings imposed before entry into Canaan (v 33f), e.g., are paralleled by the 40 years set aside for the destruction of all the אנשי המלחמה in CD 20:14. Note too זנות (v 33); cf. CD 2:16, עני זנות, and 4:17, הזנות.

[20]   There are further contacts between Dt 29 and other portions of CD 1-8, as will become obvious as we proceed. For now, it can be noted that CD 2:14, עיניכם לראות, is reminiscent of Dt 29:3, ועינים לראות, while Dt 29:18 utilizes the idiom שרירות לב, as does CD 2:17. Moreover, after mention of הדור האחרון in Dt 29:21 comes reference to the נסתרת and the נגלת in Dt 29:28; cf. CD 3:14.

4.2.2 Nevi'im in CD 1:1-2:1

The prophetic passages reflected in CD 1:1-2:1 do not fall into neat categories in the way that those from the Pentateuch seem to do. Hence, we must work our way through them.

The language of CD 1:1,2 is reminiscent of that in Is 51:1,7, Jer 25:31, and Hos 4:1. The first of these, שמעו אלי רדפי צדק...שמעו אלי ידעי צדק, belongs to a context addressing the exiles, promising a return to the land for those who are responsive; those who are not will "lie down in torment". This phrase is from Is 50:11, words of which are strongly alluded to in CD 5:13f. Jer 25:31, בא שאון עד קצה הארץ כי ריב לה׳ בגוים נשפט הוא לכל בשר הרשעים נתנם לחרב נאם ה׳, comes from an oracle against Judah and other peoples: God has a ריב with those nations and with all flesh (v 31); the chapter also contains the important prophecy that Judah's punishment in exile would last 70 years (25:12), as well as a reference to נבוכדנצאר מלך בבל עבדי in 25:29. Both aspects are reflected in CD elsewhere.[21] As for Hos 4:1, it reads as follows:

שמעו דבר ה׳ בני ישראל כי ריב לה׳ עם ישבי הארץ כי אין אמת ואין חסד ואין דעת
אלהים בארץ :

The wider context in which this is placed contains imagery about the prophet's unfaithful wife. More specifically, Hos 3:4 and 4:16 are cited in CD at 20:15 and 1:13, respectively, indicating the likelihood of influence from an intervening verse at this point in the Admonition.

In 1:3 we are reminded of passages from Ez. First of all, במועלם אשר עזבוהו is probably an echo of Ez 20:27. Any doubt about this is removed by the fact that the refrain in Ez 20:11,13,21 is clearly reflected in CD 3:15-16. Further, Ez 20 contains a critical survey of Israelite history, parallel to other biblical texts and to the historical sections of CD itself. הסתיר פניו brings to mind Ez 7-11 and Ez 39. Ez 7-11 describe God's desertion of Jerusalem, due to the people's sins and defilement of the מקדש. Thus, the basic idea behind the phrase in CD 1:3, הסתיר פניו מישראל וממקדשו, is reflected in each of Ez וכבוד אלהי ישראל נעלה (9:3), לרחקה מעל מקדשי (8:6), והסבותי פני מהם (7:22), and ויעל כבוד ה׳ מעל תוך העיר (11:23), מעל הכרוב. These biblical contexts show that וממקדשו makes sense as an integral part of CD 1:3 as it now stands.[22] CD 1:3 also echoes the phraseology of Ez 39:23 and 39:29

---

21   See CD 1:5-6, where Nebuchadnezzar is mentioned and "390 years" is usually connected to an interpretation of the prophet Jeremiah's "70 years".

22   We saw in chapter 2 that numerous scholars have proposed on metrical grounds that the phrase is an addition, as in the case of M. Boyce, 'The Poetry of the Damascus

(containing ואסתר פני מהם and עוד פני מהם and ולא אסתיר, respectively). Verse 23
is part of a short summary of Israel's sin, exile, punishment and restoration,
the first of which provokes God into hiding his face from them (the reason is
על אשר מעלו בי; cf. CD 1:3), while verse 29 promises that God will never
remove his countenance again after they have been restored anew in the land.

CD 1:4-7 continues with positive language. Thus, in 1:4 we hear of the
שארית. We may point foremost to Mic 2:12, a context focused on the end of
the exile, as a definite contact with our document, since Mic 2:6 and 2:11 are
reflected in CD 4:20 and 8:13, respectively. In CD 1:5, we encounter the
apparently central, but rather elusive, "390 years". Most scholars link this
number with Ez 4, where Ezekiel is told to lie on his left side for 390 days to
represent punishment for the House of Israel; 40 days are required on his
other side for Judah. Ez 4:5 reads:

אני נתתי לך את שני עונם למספר ימים שלש מאות ותשעים יום ונשת עון בית ישראל:

Whatever the precise exegetical significance of שלוש מאות ותשעים for our
writer, it is assuredly connected to the wider framework of CD's dependence
on the early chapters of Ez and the concomitant theme of the exile.[23]
Turning to CD 1:6, and having already referred above to Jer 25, we find a
reflection of both Jer 25:9 and Jer 27:6, the latter of which reads:

ועתה אנכי נתתי את כל הארצות האלה ביד נבוכדנצאר מלך בבל עבדי...:

In this context, Jeremiah warns that all must acknowledge Nebuchadnezzar as
king, while the remainder of the temple vessels will be taken to Babylon עד
יום פקדי אותם (v 22; cf. פקדם in CD 1:7). CD 1:7 moves on to consider
God's raising up (ויצמח) of a שורש מטעת, which seems to be a designation
adapted from Is 60:21, נצר מטעו. That biblical context includes the notions
of being righteous and of inheriting the land (cf. CD 1;7f, לירוש את ארצו), as

---

Document and its Bearing on the Origin of the Qumran Sect', *RQ* 14 (1989), pp.
615-628. However, the background of the employment of scripture in CD 1:1-2:1
suggests otherwise, for וממקדשו connects with our author's underlying interest in
Ez 7-11, especially the citation of Ez 9:4 in CD 19:11. Note also that Ez 9:8 and
11:13 contain the expression שארית ישראל (cf. CD 1:4), while Ez 11:16 describes
God himself as a מקדש מעט for the Israelites (cf. CD 1:3).

[23]   Note, moreover, the presence of the following turns of phrase in Ez 5:
       not walking in the חקים (vv 5,6);
       reference to a defiled sanctuary (v 11, את מקדשי טמאת);
       God's anger (v 13, חמה, אף);
       desolation (v 14, חרבה).
With these compare the frequent use of the הלך idiom in CD 2:14-4:12a; the
occurrence of וממקדשו in CD 1:3 and the defilement of the sanctuary in CD 4:18;
the repetition of אף and חמה in 1:1-2:1 and 2:14-4:12a; and חרבן in 5:20.

well as use of the צמח idiom which connotes the idea of geographical and spiritual restoration. Although we shall not appeal to this scriptural passage again, it has been included in the highlighted text above in view of such linguistic and thematic linkage with CD 1:1-2:1.

CD 1:8-12 contains language that is more specific and which details the development of a particular group, related in some way to the שארית and/or שורש of CD 1:4,7. In Is 59, as well as a story-line generally similar to that recounted in CD 1:1-2:1 and the other historical sections, we find the source of the allusive wording of CD 1:8-9 at verse 10, נגששה כעורים קיר וכאין עינים כמתים, נגששה כשלנו בצהרים כנשף באשמנים, and verse 12, כי פשעינו אתנו ועונתינו ידענום. Other connections between Is 59 and the Admonition support this observation.[24]

Hos 10:12 is the source for מורה צדק in CD 1:11. Hos 9-11 forms a wider background to this borrowing of scriptural language, for these chapters stress that, even though God has loved and cared for his people, they persisted in their rebellious ways; he will therefore punish them with the loss of king, children, places of worship, and land. Further, that Hos 10:12, וירה צדק לכם, stands behind מורה צדק is corroborated by the presence of טוב הצואר in CD 1:19, which certainly reflects Hos 10:11.[25] Moreover, it is likely that the final phrase in Hos 10:12 was taken as a personal reference to the מורה צדק, and that a link was made with Is 30:20,21, part of a promise of restoration in verses 18-25. These two verses in Is 30 read as follows:

ונתן לכם אדני לחם צר ומים לחץ ולא יכנף עוד מוריך והיו עיניך ראות את מוריך :
21ואזניך תשמענה דבר מאחריך לאמר זה הדרך לכו בו כי   תאמינו וכי תשמאילו:

Two factors render it difficult not to conclude that our author was aware of both of these biblical occurrences of מורה-like terminology. First, Hos 10:11 (containing טוב צוארה) is reflected in CD 1:19, as just mentioned; secondly, Is 30 exerts influence at two other points in this first historical section, as we shall see.

In CD 1:13ff, the language remains personal and detailed but becomes negative. הם סרי דרך in 1:13 is reminiscent of Is 30:11, סורו מני דרך, describing the false prophets that Isaiah criticizes. Other connections between Is 30 and the Admonition, especially 1:18f, make another link likely here. Staying with CD 1:13, we find the first explicit biblical quotation, taken

---

24   Thus, Is 59:5 informs CD 5:13f, and Is 59:20 probably stands behind CD 20:17.

25   The presence of בטוב הצואר is a case similar to "390 years" in CD 1:5f, inasmuch as its biblical origin is assured but its precise exegetical significance is not clear; we must be satisfied with noting that טוב הצואר connects to a wider framework of use of Hos in the Admonition.

from Hos 4:16, in the Admonition. We have already commented on the fact that the significance of the utilization of this biblical verse may lie, not so much in its suitability to the specific points being argued in CD 1:13ff, but in its relation to other points of contact between Hos and CD 1-8 or 19-20.

The description of enemies continues with reference in CD 1:14 to the איש הלצון, an epithet probably derived from Is 28:14. His followers are accused of removing the גבול (CD 1:16), and it is difficult not to conclude that Hos 5:10 may be in mind, especially since this verse is certainly used in CD 8:3/19:15. An allusion here is further corroborated by the presence of צו in both Hos 5:11 (see CD 4:19) and Is 28:10,13.[26] If these points are sound, the names and descriptions of the enemies of our writer were derived from a network of interrelated scriptural passages - passages on which he has also drawn more generally for other allusions and quotations.

The list of faults enumerated in CD 1:18 uses words that can only be from Is 30:10. This receives some confirmation by the fact that Is 30:1, beginning הוי בנים סוררים, evidences another interesting linguistic link with CD 1:1-2:1, this time with the negative language of 1:13. The picture painted of the opponents reaches its end in CD 1:20ff, where Is 24:5 is reflected, as seems likely given that Is 24:17 is quoted in CD 4:14f.

As can be seen, there are a considerable number of important allusions to the Prophets in CD 1:1-2:1. Clusters of texts from a specific prophetic book tend to reappear as influential: Is 30, Jer 25-27, Ez 7-11 and Hos 4-5, 10-11. Such passages often interconnect in relation to their influence in other parts of CD. Moreover, the prophetic contexts to which we have referred have to do with the exile in some way - the situation preceding it, the event itself, life away from the land, promise and fulfilment of restoration, or a mixture of these.

4.2.3 Ketuvim in CD 1:1-2:1

Let us now consider the relationship between this portion of CD and the Writings. Of obvious interest here are Dn 9 and Ezr 9, as well as Ps 94 and Ps 106.

---

26   Note also that some ancient versions appear to have read לשם צאה for לשמצה at Ex 32:25. In view of the reference to צאה in Is 28:8, as well as to צו in Is 28:10,13, it is tempting, if speculative, to imagine that these scriptural passages were linked in the mind of our writer. See below, p. 125, note 57.

Dn 9 appears to evince more than superficial connections to CD 1:1-2:1. In view of CD 1:3, במועלם אשר עזבוהו, the last phrase in Dn 9:7 is especially noteworthy:

הארצות אשר הדחתם שם במעלם אשר מעלו בך: ...

More generally, Dn 9 pictures Daniel confessing both his own and his people's sin, asking God to lay aside his anger and restore the people and Jerusalem. The angel Gabriel appears and explains the meaning of the "70 years" of Jer 25:11,12 and 29:10. The significance of the interpretation of this period of time in Dn 9:24-27 is fairly straightforward, although the import of the "seventy weeks" for the writer of CD is another matter.[27]   In any case, given our interest in the framework of biblical associations beneath CD 1:1-2:1, we can now see that it may well include Dn 9, especially if other phrases from that scriptural context inform the language of the Admonition elsewhere.[28]

Ezr 9 has an overall similarity of form and content to Dn 9 in that both involve confession and supplication, and recount a basic story-line about the exile. There are also a few items of common vocabulary.[29]   More especially, the שארית language of Ezr 9:8 reminds us of CD 1:4 and, in the form of Ezr 9:14, לאין שארית ופליטה, this biblical chapter reappears as influential at CD 2:6. Talk of 'inheriting the land' in CD 1:7ff is reminiscent of Ezr 9:12, as well as Ps 37:29 (in which it is a refrain in vv 9,11,22,29,34). The fact that Cave 4 revealed a Pesher on Ps 37, interpreting the צדיקים and רשעים of the biblical text as the sectaries and their opponents, suggests that we are justified in seeing a possible allusion here in the Admonition.[30] Moreover, Ps 94 is of a similar type and was certainly drawn upon by our author.

In fact, the words of Ps 94:21 in CD 1:20 indicate that this scriptural verse lies behind CD at this point, as is confirmed by the unmistakable reflection of Ps 94:6 at CD 6:17 and by the possible utilization of 94:2 in CD 7:9. We may suppose that, because this scriptural text (like Ps 37 in 4QpPs37) is expressed in general terms about the righteous and the wicked, it was applied to the group behind our document and their opponents.

---

[27]   One way of explaining CD's understanding is to combine figures in the document (1:5, "390 years"; 1:10, "20 years"; 20:15 "40 years") and add an extra 40 years for the life of the מורה, giving a total of 490 years, i.e., 7x70 years.

[28]   Cf. CD 7:6/19:1 and Dn 9:4, שמר הברית והחסד לאהביו ולשמרי מצותיו; for CD 1:17, see Dn 9:11, האלה והשבעה. On the other hand, some caution regarding a young work like Dn may be in order, as was suggested in chapter 2.

[29]   Thus, Dn 9:6 and Ezr 9:11 have עבדיך הנביאים; Dn 9:21 and Ezr 9:4 read מנחת ערב and מנחת הערב, respectively.

[30]   For a short overview of 4QpPs 37, see Schürer, III.1, pp. 438-439.

There is another class of Ps also reflected in CD 1:1-2:1, which recounts God's great deeds throughout history, with elements such as Israel's rebellion despite God's goodness, confession of such sin by the psalmist, prayer for help, and reference to major events in Israelite history (Moses' dealings with Pharaoh, for instance, the 40 years desert wanderings, or the entry into the land). Ps 106 is of this type and tells of the ups and downs of Israel's past. There are a number of connections with CD 1:1-2:1, as well as with other portions of the document.[31] In particular, CD 1:21, ויחר אף אל בעדתם, can be construed as a combination of Ps 106:18, ותבער אש בעדתם, and 106:40, ויחר אף ה' בעמו. Also, it is important to note that CD 1:4's reference to God's remembrance of the covenant recalls Ps 106:45, ויזכר להם בריתו, along with a number of other biblical contexts

Finally, it will be observed that a reference to another Ps of this kind, Ps 107:40, has been included in our highlighted arrangement of CD 1:1-2:1, because words from this biblical verse appear verbatim in CD 1:15. However, their employment by our author does not connect to any other use of Ps 107 in the Admonition. Although it is tempting to hypothesize that it signifies another deliberate allusion to one of the historical Pss, without further evidence, therefore, it must be deemed to be a case of linguistic imitation.

In conclusion, it can be seen that the passages from the Writings which appear to have had a bearing on CD 1:1-2:1 share characteristics with the pentateuchal or prophetic contexts considered above. In other words, they concentrate on a certain type of more or less extensive historical cycle, and, as far as the Ketuvim are concerned, this includes Ps 106, describing a large chunk of Israelite history, and Ezr 9, centring on the exile.

4.2.4 Summary

Our purpose has been to show that a large percentage of the vocabulary in CD 1:1-2:1 is paralleled by the same or similar in parts of scripture. Even with the exclusion of numerous unlikely or unclear instances which have not been discussed and allowing for some misjudgement on our part in individual cases, language from the bible certainly suffuses this portion of the document.

---

31   Ps 106:6f contains a confession similar to those in numerous other biblical texts (e.g., Dn 9 and Ezr 9), as also to CD 3:12ff and 20:28ff; further, Ps 106:25 is reflected in CD 3:8. On a wider front, see G.J. Brooke, 'Psalms 105 and 106 at Qumran', *RQ* 14 (1989), pp. 267-292.

The Torah is reflected in phraseology from Ex 32/Dt 9, Lv 26, and Nu 14, as well as Lv 26 and Dt 28-32. We have noted that the use of these contexts is connected to dependence on them in other sections of CD 1-8 and 19-20. For example, Dt 9 retells the incident of the golden calf (narrated in Ex 32) and is influential in CD 8:14f. Of further interest is a pattern of events that comes across from these passages of the Pentateuch; to an extent, CD 1:1-2:1 appears to be modelled on such a story-line, involving rebellion, punishment and the restoration of a faithful remnant. Turning to the Prophets, we find a somewhat more complicated picture. Nonetheless, certain passages stand out. We noted that Hos 4:16, quoted in CD 1:13, is only one element in a number of allusions to Hos in CD 1:1-2:1 and elsewhere. There were also numerous other contexts, either individual chapters or clusters of chapters, that were prominent: Is 30, Is 59, Jer 25-27, Ez 3-5, and Ez 7-11. Each of these provides a number of allusions or quotations in CD, whether in 1:1-2:1, elsewhere in the document, or in both. As for the Writings, Ps 106, Dn 9, and Ezr 9 proved significant, paralleling in a number of ways what was found in relation to the Torah and Nevi'im. Of especial note was CD 1:3, במועלם אשר עזבוהו, informed apparently by biblical phraseology from three separate contexts (i.e., Lv 26, Ez 20, Dn 9). Similarly, we saw that Ex 32/Dt 9 and Is 30, as well as the obvious Hos 4:16, lie behind the סרר/סור language in CD 1:13f.

These observations confirm our reluctance to exclude as secondary certain words or phrases in CD 1:1-2:1. Thus, while we have deliberately not engaged in detailed exegesis nor in attempts to identify the precise historical or theological referents in this portion of the Admonition, reference to the מורה צדק in 1:11 connects to a framework of scriptural allusions in this and other portions of CD, as does the brief interpretative citation of Hos 4:16 in 1:13f. Such data lead us to different conclusions than those of some scholars.[32] Indeed, it may be conjectured that considerable care went into forming the narrative of CD 1:1-2:1, whatever is to be made of the historical problems outlined above.[33] Further analysis of the rest of CD 1-8 (2:2-13, 2:14-4:12a, 4:12b-5:15a, 5:15b-6:11a, 6:11b-8:19) and 19-20 is now required in order to determine whether the same applies to the remainder of the Admonition. Hence, consideration will now be given to the second and

---

[32]   As remarked earlier, Davies, p. 200, suggests that מורה צדק is not original; Boyce, pp. 35-41, argues that 1:12b-14a is additional like all midrashic portions of the Admonition. Others routinely suggest וממקדשו and "390 years" (in CD 1:3 and 1:5f, respectively) are secondary glosses.

[33]   See above, pp. 53-55.

third historical sections (2:14-4:12a and 5:15b-6:11a) and, in the next chapter, we shall analyse what may be called CD's intervening midrashic portions - those parts engaged in more overt citation and interpretation of biblical passages.

4.3 Scripture in CD 2:14-4:12a

This is the most extensive of the historical sections in the Admonition. Its greater length is due to the fact that, while CD 1:1-2:1 opens its narrative immediately prior to the exile, 2:14-4:12a runs through the history of the world and of Israel from the Watchers onwards in 2:18ff, although the description of the period in the land after the conquest is rather curtailed (CD 3:9ff). For the most part, CD 2:14-3:12a is straightforward, in that the persons and events referred to are easily identified. However, the transition in 3:12ff from the account of the wider history of Israel to that of the sect is more problematic, and it is further complicated by the need to restore parts of the text which have dropped out or suffered corruption as evidenced in the Cairo Genizah MSS.

In CD 2:14ff we come across the third and final formula in the Admonition, similar to the formulae in 1:1f and 2:2f. This means that the scholar has to tackle the large block of material from 2:14 to 8:21 and decide how to relate it to the words in 2:14-16. However this is to be done, it is in any case reasonable to attempt to handle CD 2:14-4:12a in terms of its present inner shape and consistency as one of the historical sections in the final form of the Admonition. Within 2:14-4:12a we find that 3:12a/12b constitutes a break, since it marks a change in emphasis; the writer moves to a positive description of the מחזיקים במצות אל as a climax, in contrast to that narrated in 2:14-3:12a, which is overwhelmingly negative. This and the division at 4:12a/12b need only be deemed to initiate new paragraphs, as it were, inasmuch as these points function as markers in a similar way to, if less precisely than, the formulae in 1:1f, 2:2f, and 2:14ff.

In fact, the words of 2:14ff are more like those in 1:1f than 2:2ff, since the declared aim in the present passage and in 1:1 is to grant understanding of the מעשי אל and the lessons to be learned therefrom. Yet, whereas in 1:1f that of which the readers are informed is chiefly the present ריב between God and כל בשר, with the sect as the only means of deliverance from it, the description here is broader, although related in its desired effect upon the reader. In other words, both sections seek to shed light on the contemporary situation but 2:14ff has a long preamble on the ancients. Thus, by knowing what went wrong with previous generations, as far back as the Watchers, as well as why and to what effect, the reader can choose aright so as to avoid the same fate. The form of such a choice, with its concomitant mode of behaviour, is not yet intimated in detail, though a hint is given in 3:2-4a in the the brief, almost parenthetical, mention of Abraham, Isaac and Jacob.[34]

The descriptions that follow the introductory rubrics, especially the rebellion and punishment in 2:16-3:12a, whilst involving God's actions, are more specifically concerned with the errors of men. Divine anger follows secondarily from such offences, so that God is only referred to in his reaction to wickedness (as in 2:21), or as the presumed cause of the misfortune which overtakes those responsible for evil (2:17). Indeed, it is noteworthy that this negative historical survey reaches its climax in the exile of the sixth century BCE. Immediately after this, it would seem from 3:12ff, comes God's rescue of, and revelation to, the (potentially or actually?) righteous. The divine initiative continues as the focus of attention in 3:14ff, where God's establishment of a faithful group of followers and his revelation to them of the נסתרות אשר תעו בם כל ישראל is recounted as something of a contrast to the description of a history of sin and its consequences in 2:16ff. In point of fact, the community's reception of the נסתרות is what constitutes our author's primary message, for which he has already laid the foundations in 2:14-3:12a, heightening the importance of such revelatory activity by God in the community. This confirms our delineation of the text, as well as our assertion that the introductory formula in 2:14ff is intended to cover at least the whole of 2:14-4:12a.

Returning to 2:14-3:12a, the fact that the author is dealing with events that lead up to the exile makes the interpreter's task relatively easy, because, in contrast to 1:1-2:1, the problem of ambiguity is less pressing. The contemporary situation is being addressed but not, it appears, recent events. The main point, summed up in 3:10b-12a, is that sin incurs guilt, which leads to divine wrath and a forfeiting of the covenant's blessing, even of the covenant itself. The writer hammers home his point by repeating certain

---

34   We discover more on this aspect in CD 4:12b-5:15a (criticizing outsiders for behaviour contrary to the laws of the sect) and in CD 6:11b-7:8 (describing some of the obligations on the sectaries). But even in these portions of the Admonition, it is to be suspected that much of the language about good or bad behaviour is formal, even clichéd. Certainly, biblical phraseology is frequently employed, as we shall have occasion to notice in the next chapter.

words and phrases.[35] He is then able to offer some hope by describing the community which remained (or became?) faithful and is now embodied in his own group. Nevertheless, even this option has its negative side, for, unless a person is already a member or inclined to join, he is inevitably lost. In 3:12ff, God's activity as it concerns the sect and its creation is detailed; they were those who "held fast" to his Law. When the מעשי אל are acknowledged - not just God's vengeance on those who forsake him but also, as we now learn, his establishing the community - a person is in a position to be able to choose את אשר רצה and to reject כאשר שנא and to walk תמים בכל דרכיו (2:14-16a). Our author narrates the formation of the group with whom God created, or re-created, the covenant, after the destruction of which earlier generations' faithlessness was the cause. With them God decided to deal afresh, and with their successors, it is implied, he still deals.

The reason, the general circumstances and the results of the formation of this community are described in 3:12b-20b. This is followed by a telescoped quotation from Ez 44:15 in 3:20c-4:2a, interpreted in terms of the make-up of that group in 4:2b-4a. Next comes the announcement in 4:4b-6a of a list of various details about the people involved; unfortunately, the list seems to have dropped out of the Admonition as we now have it. After another textual problem in 4:6b, the reader is assured of the continuing validity of the promises made to earlier members, culminating in a warning in 4:10b-12a that the approaching consummation of the age will spell the end of any opportunity to belong to the party of God's favour.

In view of this brief survey of the contents of CD 2:14-3:12a and 3:12b-4:12a, it does indeed seem sensible to keep both together for description and evaluation. Despite the obvious change of emphasis in 3:12ff, what follows is still intended to be a continuation of the same story. Since, in order to see, understand, and choose appropriately, a person has to be informed about the sect, as well as the rebellion against which it was formed, it is also best to take the introductory formula in 2:14ff as extending right up to 4:12a. Whilst "And in all these years" in 4:12b is obviously connected to what precedes it,

---

[35]   Such motifs in the narrative are pointed out by Davies, pp. 79-80:
  1. keeping the commandments of God;
  2. not walking in stubbornness of heart;
  3. not following one's own desires;
  4. the anger of God being aroused;
  5. the succession of rebellion through children ending every episode.

the new context there is not concerned so much with the מעשי אל as with what might be called the מעשי בליעל, at least up to 5:15a.[36]

If what has been stated so far is correct, this section of CD places the sect's formation directly, or fairly soon, after the Babylonian devastation. There is no other way of taking the words אשר נותרו מהם, placed after the clear-cut reference to the latter event in 3:10ff. Also to be noted is the absence of the מורה צדק in the narrative, although even CD 1:11 places his appearance some interval of time after the founding of both the שארית and the שורש מטעת. If 4:2ff refers to three consecutive groupings of successors within the community since its beginning, then the שבי ישראל are the founders of the sect. However, it is difficult to deduce much more than this, since, as we have seen, scholars variously take the latter phrase, in association with דמשק and היוצאים מארץ יהודה, as denoting either "repentants of Israel" who left Jerusalem and the temple in the second century BCE in order to take up a monastic-like residence at Qumran, or as designating exiles of the sixth century BCE, the "returnees of Israel" or "captivity of Israel", with whom God re-established the covenant. Nevertheless, if the exilic origins attributed to the community in this and other parts of the Admonition are a fair representation of what the text claims, then an exilic connotation for the epithet שבי ישראל is to be preferred. This is especially so given that, after the exile and formation of the community, there is no mention of any positive or negative dealings between God and Israel in 3:12b-4:12b, apart from the brief reference to the contemporaries in the sect hinted at in 4:2ff.

Before continuing, it is appropriate to include the Hebrew of CD 2:14-4:12a as follows:

ועתה בנים שמעו לי ואגלה עיניכם לראות ולהבין במעשי

15   אל ולבחור את אשר רצה ולמאוס כאשר שנא להתהלך תמים

בכל דרכיו ולא לתור במחשבות יצר אשמה ועני זנות כי רבים

תעו בם וגבורי חיל נכשלו בם מלפנים ועד הנה בלכתם בשרירות

לבם נפלו עידי השמים בה נאחזו אשר לא שמרו מצות אל

ובניהם אשר כרום ארזים גבהם וכהרים גויותיהם כי נפלו

20   כל בשר אשר היה בחרבה כי גוע ויהיו כלא היו בעשותם את

רצונם ולא שמרו את מצות עשיהם עד אשר חרה אפו בם

---

[36]   However, attempting to set a limit to the material covered by the appeal for attention in 2:14ff is somewhat artificial when the text of CD 1-8 is viewed as a whole, for, as a general call to attention, these lines would allow a wide variety of literary types to be placed after them. Thus, 2:14ff extends over the rest of the Admonition, although, after two or three columns, the hearer or reader will normally have forgotten about these specific rubrics.

בה תעי בני נח ומשפחותיהם בה הם נכרתים 1
אברהם לא הלך בה ויעל אוהב בשמרו מצות אל ולא בחר
ברצון רוחו וימסור ליישחק וליעקב וישמרו ויכתבו אוהבים
לאל ובעלי ברית לעולם   בני יעקב תעו בם ויענשו לפני
משגותם ובניהם במצרים הלכו בשרירות לבם להיעץ על 5
מצות אל ולעשות איש הישר בעיניו ויאכלו את הדם ויכרת
זכורם במדבר להם בקדש עלו ורשו את רוחם ולא שמעו
לקול עשיהם מצות יוריהם וירגנו באהליהם ויחר אף אל
בעדתם ובניהם בו אבדו ומלכיהם בו נכרתו וגיבוריהם בו
אבדו וארצם בו שממה בו הבו באי הברית הראשנים ויסגרו 10
לחרם בעזבם את ברית אל ויבחרו ברצונם ויתורו אחרי שרירות
לבם לעשות איש את רצונו   ובמחזיקים במצות אל
אשר נותרו מהם הקים אל את בריתו לישראל עד עולם לגלות
להם נסתרות אשר תעו בם כל ישראל   שבתות קדשו ומועדי
כבודו עידות צדקו ודרכי אמתו וחפצי רצונו אשר יעשה 15
האדם וחיה בהם   פתח לפניהם ויחפרו באר למים רבים
ומואסיהם לא יחיה והם התגוללו בפשע אנוש ובדרכי נדה
ויאמרו כי לנו היא ואל ברזי פלאו כפר בעד עונם וישא לפשעם
ויבן להם בית נאמן בישראל אשר לא עמד כמהו למלפנים ועד
הנה המחזיקים בו לחיי נצח וכל כבוד אדם להם הוא כאשר 20
הקים אל להם ביד יחזקאל הנביא לאמר הכהנים והלוים ובני
צדוק אשר שמרו את משמרת מקדשי בתעות בני ישראל 1
מעליהם יגישו לי חלב ודם   הכהנים הם שבי ישראל
היוצאים מארץ יהודה והנלוים עמהם   ובני צדוק הם בחירי
ישראל קריאי השם העמדים באחרית הימים הנה פרוש
שמותיהם לתולדותם וקק מעמדם ומספר צרותיהם ושני 5
התגוררם ופירוש מעשיהם   הקודש שונים אשר כפר
אל בעדם ויצדיקו צדיק וירשיעו רשע וכל הבאים אחריהם
לעשות כפרוש התורה אשר התוסרו בו הראשנים עד שלים
הקק השנים האלה כברית אשר הקים אל לראשנים לכפר
על עונותיהם כן יכפר אל בעדם ובשלום הקק למספר השנים 10
האלה אין עוד להשתפח לבית יהודה כי אם לעמוד איש על
מצודו נבנתה הגדר רחק החיק

There are several problems with the text that deserve our attention.[37] Although the word appears as עידי, it is clear that עירי is intended in 2:18. More generally, there is a frequent ambiguity between *yod* and *waw* throughout this historical section. This applies, for example, to the

---

37   Note that CD 4:8 does not contain the reading הראשונים, as in Broshi, p. 17, but הראשנים.

alternation of שלים and שלום in 4:8,10, although the meaning is clear, while
החיק in 4:12 is obviously intended to represent החוק. Turning to 3:4, לפני
must surely be a mistake for לפי, and הבו in 3:10 probably signifies חבו.
More important are the elements that appear to be missing from CD 3:7, 4:3
and 4:6. However, scholars are almost universally agreed as to the correct
restorations at these points, and these will be mentioned individually below as
we analyse the text.

Of greater significance still is the difficulty of relating the overall story
contained in 2:14-4:12a, but particularly in 3:10-21, to that in the first
historical section of CD. On its own, CD 2:14-4:12a is easier to follow than
1:1-2:1, notwithstanding the vagueness of the referents in 3:16ff and their
relation to those in 4:2ff. The story-line would appear to present the
formation of the repentant מחזיקים into a specific group at some point in time
after the exile. There is no reason to think this took place a long time
thereafter, as is the case for the שורש מטעת in CD 1:5ff, which was founded
some 390 years after Nebuchadnezzar's devastation of Jerusalem. Thus, it is
only when CD 1:1-2:1 and 2:14-4:12a are placed in the same document that
the main difficulty arises. As a result, it is not necessary for us to work our
way through the detail of the story of this second historical section.

However, a new perspective is gained by viewing the use of scripture in
CD 2:14-4:12a, as was also the case for CD 1:1-2:1. Once more, the text
would appear to be carefully planned, and the overlap between the first two
historical sections is so substantial in this regard that the value of appealing to
sources or previous redactions of the Admonition is to be seriously
questioned. The text is set out below (pp. 75-76), therefore, with the bible
references highlighted, and we shall now proceed to examine this layout in
greater detail.

4.3.1 Torah in CD 2:14-4:12a

It is immediately noticeable that a good number of texts referred to in
connection with CD 1:1-2:1 reappear here. On the other hand, due to the
wider limits of the story in CD 2:14-4:12a, the influence of some hitherto
unmentioned scriptural contexts is perceptible. As well as this unmistakable
biblical borrowing, however, some apparent scriptural usage is less certainly
present in this section.[38]

---

38   Instances of little or unclear force in this regard may be listed as follows and
      otherwise left to one side:

Of certain interest are our author's introductory words in 2:14-16, concluding with an exhortation not to "go after the thoughts of the guilty inclination". These words are reminiscent of Nu 15:39, commanding the wearing of tassels:

והיה לכם לציצת וראיתם אתו וזכרתם את כל מצות ה' ועשיתם אתם ולא תתרו אחרי
לבבכם ואחרי עיניכם אשר אתם זנים אחריהם:

Indeed, both תור and זנות/זנה are present in Nu 15:39 and CD 2:14f alike. A connection between this verse and CD 2:16 is confirmed, moreover, by the fact that Nu 13ff and Nu 16 are important biblical contexts drawn upon elsewhere in our document. The former was considered in association with CD 1:1-2:1, inasmuch as Nu 14:23 informs the language of CD 1:2, בכל מנאציו. Nu 16 goes on to recount the rebellion of Korah, Dathan and Abiram, as well as God's resultant anger, which is calmed only by the pleas of Moses and Aaron (vv 21ff, 45ff). The importance of these two pentateuchal rebellions may explain how the idiom from Nu 15, a legal section in between these two blocks of text, could be on the mind of our author and reflected here.

CD 2:17-3:5 concerns persons and events in prehistoric times and in the life of ancient Israel. There are two occurrences of שרירות with לב in these lines (see CD 2:17; 3:5), as well as a third in 3:11. Use of this expression almost certainly relates to Dt 29:18, והתברך בלבבו לאמר שלום יהיה לי כי בשררות לבי אלך, which describes the Israelite tempted to break his side of the covenant. Indeed, as we have remarked before, the whole of Dt 28-30 is important for CD 1:1-2:1 and will be seen to be equally so vis à vis those

---

For להתהלך תמים (CD 2:15), see Gn 17:1, התהלך...והוה תמים, introducing a context recounting the establishment of the covenant between God and Abraham, marked by circumcision. In view of the mention of Abraham's exemplary character in CD 3:2f, as well as the recurrence of הקים and ברית in both the biblical narrative and CD 3:13, it is with some reluctance that Gn 17:1 was not included in the highlighted text set out above;

כל דרכיו (CD 2:16) might be taken to reflect Dt 10:12, ללכת בכל דרכיו, concerning Israel's required response to the covenant. Although the immediately predecing block of material, Dt 9:1-10:11, shows its influence elsewhere in CD (in CD 3:7 with regard to Dt 9:23, and in CD 8:14 with a citation from Dt 9:5), lack of firm corroboration means this reference must be left to one side;

Finally, given that the יצדיקו צדיק phraseology of CD 4:7 is reminiscent of that in CD 1:19, where it was employed negatively of the enemies of the sect, we may note the similarity of the language in Dt 25:1. However, we have no other evidence to show that this was a particularly significant context for our author.

portions of CD to be dealt with in the next chapter.[39]   The wording in CD
3:20, כל בשר...בחרבה...גוע, appears to be a mixture of vocabulary present in
Gn 6:17 and 7:22. On balance, this probably constitutes an allusion, the point
of contact with CD lying in the fact that Gn 6-7 deals with part of a
momentous pentateuchal episode of rebellion, namely, the Flood.   The בני נח
ומשפחותיהם, mentioned in CD 3:1, are also referred to in Gn 10:32, אלה
משפחת בני נח, and we may hypothesize that this context also lies behind the
language chosen by our author in that it contains the tower of Babel
narrative, yet another rebellious story chronicled within the Torah.   In
addition, specific incidents are probably in view when our writer states תעו
בני נח and בני יעקב תעו בם in CD 3:1 and 3:4, respectively, but our
document's silence leaves us ignorant of what precisely they may have been.[40]

     The descendants of Jacob in Egypt are criticized in CD 3:6. לעשות איש
הישר בעיניו and ויאכלו את הדם are similar to Lv 17:10 and 19:26 and to Dt
12:8, 12:16, and 12:23ff. The passages from Lv concern the eating of blood
and its relevant punishment; Dt 12 outlines the importance of having one
sanctuary in the land (i.e., in Jerusalem) and of the necessity of refraining
from eating blood once resident in Canaan (vv 16, 23ff).   Only upon
compliance with these two requirements will it go well with Israel in the land,
so that a man should not, therefore, do כל הישר בעיניו (v 8). We may note
also that Lv 17 marks the beginning of what modern scholars term the
Holiness Code, which is influential in the language employed in parts of CD
6:11b-8:21. Similarly, Dt 12 follows on immediately from the curses and
blessings described in Dt 11, a context which bears a striking resemblance to
Dt 28ff, on the importance of which we have just remarked.[41]

---

[39]   With the specific phraseology in CD 2:17; 3:5; 3:11, cf. 1QS 1:13,14, which is also
clearly based on Dt 29:18.

[40]   See, e.g., Gn 9:20ff; 11:1ff; and Gn 34:22; 37; 38:12; 49:5. Especially interesting
are the expansions of these stories in Jub, where the morally or cultically
questionable aspects of the activity of the sons of Jacob are toned down.

[41]   The Holiness Code is important in CD, both for 1:1-2:1, as manifest in the influence
of Lv 26, and elsewhere. Whilst it would hardly have been viewed in the Second
Temple period as a once independent legal source, as if from a modern critical
viewpoint, it will have been seen to constitute a discrete unit within the text of Lv.
Regarding Dt 11-12 and 26ff, both contexts have overlapping material, especially
curses and blessings, so that we may well envisage that one context would have
easily connoted the other for any Second Temple writer meditating on the
scriptures.

	Hebrew text	References
	ועתה בנים שמעו לי ואגלה עיניכם לראות ולהבין במעשי	*Is 51:1,7*
15	אל ולבחור את אשר רצה ולמאוס כאשר שנא להתהלך תמים	Nu 15:39 *Ez 6:9*
	בכל דרכיו ולא לתור במחשבות יצר אשמה ועיני זנות כי רבים תעו בם	Dt 29:18 *Jer 23:17* **Ps 81:13**
	וגבורי חיל נכשלו בם מלפנים ועד הנה בלכתם בשרירות לבם נפלו	*Am 2:9*
20	עירי השמים בה נפלו בה נאחזו מלאכי השמים כי הלכו בשרירות	Gn 6:17 7:22
	לבם ולא שמרו את מצות אל בניהם אשר נפלו בה	
1	בהם בניהם אשר כרום ארזים גבהם וכהרים גויתיהם כי נפלו	Gn 10:32
	כל בשר אשר היה בחרבה כי גוע ויהיו כלא היו בעשותם את	*Is 41:8* **2 Chr 20:7**
	רצונם ולא שמרו את מצות עשיהם עד אשר חרה אפו בם	
5	בניהם תעו בה בחירי ישראל ויחזיקו במעשיהם ויכלו	Dt 29:18 *Jer 23:17 Ez 20:5* **Ps 81:13**
	ואחזו בם בדעת את בני יעקב אבותינו ויתהלכו בה ויכרתו	Dt 12:8 Lv 17:10 Dt 12:23 *Ez 33:25*
	ברית אל לאבותם להודיעם בדעת עליון ויכרתו	Dt 9:23 **Ps 106:25**
	אל עם ישראל וישם להם בלבבם ויעשו ויבנו להם בית נאמן	**Ps 106:25** Ps 106:18,40
10	בישראל כמהו מלפנים עד הנה כי הם קדש לישראל מעל	Lv 26:33 *Ez 33:25,28* **Ps 78:62 2 Chr 36:21**
	וילכו אחרי שרירות לבם להתהלך איש ברצון נפשו	Nu 15:39 Dt 29:18 *Jer 23:17* **Ps 81:13**
	ויתגוללו בחטאת אדם ובדרכי נדה ויאמרו כי לנו היא	*Is 56:4*
	ואל בדעת לבם בסתרות הנסתרות אשר תעו בם לישראל	Dt 29:28 **Neh 9:14**

Quotation and Allusion in CD 2:14-3:14

Lv 18:5 Ez 20:11,13,21 **Neh 9:29**	
Ez 11:15	
1 Sa 2:35	
Dn 12:2	
Ez 44:15	
Is 59:20	
Nu 18:2 Is 56:6	
Nu 16:2	
Hab 2:1	
Mic 7:10	

15

20

1

5

10

Quotation and Allusion in CD 3:15-4:12a

It is necessary to restore the text in CD 3:7 in order to make sense of it.
Most scholars agree on a reading along the following lines:[42]

ויאמר להם בקדש עלו ורשו את הארץ ויבחרו ברצון רוחם ולא שמעו...

The relevant biblical story is recounted in Nu 13f, and is summarily referred
to in Dt 9:22-24, which states:

ובתבערה ובמסה ובקברת התאוה מקצפים הייתם את ה': 23ובשלח ה' אתכם מקדש
ברנע לאמר עלו ורשו את הארץ אשר נתתי לכם ותמרו את פי ה' אלהיכם ולא האמנתם
לו ולא שמעתם בקלו: 24ממרים הייתם עם ה' מיום דעתו אתכם:

After Moses' review of the golden calf incident, these verses discuss what
happened at Kadesh-barnea, before returning to the former topic in verse
25ff. In view of this passage, on which we commented in association with Ex
32 in our analysis of CD 1:1-2:1, it is reasonable to restore the text of CD 3:7
as above.[43] We see again the use of scriptural contexts that are becoming
increasingly familiar, especially Dt 9. Clearly, the whole of Nu 13-14 is also
important for CD 3:7ff. Indeed, there is a cluster of events and texts which
appear to be interconnected, even if in a somewhat jumbled fashion, in both
the first and second historical sections: Ex 32, Nu 13f, and Dt 9.

CD 3:10,11 refers to the desolation of the land and going after a שרירות
לב; see again Lv 26:32f, Nu 15:39 and Dt 29:18. The latter we have already
referred to above in connection with CD 2:17. Nu 15:39 contains the verb
תור, already familiar from CD 2:16, while Lv 26:32f, ...והשמתי את הארץ,
והיתה שממה, appears in the generally relevant context of Lv 26, which we
highlighted in association with CD 1:1-2:1 and which will reappear before we
have completed our study of the Admonition

In CD 3:14, we return to another common scriptural context. Dt 29:28
mentions the נסתרת, to which only God is privy, over against the נגלת, which
he revealed to Israel. Although this is not the case in CD, in which God is
reckoned to have revealed the נסתרות to his chosen remnant, the identical
term is almost certainly connected to Dt 29.[44] It is worth recounting the
story in Dt 29:21-28 at this point:

ואמר הדור האחרון בניכם אשר יקומו מאחריכם והנכרי אשר יבא מארץ רחוקה וראו
את מכות הארץ ההוא ואת תחלאיה אשר חלה ה' בה: 22גפרית ומלח שרפה כל ארצה
לא תזרע ולא תצמח ולא יעלה בה כל עשב כמהפכת סדם ועמרה אדמה וצביים אשר
הפך ה' באפו ובחמתו: 23ואמרו כל הגוים על מה עשה ה' ככה לארץ הזאת מה חרי

---

[42] Vermes, p. 160, postulates use of the root דבר, not אמר, since the confused state of
the text can then be explained through haplography; Boyce, p. 87, argues likewise.

[43] The restoration of ויבחרו ברצון seems safe in that it is the sort of language CD
utilizes elsewhere; see, e.g., CD 3:4f, ולא בחר ברצון רוחו.

[44] It is worth recollecting that we referred to הדור האחרון (Dt 29:21) in association
with CD 1:1-2:1 (CD 1:12, דור אחרון).

האף הגדול הזה: 24ואמרו על אשר עזבו את ברית ה׳ אלהי אבתם אשר כרת עמם
בהוציאו אתם מארץ מצרים: 25וילכו ויעבדו אלהים אחרים וישתחוו להם אלהים אשר
לא ידעום ולא חלק להם: 26ויחר אף ה׳ בארץ ההוא להביא עליה את כל הקללה
הכתובה בספר הזה: 27ויתשם ה׳ מעל אדמתם באף ובחמה ובקצף גדול וישלכם אל
ארץ אחרת כיום הזה: 28הנסתרת לה׳ אלהינו והנגלת לנו ולבנינו עד עולם לעשות את
כל דברי התורה הזאת:

Dt 29 overall is a warning from Moses that the people should stay faithful to
the covenant. Otherwise, all the curses of 'the book' will befall them, with
resultant deportation. There then follows the expression in verse 28
regarding the נסתרת and נגלת. After this, in 30:1-7, we read:

והיה כי יבאו עליך כל הדברים האלה הברכה והקללה אשר נתתי לפניך והשבת אל
לבבך בכל הגוים אשר הדיחך ה׳ אלהיך שמה: 2ושבת עד ה׳ אלהיך ושמעת בקלו ככל
אשר אנכי מצוך היום אתה ובניך בכל לבבך ובכל נפשך: 3ושב ה׳ אלהיך את שבותך
ורחמך ושב וקבצך מכל העמים אשר הפיצך ה׳ אלהיך שמה: 4אם יהיה נדחך בקצה
השמים משם יקבצך ה׳ אלהיך ומשם יקחך: 5והביאך ה׳ אלהיך אל הארץ אשר ירשו
אבתיך וירשתה והיטבך והרבך מאבתיך: 6ומל ה׳ אלהיך את לבבך ואת לבב זרעך
לאהבה את ה׳ אלהיך בכל לבבך ובכל נפשך למען חייך: 7ונתן ה׳ אלהיך את כל
האלות האלה על איביך ועל שנאיך אשר רדפוך:

There appears to be a connection between the pattern here in Dt, with 29:28
at its centre-point, and that in CD 3:10-3:21ff. This is evident in various
common items of vocabulary and in a general parity of story-line. To the
latter phenomenon we shall return presently.

CD 3:15, אשר יעשה האדם וחיה בהם, is found almost verbatim in Lv 18:5.
This is a case where it is difficult to define our document's use of scripture,
for our author's utilization of the biblical phrase seems too strong to be
deemed mere allusion, although the lack of any formula precludes it as a
quotation.[45] In any case, the scriptural text reads:

ושמרתם את חקתי ואת משפטי אשר יעשה אתם האדם וחי בהם אני ה׳:

This follows on from laws regarding blood-eating (and the consumption of
טרפה) in Lv 17, and forms part of a general exhortation to obey the
commands in 18:1-5. Lv 18:6ff contains laws against incest. Even here,
therefore, we can detect inter-scriptural connections perceived by our author
as significant, since both blood-eating and זנות/ערוה were important issues, at
least formally, for him.[46]

Finally, turning to CD 4:3 with its pun on the root לוה, we may postulate a
probable connection with Nu 18:2, מטה לוי...וילוו עליך. This was included in

---

[45]   Again, the equivalent in modern terms would be to place the words in inverted
        commas, although it should be noted that the phrase also echoes Ez 20:11,13,21 and
        Neh 9:29.

[46]   For accusations of זנות and ערוה (עריות) levelled against opponents, see CD 4:20-
        5:11.

the highlighted text above, since Nu 18 will reappear as influential later on. Similarly, קריאי השם in CD 4:4 may reflect Nu 16:2, נשיאי עדה קראי מועד אנשי שם, although those so designated in the biblical text are involved in rebellion (cf. the transformation of Am 5:27 in CD 7:14ff). Nonetheless, there are good reasons to think that this context too was in the author's mind, as we shall see in relation to CD 2:2-11.

4.3.2 Nevi'im in CD 2:14-4:12a

Turning now to the Prophets, it is difficult to judge the extent or nature of the influence of some biblical passages upon this section of CD.[47]   Apart from the repetition in CD 2:14 of a probable allusion to Is 51:1,7, already recorded in relation to CD 1:1, the first noticeable connection is between CD 2:16 and Ez 6:9. Ez 6:8-10 reads:

והותרתי בהיות לכם פליטי חרב בגוים בהזרותיכם בארצות: 9וזכרו פליטיכם אותי בגוים אשר נשבו שם אשר נשברתי את לבם הזונה אשר סר מעלי ואת עיניהם הזנות אחרי גלוליהם ונקטו בפניהם אל הרעות אשר עשו לכל תועבתיהם: 10וידעו כי אני ה׳ לא אל חנם דברתי לעשות להם הרעה הזאת:

This is part of a wider oracle contained in Ez 6:1-14 against the Mountains of Israel, emphasizing that punishment will come upon Israel for his idolatry, a fact which will only be fully recognized by the people when they are "among the nations". There are some general links of vocabulary in these verses with CD 2:14-4:12a which are obvious: זכר, חרב, זנה, פליטים.   In CD 2:16, however, עני זנות is used as part of a general warning to pay heed to the lessons to be learned from the broad sweep of Israelite history, as is about to be described. Similarly, the whole of CD 2:17-3:1 employs vocabulary from scripture, which often has a more specific meaning in its own biblical context but which our author uses more generally or transfers to another subject. An

---

47   The following do not help a great deal, providing merely a general linguistic background for our author, or else would constitute somewhat speculative connections:

והיו כלא היו (CD 2:20) is found in the same form in Ob 16;

Jos 24:14 and Ez 23:3 designate as sinful Israel's time in Egypt (cf. CD 3:5), although no other links with the Admonition are noticeable;

Ju 17:6; 21:35 contain איש הישר בעיניו phraseology (as in CD 3:6) but evince no other connections with CD 1-8 or 19-20;

Jos 5:4, הזכרים...במדבר, contains the story of the circumcision of Israelites in the wilderness and, at least in the most general way, may inform CD 3:7, זכורם במדבר;

Jer 32:23 uses language similar to CD 3:7 in criticism of Israel's sin.

instance of this can be seen in the adoption of words from Am 2:9 in CD
2:19. As we shall see when considering CD 6:11b-8:21 in the next chapter,
however, this virtual replication of words from the biblical verse does not
represent mere linguistic imitation on the part of our author but, inasmuch as
it seems to tie in with other dependence on Am in the Admonition, deliberate
allusion.

In CD 2:17 and 3:5 and 11, we find the שררות לב idiom which echoes a
number of passages from Jer, including Jer 7:24, 9:14, 11:8, 13:10, and
23:17. These refer to the stubbornness of the people, who refuse to follow
God yet think all is well; Jeremiah, unlike the false prophets who fill them
with "vain hopes" (23:16), warns them that they will be punished. We may
well imagine that this scenario could easily be taken as a cipher for the
situation of a later period, viewed through sectarian eyes. In any case, the
Admonition employs the motif as a designation of all sinners throughout all
periods of history up to the exile. Since it belongs to a chapter that lies
behind other portions of the Admonition, Jer 23:17 is of greatest interest
here:

אמרים אמור למנאצי דבר ה׳ שלום יהיה לכם וכל הלך בשררות לבו אמרו לא תבוא
עליכם רעה:

Now, it is plain that a verbal connection already exists between Dt 29:18 and
Jer 23:17 in that both contexts warn against a שררות לב. The writer of CD 1-
8 seems to have noted this himself, however, and cross-referenced it to other
inter-scriptural links of his own. Thus, see below on CD 5:20, ויתעו את
ישראל, and its similarity to Jer 23:13.

The language in CD 3:2 is informed by Is 41:8, describing Abraham as
"God's friend". This designation appears fairly straightforward, and the
biblical text reads:

ואתה ישראל עבדי יעקב אשר בחרתיך זרע אברהם אהבי:

Presumably, the writer of CD connects Abraham's designation אוהב with his
righteousness, with which he may equate, or in which he may include,
obedience to the Law, since the context in CD at this point concerns
behaviour according to God's commands.[48]

Ez 20 is the next passage of significance, both to CD 3:5 and 3:15. The
first portrays Israel's state of impiety in Egypt. This is reflected in Ez 20:5ff,
where it is said that God showed himself to the people while they were in

---

[48] Indeed, already in Jub we find the Patriarchs anachronistically obeying the demands
of the Torah.

Egypt, but they did not walk in his חקים.[49] CD 3:15 contains a virtual quotation of the refrain found in Ez 20:11,13,21 (אשר יעשה אותם האדם וחי בהם). In addition, it is worth noting again verse 27, which, in accusing "your fathers" (במעלם בי מעל), probably lies behind CD 1:3 (במועלם אשר עזבוהו). These individual correspondences between CD 3:5,15 and Ez 20 are strengthened when it is further realized that both also contain a similarly negative account of Israelite history down through the ages, as we remarked in association with CD 1:1-2:1.

Regarding the language of CD 3:10, וארצם בו שממה, two further passages from Ez are of interest. Ez 33:25, על הדם תאכלו...והארץ תירשו, speaks of the negative consequences of eating blood, especially the resultant devastation of the land, and it is tempting to link this passage with our author's choice of words here, as well as in CD 3:6. Ez 33:38, ונתתי את הארץ שממה, would lend support to this suggestion, and both, therefore, are included in the highlighted text set out above.[50]

Turning our attention to CD 3:12 amd 4:3, ובמחזקים and והנלוים, possible parallels may be found in Is 56:4 and 56:6, respectively. Is 56:4 contains the word מחזיקים regarding eunuchs, while the verb in the *hiphil* is employed in 56:2 of the Israelite who keeps justice and righteousness and holds fast to the Sabbath; this is not dissimilar to CD 3:13 mentioning the שבתות קדשו to be observed by the מחזיקים. We may note too that Is 56:3,6 refers to the foreigner who "has joined himself to the LORD" (הנלוים, הנלוה). Somewhat speculatively, perhaps, we may suggest from these points that the text of CD 3:12 and 4:3 echoes Is 56:2-6 by employing both המחזיקים and הנלוים.

Moving on to CD 3:18, our writer maintains that those who were "defiling themselves" were also saying לנו היא.[51] This expression is probably influenced by Ez 11:14-15, which states:

ויהי דבר ה׳ אלי לאמר: [15]בן אדם אחיך אחיך אנשי גאלתך וכל בית ישראל כלה אשר
אמרו להם ישבי ירושלם רחקו מעל ה׳ לנו היא נתנה הארץ למורשה:

Understanding this in its own context is not problematic but it is difficult to know what the exact significance of לנו היא was for the writer of CD.[52]

---

49   Such a characterization of the Israelites in Egypt is relatively rare in literature of the Second Temple period outside CD; cf., indeed, Wisd 10:15, "A holy people and blameless race wisdom delivered from a nation of oppressors".

50   Jer 12:11; Ez 35:12; 36:34 speak similarly of the coming devastation of the land, due to transgression, but otherwise seem of little import.

51   If Ez 11:15 is being connoted here, then it may be best to take the כי as introducing the words spoken, rather than as part of them, like the Greek οτι.

Suffice it for us to note, however, that it relates to CD's employment of the first chapters of Ez, in much the same way that the presence of שלוש מאות ותשעים in CD 1:5f (drawn from Ez 4:5) does.

We are told in CD 3:19 that God "raised for them a sure house in Israel the like of which had not stood from of old until now". This language reflects 1 Sam 2:35, which reads:[53]

והקימתי לי כהן נאמן כאשר בלבבי ובנפשי יעשה ובניתי לו בית נאמן והתהלך לפני
משיחי כל הימים:

For the background of the misbehaviour of Eli's two sons against which this verse is set, the story best speaks for itself (vv 27-34):

ויבא איש אלהים אל עלי ויאמר אליו כה אמר ה' הנגלה נגליתי אל בית אביך בהיותם
במצרים לבית פרעה: ²⁸ובחר אתו מכל שבטי ישראל לי לכהן לעלות על מזבחי
להקטיר קטרת לשאת אפוד לפני ואתנה לבית אביך את כל אשי בני ישראל: ²⁹למה
תבעטו בזבחי ובמנחתי אשר צויתי מעון ותכבד את בניך ממני להבריאכם מראשית כל
מנחת ישראל לעמי: ³⁰לכן נאם ה' אלהי ישראל אמור אמרתי ביתך ובית אביך יתהלכו
לפני עד עולם ועתה נאם ה' חלילה לי כי מכבדי אכבד ובזי יקלו: ³¹הנה ימים באים
וגדעתי את זרעך ואת זרע בית אביך מהיות זקן בביתך: ³²והבטת צר מעון בכל אשר
ייטיב את ישראל ולא יהיה זקן בביתך כל הימים: ³³ואיש לא אכרית לך מעם מזבחי
לכלות את עיניך ולאדיב את נפשך וכל מרבית ביתך ימותו אנשים: ³⁴וזה לך האות
אשר יבא אל שני בניך אל חפני ופינחס ביום אחד ימותו שניהם:

The בית נאמן in the biblical text signifies the ending of an unfaithful priesthood and its replacement by a trustworthy one.[54] In the narrative of 1,2

---

[52]   We noted the wider context of Ez 11 in association with CD 1:1-2:1; see above, p. 60. Scholars often attempt to use the phrase, כי לנו היא, in association with other data, to facilitate historical reconstructions. Boyce, p. 125, e.g., makes two possible suggestions as to the meaning לנו היא. It could, he says, claim possession of the land at the time of the Maccabean Revolt, or at 142 BCE, when Simon won independence; an initially positive acclamation, it became negative due to the strife that took hold of the Hasmonean dynasty. Alternatively, he suggests, it may mean "This [course of action] is for us", in the sense of doing something according to desire and referring, perhaps, to disputes over the calendar or priesthood (cf. the נסתרות of 3:14 or the midrash on Ez 44:15 in 3:20ff).

[53]   For other occurrences of בית נאמן, see 1 Sam 25:28; 2 Sam 7:16; 1 Ki 11:38. These do not seem to be of significance to our study, for they refer to the secure future of the Davidic dynasty.

[54]   בית נאמן is applied to the community analogously, in that the sect is the continuator of God's covenant since Israel's apostasy, but also more literally, in that Zadok's line is of particular importance. Note that 1 Sam 2:35 is taken as referring to a new dynasty which will be faithful to the Law and to God, not in terms of the establishment of a temple itself for the dynasty concerned. These points are relevant to scholarly debates as to whether the group behind CD had abandoned participation in the temple cult or not - a debate into which we cannot enter. See P.R. Davies, 'The Ideology of the Temple in the Damascus Document', *JJS* (1982), pp. 287-301;

Sam and 1,2 Ki, this finds fulfilment in the exclusion of Abiathar and his replacement by Zadok (see 1 Ki 2:27,35). The latter figure is, of course, important for the writer of CD and for the sectarian DSS in general.[55] Moreover, in view of other passages we have examined, it is reasonable to suppose that allusion to 1 Sa 2:35 can be largely explained by its association with a major incident of rebelliousness in the bible.[56]

We come to one of the most important quotations in CD at 3:21c-4:2a. These lines contain a condensed citation of Ez 44:15. In the MT this reads:

והכהנים הלוים בני צדוק אשר שמרו את משמרת מקדשי בתעות בני ישראל מעלי המה
יקרבו אלי לשרתני ועמדו לפני להקריב לי חלב ודם נאם אדני ה' :

As well as the telescoping of this scriptural verse, we can note in particular an extra "and" before both הלוים and בני צדוק. The whole basis of the interpretation of the passage in the following lines depends on these additions, and the author may have deliberately changed his text.[57] The biblical verse, featuring the בני צדוק once more, is used to prove that the community was raised up to inherit the covenantal promises. If כאשר הקים is intended to relate the scriptural text to the promises of blessing just mentioned in CD 3:20, then the idea, as in 3:12f, is that fidelity to the Torah

---

D.R. Schwarz, 'To Join Oneself to the House of Judah (Damascus Document VI.11)', *RQ* 10 (1981), pp. 435-446. See also J. Murphy-O'Connor, 'The Essenes and their History', *RB* 81 (1974), p. 229f, for the Teacher as an interim High Priest before the accession of Jonathan Maccabee in 152 BCE; this was originally propounded by H. Stegemann, *Die Entstehung der Qumrangemeinde*, Bonn (1971), but has not met with general acceptance. More recently, note M.O. Wise, 'The Teacher of Righteousness and the High Priest of the Intersacerdotium: Two Approaches', *RQ* 14 (1990), pp. 587-613.

[55] Many scholars posit an essential Zadokite element in the formation or development of the Essene/Qumran sect. However, for the בני צדוק as less important in the sectarian DSS than usually thought, see P.R. Davies, *Behind the Essenes: History and Ideology in the Dead Sea Scrolls*, Atlanta (1987), pp. 51-72. Certainly, their precise role within the community responsible for the DSS requires re-evaluation in view of the divergent readings found in 4QS^d, replacing 1QS's references to הכהנים בני צדוק with הרבים; for details, see G. Vermes, 'Preliminary Remarks on the Unpublished Fragments of the Community Rule from Qumran Cave 4', *JJS* 42 (1991), pp. 250-255.

[56] Another possible connection between this portion of 1 Sa and CD may be evident in the presence of (ה)נגלה in both 1 Sa 2:27 and CD 5:5. See the next chapter on CD 5:5.

[57] Alternatively, he may have been using a variant reading. In any case, Boyce, p. 130, points out that, without the shortening of the citation and resultant omission of המה יקרבו אלי לשרתני ועמדו לפני, the additional *waws* would have rendered הם unclear (assuming מעליהם should properly read מעלי הם).

is rewarded. In any case, our next chapter will show that the citation here, rather like Hos 4:16 in CD 1:13f, is part of a wider dependence upon this context in Ez, even if identification of the historical referents in CD 4:2ff is fraught with uncertainty.[58]

One of the elements in the quotation, "the priests", is defined in CD 4:2 as the שבי ישראל. Is 59:20 may prove helpful here:

ובא לציון גואל ולשבי פשע ביעקב נאם ה':

Rabin maintains that the phrases שבי ישראל and שבי פשע in CD are abbreviations for these words in Is 59:20.[59] In addition, our observations above on the relation between Is 59 and CD 1:1-2:1 show that this biblical context exercised a wider influence on CD.

It is usually thought that the final words in this section of CD, 4:11-12, reflect the language in Hab 2:1 and Mic 7:10.[60] The מצוד imagery is used to convey the picture of a person standing before God in judgement; only those who belong to the בית יהודה (i.e., the sect) will be acceptable.[61]   The phraseology from Mic 7:11 refers to the "wall" dividing community members from those outside; originally concerned with the restoration of Jerusalem, the scriptural text has been redirected by the author towards the eschaton and/or the time immediately preceding it.

4.3.3 Ketuvim in CD 2:14-4:12a

A number of possible scriptural echoes from the Writings in this second historical section do not seem important upon closer examination.[62]   The

---

[58]   See especially CD 4:18 and 6:17, employing Ez 44:7 and 44:23, respectively.

[59]   See Rabin, p. 13, as well as CD 2:5, שבי פשע; CD 20:17, שבי פשע יעקב; and CD 6:5, שבי ישראל.

[60]   Davies, p. 104, argues that CD's interpretation of מצוד from Hab 2:1 is very different from that in 1QpHab 6:12ff. Boyce, p. 147, maintains that it is, in fact, similar. Inasmuch as the biblical text is used eschatologically for a contemporary situation, Boyce is right; Davies, however, correctly points out that 1QpHab's image is one of waiting to receive a vision from God, whereas in CD 4:11f the picture is of a person left to his own devices before God in negative judgement.

[61]   For בית יהודה as a cipher for the sect, see D.R. Schwarz, 'To Join Oneself to the House of Judah', *RQ* 10 (1981), pp. 435-446.

[62]   The following should be mentioned in this regard:
שמעו...בנים at the beginning of CD 2:14 reflects typical Wisdom language, such as that found in Pr 4:1, שמעו בנים מוסר אב;
Pr 3:18 employs the word מחזיקים in reference to those who possess Wisdom; cf. CD 3:12.

reason for this has to do largely with the nature of much of the material in this section of the bible and the fact that it has a tendency to be employed by way of linguistic imitation, which, while interesting, is not of great significance. However, certain passages do stand out.

Firstly, there is a plausible connection between our text at 2:17 and 3:11, both of which contain the idiom שרירות לב, and Ps 81:13, which uses the same phrase. Not only is Ps 81 a historical Ps, like 106, and, therefore, eminently suitable for use by our author, but we may also note two other links with CD. First, the rebellion at Meribah is mentioned (v 80), and we have remarked before that this theme was prominent within CD in the form of its utilization of Nu 13ff. Secondly, the שמע לקול phraseology (v 12) may constitute a loose link with CD 3:7f, ולא שמעו לקול עשיהם (cf. Ps 106:25). Another significant passage seems to be 2 Chr 20:7, mentioning Abraham as God's friend. Since CD 3:2's evaluation of the Patriarch is based on such precedents, as well as on Is 41:8, it is included in the highlighted text above, and may receive some small corroboration as influential here due to the fact that the מקדש is mentioned in the following verse (cf. CD 1:3, וממקדשו).

Another relevant biblical passage has already been referred to elsewhere, namely, Ps 106. Words from this Ps are reflected in CD 3:7,8, particularly in the form of וירגנו באהליהם, which is almost a citation. As indicated in relation to CD 1:1-2:1, Ps 106 rehearses the history of Israel from the entry into Canaan, stressing the people's faithlessness, despite God's patience and care. וירגנו באהליהם and לא שמעו בקול ה׳ in Ps 106:25 and וירגנו באהליהם and לא שמעו לקול עשיהם in CD 3:7f describe the same series of interconnected events, showing once more that Ps 106 was on the author's mind. Staying with the Psalter, Ps 78:62, ויסגר לחרב עמו, uses language parallel to that in CD 1:17, as already noticed, as well as 3:10, ויסגרו לחרב.

2 Chr 36:21 refers to the land being desolate, in fulfilment of Jeremiah's '70 year' prophecy and in receipt of the sabbaths it never had in the pre-exilic period. Although it is not possible to be sure that a connection exists with CD 3:10, ארצם בו שממה, it seems probable in view of the fact that we have referred to this important prophecy before. Moreover, 2 Chr 36 will reappear when we tackle CD 6:11b-8:21 in the next chapter.

Parallel to the employment of scripture we identified in CD 1:1-2:1, Neh 9:14,29 is reflected in CD 3:14,15. Like the above-mentioned Ps 106 and resembling Ezr 9, Neh 9 recounts Israelite history from the sojourn in Egypt to the return from the Babylonian exile, telling of the people's manifold failings over against God's continued faithfulness. Verse 14f, regarding the statutes and the ordinances, especially את שבת קדשך, and verse 29, אשר יעשה האדם וחיה בהם, are points of contact with the section of CD under

consideration; see CD 3:13, שבתות קדשו, and CD 3:15f, אשר יעשה האדם
וחיה בהם.

Although the connection itself seems rather slight, it is worth noting the
parallel between לחיי נצח in CD 3:20 and לחיי עולם in Dn 12:2. The latter, in
the context of verses 1-4, reads:

> ובעת ההיא יעמד מיכאל השר הגדול העמד על בני עמך והיתה עת צרה אשר לא נהיתה
> מהיות גוי עד העת ההיא ובעת ההיא ימלט עמך כל הנמצא כתוב בספר: ²ורבים מישני
> אדמת עפר יקיצו אלה לחיי עולם ואלה לחרפות לדראון עולם: ³והמשכלים יזהרו כזהר
> הרקיע ומצדיקי הרבים ככוכבים לעולם ועד: ⁴ואתה דניאל סתם הדברים וחתם הספר
> עד עת קץ ישטטו רבים ותרבה הדעת:

Although some caution is advisable, Dn may well exercise an influence on the
Admonition elsewhere.[63] If CD 3:20 is dependent on Dn 12:2 for לחיי נצח,
this would suggest a belief in resurrection and the afterlife of a more defined
type than has often been assumed in relation to the sectarian DSS.[64]

4.3.4 Summary

Our examination of the use of scripture in CD 2:14-4:12a has yielded
observations similar to those gleaned from our analysis of CD 1:1-2:1.
Influence from biblical texts is varied, ranging from the apparently superficial
to that involving an obvious amount of interconnected thought on the part of
our writer in a conscious and deliberate manner. Although, at times, it may
be difficult to discern into which class certain particular cases belong, this
does not detract from the cumulative impact of the overall phenomenon we
have been describing.

As with CD 1:1-2:1, the most interesting use of the Pentateuch was that
which employed contexts concentrating on events of major moment in Israel's
history. The same scriptural texts reappeared: Ex 32, Lv 17-26, Nu 13-16,
and Dt 9,12,28ff. Additional passages came from contexts dealing with pre-
and early Israelite history, for which there is no parallel in the narrative of
1:1-2:1. Similarly, the main prophetic texts which the writer alludes to or
quotes involve the usual nexus of events and evaluations associated with the

---

[63]   See above on CD 1:3, במועלם אשר עזבוהו (cf. Dn 9:7), and below on CD 2:4, ארך
אפים (cf. Dn 9:9).

[64]   See, e.g., Schürer, II, pp. 582-583. 1QS 4:8,23 contains both, and 1QH 17:14,15
only the second, of the phrases חיי נצח and כבוד אדם. See too *BJ* 2.154-158 for
Josephus' view of Essene beliefs about the after-life, as well as the recently released
4Q521 with its reading ומתים יחיה, "and the dead he [God] will resurrect". For a
preliminary account of the latter, consult EW, pp. 19-23.

exile, its causes and future termination/restoration.   In particular, we
considered passages from Is, Jer, and Ez, including not a few which had been
mentioned in connection with CD 1:1-2:1.   As was found to be the case in the
previous historical section, a pattern in the use of the Writings was less
readily ascertainable.   Nevertheless, it was difficult not to conclude that some
use of Ps 106, one of the historical Pss, was being made.   Neh 9 also proved
interesting, being parallel to the presence of some influence from Ezr 9 in CD
1:1-2:1.   More specifically, of particular note was CD 3:15, אשר יעשה האדם
וחיה בהם.   This reflects language from each of Lv 18:5, Ez 20:11,13,21, and
Neh 9:29, all of which have other connections to the Admonition.   Similarly,
שרירות לב in CD 3:17 echoes the same idiom found in Dt 29:18, Jer 23:17,
and Ps 81:13.

More generally, a primary reference for our author seems to have been the
exile, both in terms of the event itself and of incidents prior to it which exhibit
parallel causes and effects.   Further, the situation after the exile would appear
to be a continuation of it in some sense, at least for those outside the sect.
This is suggested by the mass of exilic imagery and the prominence of certain
scriptural passages, in combination with the story-line in this second historical
section which, while it assumes that the sect experiences a kind of foretaste of
salvation, also makes it clear that the restoration of all things will not come
about until the eschaton (see 4:11-12a).

A final point may be made at this juncture concerning the historicity of one
element in the narrative of CD 2:14-4:12a.   In our analysis above, we dealt
briefly with the idea of blood-eating leading to the loss of possession of the
land, in association with Lv 17:10 and Dt 12:23 and as fulfilled in the exile
according to Ez 33:25; we saw that these passages are influential in CD 3:6.
However, at that point in his narrative our author is dealing with the Israelites
in the wilderness before entry into Canaan, not with the period immediately
prior to the exile.   Indeed, numerous scholars have noted the unexpected
reference to blood-eating here, whereas other rebellious incidents from the
Pentateuch would readily spring to mind as more appropriate, especially that
pertaining to the golden calf narrative of Ex 32/Dt 9.[65]   It would appear,
therefore, that, because the generation of the Israelites in the desert was
denied possession of the land, our writer, on the basis of the aforementioned
biblical passages, has deduced that one of the crimes responsible for such a

---

[65]   See, e.g., Knibb, p. 31. However, we have seen that Ex 32 was probably in the mind
of the author of CD as well, and this is analogous to 1QpHab 11:9-14, where (as we
noted above, p. 19, note 26) an analysis of the Pesher following the biblical citation
shows the writer was aware of two readings in Hab 2:16, הערל and הרעל.

fate 'must' have been the eating of blood. This would seem to constitute an instance of what might be called the 'creation of history'.

4.4 Scripture in CD 5:15b-6:11a

We have already argued that it is reasonable to include 5:15b-6:11a among the other sections we have designated 'historical'. Like them, this passage narrates events outlining the origins of the group commended in the Admonition but it is, unfortunately, more difficult to delineate perimeters for the relevant material belonging to this third historical section. Although CD 5:15ff returns to a style familiar from 1:1-2:1 and 2:14-4:12a, the change takes place in a gradual way that is not clear-cut, partly explaining the different ways in which scholars divide up the document here.[66]

Notwithstanding this imprecision, to start at 5:15b makes sense. It is clear, as we shall see in a subsequent chapter, that CD 4:12b-5:15a concerns itself with a description of Judaism outwith the sect "during all those years" (4:12b), that is, during the previously mentioned "number of those years" (4:10). By 4:12ff, the downfall of the majority of Israel has been described, with the creation of the community to take its place, and in what follows the author attacks the remaining Judaism outside, showing it to be a sham controlled by the devil.[67] Then a break occurs in the text at 5:15a/b, for, from 5:15b, we are again thrown back in time, presumably in order to learn about the present.[68]

---

[66] Thus, J. Murphy-O'Connor views his original Essene Missionary Document to end at CD 6:2, characterizing 5:14b-6:2 as "Warnings" and 6:3-11a as "The Well Midrash"; see 'An Essene Missionary Document? CD II,14-VI,1', *RB* 77 (1970), p. 222f, and 'A Literary Analysis of Damascus Document VI,2-VIII,3', *RB* 78 (1971), p. 228f. He has, however, reworked his opinions, and now considers the section as running to 6:11; see 'The Damascus Document Revisited', *RB* 92 (1985), pp. 223-246. Davies, pp. 243-251, views 4:12b-7:10a a large section on "Laws". Like ourselves, Knibb, p. 44ff, treats 5:15b-6:11a as a unit, calling it "God's remembrance of the Covenant". Vermes, p. 162ff, deals with 4:12-6:2, "The Wickedness of Israel at the time of the Formation of the Community", and 6:2-11, "The Exiles of Damascus and their Study of the Law".

[67] This is achieved by an interpretation of Is 24:17 in CD 4:12b-19a, concretized in terms of contemporary religious morality and purity in 4:19b-5:15a.

[68] Boyce, p. 168ff, insists on making 5:11 the beginning of another original poem but to argue for literary sources, as he does, requires a precision which is not possible, as we saw earlier in relation to CD 1:1-2:1. On the contrary, we simply seek a flow

Thus, CD 5:15b-6:11a describes briefly, in 5:15b-6:2a, the destruction which overtakes those who behave as criticized in 4:12ff, by appealing to that which happened in "former times", namely, during the Egyptian and Babylonian exiles. Whether an interpolation or not, 5:17b-19 is clearly an aside which harks back to the events of Ex 7:11.[69] After this, 5:20ff returns to the theme of the Babylonian exile, giving the writer another opportunity to rehearse the sect's origins in 6:2b-11a. This time, he stresses the community's halakhic superiority by playing on the root חקק, which is rather appropriate in view of the preceding criticism of contemporary Judaism in CD 4:12b-5:15a. Whilst we are reminded of 1:1-2:1 and 2:14-4:12a, therefore, this section is different in its legal preoccupation, although it does not argue for specific points of law or behaviour; the latter comes in the next section of the Admonition and in CD 9-16.[70] Also noteworthy and corroborative of our inclusion of CD 5:15b-6:11a in this part of our study is the fact that in CD 6:5 we find an important reference to the שבי ישראל היוצאים מארץ יהודה ויגורו בארץ דמשק, who were also mentioned in CD 4:2ff. The portion ends with an eschatological reference to a certain יורה הצדק, whose advent will bring the age of wickedness to an end.

In terms of the historical reconstruction of the community's beginnings, the mention of this figure in 6:11 is one of the major problems in understanding CD 1-8 as a consistent whole. In 6:2ff, the sect's history starts off in the past at some point after the Babylonian captivity, with the appearance of one דורש התורה, that is, the מחוקק and those who were his followers, the מחוקקות. However, the summary of the remainder of the community's expected history suggests that the laws of the דורש will be valid only until the advent of a יורה הצדק. Of course, such a figure is usually associated with the origins, not the eschatological culmination, of the life of the sect. Indeed, the

---

to the text and, if it reflects the nature of the work, acknowledging a certain looseness in this respect may be appropriate.

69   Murphy-O'Connor considers it secondary, as does J. Duhaime, 'Dualist Reworking in the Scrolls from Qumran', *CBQ* 49 (1987), pp. 32-56. Boyce, p. 177f, argues to the contrary.

70   The dual (i.e., halakhic and historical) nature of 5:15b-6:11a, and the impossibility of defining definitively such multifaceted material, led Davies, pp. 56-104, to exclude it from his 'History' section analysing CD 1:1-4:12a; but in *Behind the Essenes: History and Ideology in the Dead Sea Scrolls*, Sheffield (1987), pp. 107-134, he includes it with 1:1-2:1 and 2:14-4:12a for the purposes of a historical investigation.

דורש התורה and the מורה צדק have normally been equated, with scholars attempting to harmonize associated data in various ways.[71]

Before going any further, we shall include the Hebrew text of CD 5:15b-6:11a, which reads as follows:

כי אם למילפנים פקד   15

אל את מעשיהם ויחר אפו בעלילותיהם כי לא עם בינות הוא

הם גוי אבד עצות מאשר אין בהם בינה כי מלפנים עמד

משה ואהרן ביד שר האורים ויקם בליעל את יחנה ואת

אחיהו במזמתו בהושע ישראל את הראשונה

ובקץ חרבן הארץ עמדו מסיגי הגבול ויתעו את ישראל   20

ותישם הארץ כי דברו סרה על מצות אל ביד משה וגם

במשיחו הקודש וינבאו שקר להשיב את ישראל מאחר   1

אל ויזכר אל ברית ראשנים ויקם מאהרן נבונים ומישראל

חכמים וישמיעם ויחפורו את הבאר באר חפרוה שרים כרוה

נדיבי העם במחוקק הבאר היא התורה וחופריה   הם

שבי ישראל היוצאים מארץ יהודה ויגורו בארץ דמשק   5

אשר קרא אל את כולם שרים כי דרשוהו ולא הושבה

פארתם בפי אחד והמחוקק הוא דורש התורה אשר

אמר ישעיה מוציא כלי למעשיהו ונדיבי העם הם

הבאים לכרות את הבאר במחוקקות אשר חקק המחוקק

להתהלך במה בכל קץ הרשיע וזולתם לא ישיגו עד עמד   10

יורה הצדק באחרית הימים

There are a few minor problems with the text of MS A as set out above. אם in 5:15b would appear to have crept in by mistake, and this is confirmed by

---

[71] According to usual interpretations, the יורה הצדק cannot be the same as the מורה צדק in CD 1:11; he is either a future figure of a deliberately similar epithet, or the מורה *redivivus*. It is difficult to produce a harmonization which is both consistent and convincing, however, for the idea of a future figure, not equal with the Teacher of Righteousness but with a similar name and typologically similar role at the eschaton, does not ring true. Davies, p. 198ff, argues that the original Admonition predicted the arrival of a יורה הצדק; when someone came onto the scene who was believed by some to fulfil this role, CD 1:11's reference to the advent of the מורה צדק was added, along with other details, in a Qumran edition of the work. However, while attractive, such an appeal to sources/redaction suggests that we do not really understand the final form of the text in a way the first century sectaries would have. On the identity of the דורש התורה, S.A. Fraade, 'Interpretative Authority in the Interpreting Community at Qumran', *JJS* 44 (1993), pp. 58-62, has recently suggested that the דורש התורה in CD 6:7 may denote a communal official rather than a specific historical character, noting that 1QS envisages an ongoing communal study of the Law by an איש דורש בתורה (1QS 6:6) or by האיש הדורש (1QS 8:11f).

the preference for כי only in 4QD^a. במשיחו in 6:1 should probably read במשיחי, and it is interesting to note that both 4QD^a and 4QD^b preface the words from Nu 18:21 with a citation formula, אשר אמר משה, which is not present in CD 6:3. Finally, although ולא הושבה פארתם בפי אחד in 6:6f is best understood as translated by Knibb in the sense "and their <re>nown was not disputed by the mouth of anyone", it is not necessary to emend פארתם to תפארתם, since the noun פארה is evidenced elsewhere in the sectarian DSS.[72]

Once again, the chief problem arises when CD 5:15b-6:11a is placed alongside 1:1-2:1 and 2:14-4:12a. On its own, the story contained in this third historical section is not particularly awkward, any difficulties being limited to obscurity or ambiguity rather than contradiction. As was the case for 2:14-4:12a, however, the main focus of attention in the story-line appears to be placed not long after the exile, while 1:1-2:1 contains a competing focus of attention. Yet, as before, the highlighted text presented below (p. 92) may add a different perspective.[73]

4.4.1 Torah in CD 5:15b-6:11a

We can note a number of connections to passages from the Torah in this portion of CD, most of which we have dealt with in relation to CD 1:1-2:1 and 2:14-4:12a.[74]

Our writer is virtually quoting Dt 32:28 in CD 5:17, as part of his general interest in the last chapters of Dt.[75] Dt 31 is a warning to be faithful, and we have already noted a number of contacts with both CD 1:1-2:1 and 2:14-

---

[72] See Knibb, p. 45, and E. Qimron, *The Hebrew of the Dead Sea Scrolls*, Jerusalem (1986), p. 112.

[73] All the words and phrases highlighted are important, although it should be pointed out that יחנה ואת אחיהו in CD 5:18 is dependent on post-biblical aggadic development of the exodus story.

[74] Note that Gn 49:10 and Dt 33:21 contain biblical examples of מחקק (cf. CD 6:4f, מחוקקות...מחוקק) but otherwise appear of no relevance in the present context. Regarding the latter, however, Dt 32:28, also placed within the generally relevant block Dt 28-32, is employed in CD 5:17, as we shall see now. Note too that the Targums and other Rabbinic literature understood מחקק in Dt 33:21 as 'scribe'; see B. Grossfeld, *The Targum Onkelos to Deuteronomy*, Edinburgh (1988), p. 110f.

[75] As suggested previously, a modern equivalent to this might be to place words in inverted commas.

כי מלפנים עמד		
15	הם אל עמשיהם אמר אנה ולוליהם אבן לא עם בינות הוא	*Is 27:11*
	אמרה בני לוי וביום בקום ... איש את רעהו יצמיד בגבר לא עם ...	Dt 32:28
	... בקבץ כי ... עמד ... בקץ ... דבר קדם	Ex 7:11
	וחירות את ישראל ... הקים להם מורה צדק	
20	ויקם את יהוה ... לתעב את האדם מסבה בדרכי לבם ...	*Dt 19:14/27:17 Jer 23:13 Hos 5:10*
	ועם משה גם אהרן ביד שר האורים ויקם בליעל את ...	Dt 13:6
1	הקים ... ישעיה בן אמון ... לבני שהרה את ישראל	*Jer 23:25 2 Chr 36:15*
	החזק למועדי הברית ואת הקימות ולשרי עמד שלמים	Lv 26:45 Dt 1:13
	הם ... באר חפרוה שרים כרוה	Nu 21:18
5	אשר לא יקמו	*Is 59:20*
	...	
		Is 54:16
10		*Hos 10:12 Ezr 2:63 Neh 7:65*

Quotation and Allusion in CD 5:15b-6:11a

4:12a.[76]   Dt 32-33 contain the Song and Blessing of Moses, the former recounting how wonderfully God has acted for his people, even though they rebelled against him.   Destruction is decreed, therefore, but not total annihilation, lest those outside Israel think ill of God.   Then comes verse 28f :

כי גוי אבד עצות המה ואין בהם תבונה: 29לו חכמו ישכילו זאת יבינו לאחריתם:

According to verse 30, Israel should realize that such punishment, almost total, must come from the hand of God.   More optimistically, although God takes vengeance on his enemies, he will also restore his people.   Thus, an overall pattern similar to that in CD's historical sections emerges.   Moreover, it should be pointed out that Dt 32:33 is cited in CD 8:9f.

In CD 5:18, our author refers indirectly to Ex 7:11, namely, "the wise men and the sorcerers" of Pharaoh.   The naming of these is dependent entirely on post-biblical, aggadic development of the scriptural legend at this point.[77] We may presume that the author of the Admonition takes the opposition of Moses, Aaron and the people against Pharaoh, Jannes and his brother (backed by the Prince of Lights and Belial, respectively) as paradigmatic of the contemporary situation of his own day.

The מסיגי הגבול in CD 5:20 remind us of Dt 19:14 and 27:17, both of which may also lie behind mention of the גבול in CD 1:16.[78]   As noted in our discussion of the first historical section, the first of these may have been connected by our author to the curse announced in the latter.   In their respective biblical contexts, these passages have the sin of (projected, future) pre-exilic generations in mind, and in CD 5:20 itself, therefore, we may presume that reference to the קץ חרון is probably a mere imprecision, the whole of the period leading up to the actual desolation of the land being designated by that final event.

In 5:21, CD continues with the assertion that the מסיגי הגבול "spoke rebellion against the commandments of God".   Dt 13:6 reads:

והנביא ההוא או חלם החלום ההוא יומת כי דבר סרה על ה׳ אלהיכם המוציא אתכם
מארץ מצרים והפדך מבית עבדים להדיחך מן הדרך אשר צוך ה׳ אלהיך ללכת בה
ובערת הרע מקרבך:

---

[76]   By way of reminder, see above p. 58, note 16, for some interesting parallel items of vocabulary present in Dt 31 and encountered in association with CD 1:1-2:1 and/or 2:14-4:12a.

[77]   This biblical context was one of many considered a candidate for explication in the Second Temple period and later.   See 2 Ti 3:8, as well as the work entitled 'Jannes and Jambres' in J.H. Charlesworth, *The Old Testament Pseudepigrapha*, II, pp. 427-442.   Clearly, Ex 7 tells us virtually nothing, and the writer of CD must be dependent on such aggadic expansions of the exodus story.

[78]   It is worth pointing out that 4QD^a reads מסגי גבול for מסיגי הגבול in CD 5:20.

It is worth observing that this chapter follows on from Dt 12 with its stress on one sanctuary and the abominable nature of consuming blood, topics from a context we discovered to be relevant to our earlier examination of CD 3:6. The general theme of Dt 13 warns against those who would entice people away from God and his ways - false prophets and seers, or whole families and towns which are corrupt. The community behind CD would apply this with ease to non-sectarian Judaism, and, hence, it makes sense to understand Dt 13:6 as informing the language of CD 5:21.

CD 6:2 states that "...God remembered the covenant of the first ones". This echoes Lv 26:44-45, which says:

ואף גם זאת בהיותם בארץ איביהם לא מאסתים ולא געלתים לכלתם להפר בריתי אתם

כי אני ה׳ אלהיהם: ⁴⁵וזכרתי להם ברית ראשנים אשר הוצאתי אתם מארץ מצרים לעיני

הגוים להית להם לאלהים אני ה׳:

We have had recourse to Lv 26 a number of times already, so that its theme and vocabulary are familiar. It exemplifies the pattern of sin, punishment, purgation and restoration that is present in a number of scriptural texts, and upon which our author has drawn.

When, also in 6:2, our writer states that God raised up מאהרן נבונים ומישראל חכמים, we are reminded of Dt 1:13.[79] This reads:

הבו לכם אנשים חכמים ונבנים וידעים לשבטיכם ואשימם בראשיכם:

As Dt opens, the scene is set in the Plains of Moab and Moses recounts the departure from Sinai up to the present, showing God's guidance of his people. He refers back to the lightening of his own burden by the appointment of other officials (Dt 1:9-18; cf. Nu 11:44ff and Ex 28:13ff). Thus, mention of the חכמים and נבונים in CD may be a device not only to lend an air of authority to the text but also to imply that the sect and its leadership are the genuine heirs to Moses and his righteous followers. This, with corroboration from evidence elsewhere, might be connected to the author's claim that he and his community embody the true sucessors of those who returned to the land after the exile.

CD 6:3 contains another important reference to scripture, this time from Nu 21:18; the words as they now stand are evidently intended to be as near to a citation as possible without an introductory formula.[80] Nu 21:17,18 reads:

---

[79]   Fraade, *op. cit.*, p. 59, also recognizes that Dt 1:13 underlies the choice of words at CD 6:2.

[80]   The precise significance of the 4QD reading, which introduces the biblical text with אשר אמר מושה, in relation to the CD text is not immediately obvious. While the introductory formula could simply have dropped out of CD 6:3 accidentally, it is also possible that CD at this point represents a different edition of the text. See above, p. 43, for previous discussion of this facet of the Admonition.

אז ישיר ישראל את השירה הזאת עלי באר ענו לה: 18באר חפרוה שרים כרוה נדיבי
העם במחקק במשענתם וממדבר מתנה:

Nu 21 describes the move of the Israelites northwards into Moab and
Ammon from Kadesh; on the way the incident involving the bronze serpent
takes place (vv 4-9). Nu 21:17b-18 is a poetic fragment, dealing with a
miraculous supply of water to the people at Be'er.[81] As with other passages
from Nu which appear to have had a bearing on the historical sections in CD,
so too Nu 21 may well have been on our writer's mind inasmuch as it contains
another incident of rebellion. If correct, this seems to be the likely reason for
the use of Nu 21:17b,18 here.

By now, we almost know what to expect in considering the use of the
Torah in the historical sections of CD. Indeed, while examining CD 5:15b-
6:11a, we have referred to a number of texts which appeared as prominent in
relation to CD 1:1-2:1 and/or 2:14-4:12a. It is not surprising to see Lv 26,
and Dt 13, 19, 27 again in viewing another portion detailing the sect's origins.
New, however, is the appeal to the circumstances of Ex 7:11, as also the use
of Dt 32:28, although the broader context of the latter was familiar to us
from other borrowings from the final chapters of Dt evident elsewhere in the
historical sections. The allusion to Dt 1:13 is new as well. Of particular
interest is the interpretation of Nu 21:18 in CD 6:3ff. What appears at first
sight to be an unusual choice of passage for exegetical elaboration, in view of
its obscurity and uninterpreted brevity in Nu itself, becomes explicable in
view of our author's preoccupation with the stories of rebellion in Nu and
elsewhere.

---

[81] It is argued by some that the MT would appear to have been misconstrued at some
point in transmission. In that case, וממדבר מתנה should properly mean "a gift from
the desert", rather than "From the wilderness [they went on] to Mattanah" (NRSV;
brackets ours). Cf. Nu 21:17b,18 in REB:
   "Spring up, O well! Greet it with song,
   the well dug by the princes,
   laid open by the leaders of the people
   with the sceptre and staff, a gift from the wilderness".
With this, cf. JPSA and M. Rosenbaum, A.M. Silbermann, *Pentateuch with Rashi's
Commentary*, London (1946), II, p. 102ff, as well as Targum Onkelos' rendering:
בירא דחפרוה רברביא כרוה רישי עמא בספריא בחטריהון וממדברא אתיהיבת להון.

4.4.2   Nevi'im in CD 5:15b-6:11a

Turning to the Prophets, we have already met most of the relevant contexts that appear to have a bearing on CD 5:15b-6:11a in earlier discussions.[82]

In 5:16, the writer of CD says of Israel כי לא עם בינות הוא. This is a virtual citation from Is 27:11, which reads:

‎...כי לא עם בינות הוא על כן לא ירחמנו עשהו ויצרו לא יחננו:

Is 27 forms part of what scholars have called the Isaiah Apocalypse. After mention of God's vineyard (vv 1-5) and a promise of future blessing (v 6), verses 7-11 refer to Israel's punishment via the exile. This will act as a purge and be followed by blessing when idolatry has been removed. Meanwhile, the exiles constitute a people void of understanding. Verses 12,13 contain another oracle of final doom and triumph.

CD 5:20 refers to the מסיגי הגבול. This epithet is taken straight from Hos 5:10, an important context for our author, which is alluded to more fully in CD 8:3 and is quoted in CD 19:15f.[83] In the biblical text, Hos 5:10 belongs to a unit, Hos 4:1-8:14, bemoaning the fact that Israel has forgotten God and sought help from other gods and countries. The whole of verses 8-12 reads:

‎תקעו שופר בגבעה חצצרה ברמה הריעו בית און אחריך בנימין : ‎9אפרים לשמה תהיה
‎ביום תוכחה בשבטי ישראל הודעתי נאמנה: ‎10היו שרי יהודה כמסיגי גבול עליהם
‎אשפוך כמים עברתי: ‎11עשוק אפרים רצוץ משפט כי הואיל הלך אחרי צו: ‎12ואני
‎כעש לאפרים וכרקב לבית יהודה:

According to verse 10, it is the people's leaders who are particularly corrupt and ripe for punishment. Any doubt that this passage stands behind the usage of the epithet מסיגי הגבול in CD 5:20 is removed by the cryptic idiom הלך אחרי צו, derived from Hos 5:11 and replicated in CD 4:19.

---

82   At this point, we should note several possible but essentially unclear connections between the final historical section of the Admonition and the Prophets:

ותישם הארץ is replicated in both CD 5:21 and Ez 19:7, Ez 19 being a short chapter preceding Ez 20; the latter was in the mind of CD's author in other connections (see CD 1:3 and 3:15f);

The idea present in the reference to the משיחו הקודש (CD 5:21) may reflect a passage such as 2 Ki 17:13 but, as we shall see, 2 Chr 36:15 is more likely to have been influential in CD at this point;

Finally, note that Is 32:22 contains a prophetic example of the employment of the term מחקק.

83   Note also that 4Q424 refers to the upright man who opposes כול מסיגי גבול; see *DSSE*, pp. 278-279 and EW, pp. 166-168.

These "removers of the bound", and those under their influence, are accused of corrupting others: ויתעו את ישראל (CD 5:20). Similar phraseology is found in Jer 23:13, which says:

ובנביאי שמרון ראיתי תפלה הנבאו בבעל ויתעו את עמי את ישראל:

Jer 23:1-8 is an oracle of salvation promising that God will raise up a good shepherd to guide his people. In this respect, and in relation to CD, mention of the צמח לדוד and the ארץ צפון is noteworthy (vv 5,8).[84] Jer 23:9-40 contains oracles against prophets. Those of Samaria were bad enough (v 13) but Jerusalem's are worse, and their deeds are like those of Sodom and Gomorrah. Therefore, unsavoury punishment will be theirs. Verses 16-22 have the prophets rebuked for their false assurances, for, if they had passed on God's message aright, they would have kept his people back from sin. Verse 20, which could easily have been conected with Is 27:11 via גזרה שוה, is of particular note:[85]

...באחרית הימים תתבוננו בה בינה:

The rest of the chapter forms an attack on false prophets. As part of this, Jer 23:25 (cf. Jer 14:14) refers to those who prophesy שקר, which is an accusation levelled in CD 6:1 against those who speak סרה (5:21). Moreover, we noted Jer 23:17 in connection with CD 2:17, and Jer 25ff vis à vis CD 1:1-2:1. Hence, although our author's employment of the vocabulary of these biblical passages is complex and interconnected, it also seems consistent enough to be deliberate rather than accidental or unconscious.

Reference to the שבי ישראל in CD 6:5 reminds us both of the mention of the same group in CD 4:2 and of the biblical passage on which this epithet appears to be based, namely, Is 59:20, mentioning the שבי פשע ביעקב.

We stay with Is when, in Is 54:16, we find the source of the quotation in CD 6:8. The biblical text reads:

הן אנכי בראתי חרש נפח באש פחם ומוציא כלי למעשהו ואנכי בראתי משחית לחבל:

Is 54 is a song of assurance for Israel, promising that God will marvellously restore his people in righteousness, free from fear and strife. Indeed, God is the one who creates the חרש and the משחית and any who threaten Zion will not be of God and unable, therefore, to succeed. The significance of the citation in CD 6:8 probably relates to mention of the מחוקק, for it would appear that the כלי in Is 54:16 has been taken as a parallel to מחקק in Nu 21:18.[86]

---

[84] For צמח דוד, cf. CD 1:7; for ארץ צפון, see CD 7:14, והמחזיקים נמלטו לארץ צפון.

[85] In other words, Jer 23:20's תתבוננו echoes בינות in Is 27:11.

[86] Note too Is 54:8, בשצף קצף הסתרתי פני רגע ממך; cf. CD 1:3, הסתיר פניו מישראל.

Finally, עד עמד in CD 6:11 reminds us of Hos 10:12, to which we have already referred in relation to CD 1:11.

4.4.3 Ketuvim in CD 5:15b-6:11a

There is little influence from the Writings upon this section of CD. Regarding the reference to the משיחו קודש in CD 6:1, similar language is reflected in the idea behind 2 Chr 36:15f, which speaks for itself:

וישלח ה' אלהי אבותיהם עליהם ביד מלאכיו השכם ושלוח כי חמל על עמו ועל מעונו:
16ויהיו מלעבים במלאכי האלהים ובוזים דבריו ומתעתעים בנבאיו עד עלות חמת ה'
בעמו עד לאין מרפא:

2 Chr 36 summarizes the pattern which 1,2 Chr traces throughout history: the Israelites did what was evil in the sight of God. The cycle of sin and rebellion, despite forgiveness and restoration and a supply of prophets, meant that defeat and captivity were finally inevitable in the form of the Babylonian exile. Note that verse 21 speaks of the fulfilment of Jeremiah's prophecy of seventy years. This may act as corroboration of our suspicion that a link exists between CD 6:1 and 2 Chr 36:15, as does the likely reflection of 2 Chr 36:16 in CD 7:17f.

We find the עד עמד phraseology in CD 6:10 also present in Ezr 2:63, as well as the parallel passage Neh 7:65. These both read:

ויאמר התרשתא להם אשר לא יאכלו מקדש הקדשים עד עמד הכהן לאורים ותומים:

The governor in question here is Sheshbazzar, and the context is that of a census of the first return (Ezr 2:1-70/Neh 7:6-73). Ezr 2:59-63 deals with claimants to the priesthood who have no records of descent; they may not take part in the priestly privileges until a priest should arise who is able to use the Urim and Tummim. Murphy-O'Connor views the records now lost from CD 4:4ff as functioning similarly to ensure priestly purity.[87] Therefore, although no other echoes of either passage are evident elsewhere in the Admonition, the strength of the thematic overlap with CD at this point allows us cautiously to include them in the highlighted text arranged above.

For this portion of CD we have found it necessary to consider only three contexts from the Writings. 2 Chr 36:15 is rather like its older parallel in 2 Ki 17:13, except that the former heightens the issue as the work is brought to a close. Ezr 2:63 and Neh 7:65 both concern the hope for some special figure who will appear, possessing divinely given insight or authority to make

---

[87]   See J. Murphy-O'Connor, 'An Essene Missionary Document? CD II,14 - VI,11', *RB* 77 (1970), p. 213f.

decisions. One problem within the Admonition and in other sectarian DSS in this regard concerns the apparent expectation of more than one messianic figure, at least in some texts. Moreover, the different portions of CD may not be entirely consistent in where precisely the raising of such a figure(s) is placed historically, and, as a result, it seems difficult to harmonize the data provided by the document in this connection.[88]

4.4.4 Summary

The number of texts from scripture informing the background of CD 5:15b-6:11a is fewer than those discovered in relation to either 1:1-2:1 or 2:14-4:12a. This is partly due to the fact that CD 5:15b-6:11a is the shortest of the historical sections. Those passages of scripture that we did consider, however, have evinced the same mixture in the way they relate to the words of CD 5:15b-6:11a, and not a few had already been dealt with in relation to the two preceding historical sections: Lv 26, Dt 12ff, Dt 28ff, Is 59, Jer 23, Hos 5 and 10.

Nevertheless, we saw that CD 5:15b-6:11a has a somewhat different character. Our third historical section is concerned with the sect's legal supremacy and, more especially, the divine origin of its halakhah. The author expounds his view on this by way of an exegesis of Nu 21:18, following an account similar to, if briefer and less well ordered than, those in CD 1:1ff and 2:14ff. This means that references to persons, times and places within 5:15b-6:11a are as difficult to identify as those in the previous two historical portions of the Admonition. These historical problems of identification are exacerbated, moreover, in any attempt to combine an understanding of 5:15b-6:11a with a reading of 1:1-2:1 and 2:14-4:12a.

However, these points do not undermine our basic thesis that there is an underlying structure of biblical allusion and citation throughout the historical sections of CD. In this regard, our reference to Dt 1:13 in relation to CD 6:2 raised again the possibility of the 'creation of history' or, at least, the idealistic shaping of the presentation of more recent events under the influence of the ideal past.

---

[88] For an attempt to produce a synthesis, as well as for further bibliographical details, see G.J. Brooke, 'The Messiah of Aaron in the Damascus Document', *RQ* 15 (1991), pp. 215-230, who, *inter alia*, argues that a single messianic figure is expected throughout the Admonition, in both Ms A and Ms B. With this, cf. 1QSa 2:12 and 2:20 for the expectation of two messianic figures.

4.5 Scripture in the Historical Sections

Earlier, we proposed to examine the use of scripture in CD 1-8 and 19-20, because it was felt that this could be done with relative success without deciding between conflicting approaches to the work and to associated historical issues. Further to this, it was argued that CD 1:1-2:1, 2:14-4:12a, and 5:15b-6:11a evince similar characteristics and can, with qualifications, be viewed together as historical in orientation. Thus, while 1:1-2:1 is already marked out by the text in unambiguous terms, it is also reasonable to treat 2:14-4:12a and 5:15b-6:11a as units within the wider document. This was an argument internal to the final form of the Admonition and part of an attempt to describe the contours of the text as it now stands.

In our subsequent analysis, each portion was indeed discovered to be heavily dependent on the scriptures. One quotation and one virtual citation can be found in CD 3:21ff and 6:3f, respectively; while lacking the פשר terminology, they are pesher-like in identifying the various ingredients that make up the biblical verses. Another quotation in CD 1:14f uses a text from the bible to help identify a group and is similar. But while these instances are clearly important for any understanding of the bible in these parts of the document, they equally clearly relate to a wider body of dependence on the scriptures. Regarding Hos 4:16 (quoted in CD 1:14,15), we saw connections with Ex 32:8, Dt 9:12, and Is 30:11, all major texts for our author. Moreover, Ez 44:15 (cited in 3:21-4:2) belongs to a broad use of Ez evident in nearly every portion of the Admonition, whilst Nu 21:18 (see 6:3,4) is to be viewed against the background of our writer's preoccupation with incidents of rebellion in Nu and in the Pentateuch in general.

Arguably, our examination furthers previous treatments of scriptural usage in the sectarian DSS, which have concentrated on citations in CD 1-8, 19-20. It appears that such overt employment is rooted within the document as a whole to a greater degree than might otherwise be thought; this matches what was suggested in our introductory chapters. Indeed, each historical portion is replete with scriptural allusion, with one or two specific quotations in its midst; most of the citations and allusions interrelate, even if certain examples were beyond our scrutiny for the time being. The quotations, as well as linking with other allusions within each portion, also connect to those in other parts of the Admonition. There can be little doubt, therefore, that much of the framework of allusion that we have noted, along with the citations, is deliberately worked into the text. If this is true, the quotations seem in a sense to relate secondarily to this underlying and pre-eminent foundation of allusion. Overall, we have found ourselves referring to the same parts of the bible, and from the many passages we have examined, the following contexts stand out:

Gn 6, 7; Ex 32; Lv 17-18, 26;
Nu 13-21; Dt 1, 9, 12-13, 27-32;
Is 24, 27-28, 30, 51, 54, 59; Jer 23, 25, 27;
Ez 3-9, 11, 20, 33, 39, 44; Hos 4-5, 10; Mic 2, 7;
Pss 78, 94, 106; Ezr 9; Neh 9; Dn 9; 2 Chr 36.

Verses from each of these contexts are quoted or unquestionably alluded to in CD's historical sections and many of them will reappear when we proceed to our examination of the remainder of the Admonition.

These observations confirm our decision to attempt a reading of the Admonition as a unified piece on its own terms, laying to one side theories of redaction. In addition to a general similarity of language and style, our examination of these portions' dependence on a common body of scripture has further bolstered the fact of their interrelationship. Although each has its own distinctive contribution to make to the document, the same scriptural passages were found to be influential throughout. Even if some of the proposed allusions were speculative, most of them were not, either because they were so strong or because they connected with other citations or allusions elsewhere in the Admonition. This increases the probability of our contention that all three historical sections integrally belong to CD 1-8 in its final form, extending even to words and phrases commonly held to be secondary additions within 1:1-2:1. However, this characterization of the document clashes somewhat with some scholarly hypotheses based upon the historical problems mentioned earlier, that is, difficulties created by the coexistence of all three historical sections within one work. Our earlier remarks about cultural distance may be confirmed, therefore, in that the mind-set responsible for a text like the Admonition may not be immediately compatible with the sensibilities of modern scholars.

One further point can be made at this juncture regarding CD's story-line. Many of the above-listed scriptural contexts exhibit thematic patterns that were clearly meaningful for our writer. The pentateuchal texts employed concentrate on rebellions, punishments and subsequent restorations, culminating in the 'prophesy' of the exilic cycle. The prophetic passages used by our writer focus chiefly on the latter event, as we might expect; this is perhaps almost inevitable, considering the nature of the content of the Latter Prophets. However, it may partly explain the lack of reference to the Former Prophets, the main exception to this being the allusion to 1 Sam 2:35 in CD 3:19. The relevant contexts within the Ketuvim likewise concentrate on the exile (e.g., Ezr, Neh), or else record a general cycle of rebellion and forgiveness throughout Israelite history (Ps 106). The story-line depicted in such passages was taken very seriously by our writer and relates in some way to that outlined in CD itself. Yet, it should be emphasized that CD's historical sections do not merely retell biblical stories in biblical language; nor do they, on the other hand, recount recent events only, employing scriptural phraseology in some metaphorical or typological way to do so. Rather, these portions of the document exhibit both characteristics in their employment of the bible.

It is this that makes reading the text, especially CD 1:1-2:1, difficult for the modern person, and might bring to the fore the notion that the document's dependence on the bible has led to the 'creation of history'. If the latter is a substantial ingredient within the historical sections, however, it is difficult to posit how the effects of such a phenomenon could be identified sufficiently precisely to facilitate their removal or the recovery of 'what really happened'. In this regard, it is noteworthy, for example, that the דור אחרון in CD 1:11f, to whom the מורה צדק explained God's workings, is remarkably parallel in its function to הדור האחרן in Dt 29:21, which, rather like "those who grope for the way" in CD 1:9, asks pertinent questions about the meaning of its predicament. It is difficult not to conclude that the role of the מורה צדק in the Admonition has been constructed with Dt 29:21, *inter alia*, in view.[89] Although the historical question is rendered rather complex by this possibility, it would, of course, be rash to suggest that the Teacher of Righteousness did not exist or play an important part in the history of the community concerned. Nevertheless, in view of these and other links between CD's historical sections and narrative patterns in certain prominent biblical passages, it may be suggested that the presentation of the flow of events in our document, especially within the first and second historical sections, is largely dependent on that in Dt and in other related scriptural texts.

Before considering this possibility further in our concluding chapter, let us move on now to examine the remainder of CD 1-8 and 19-20.

---

[89]   See above, p. 59, note 20. Also, we remarked on the ambivalent status of those commended in CD 1:8ff and 3:12ff; a similar ambiguity as to the continuing or new-found righteous standing of those described can be found in Is 59 and other scriptural texts.

5 Scripture in the Midrashic Sections of the Damascus Document

5.1 The Midrashic Sections

The remainder of CD 1-8 and 19-20, not dealt with in the previous chapter, now requires examination. Unfortunately, it is difficult to put forward a category broad enough to cover all of this outstanding material. Whilst we argued that, with qualifications, CD 1:1-2:1, 2:14-4:12a, and 5:15b-6:11a could be regarded as 'historical', it is more difficult to suggest an equivalent classification able to encompass the diverse sections contained in the rest of our document. A further complication presents itself in that, from CD 7:5ff, there is a disparity in the MS evidence for the Admonition as it is attested in the Cairo Genizah texts.[1]

Nevertheless, there may be one general characterization that can be made, at least for the remaining portions of MS A. While there is mention of various persons and events, it is of a different nature than that found in the historical sections. The reason for this divergence is that the span of history dealt with is much smaller, and the author does not seek to present a flowing narrative. Nor is any attempt made to show incidents or periods as following one upon another in linear fashion over a relatively long stretch of time. In contrast, we saw that, with variation, this was the case in CD 1:1-2:1, 2:14-4:12a and 5:15b-6:11a. The feel of the text in CD 2:2-13, 4:12b-5:15a, 6:11b-8:21 and 19:1-20:34 is, therefore, more immediate, and the impression is given that the writer is involved personally in the contemporary situation addressed, for which he believes his words are especially timely.[2] Such

---

[1] From CD 7:5b on, the witnesses are two-fold: MS A and MS B. The former is usually denoted by CD 7:5b-8:21 (or VII.5b-VIII.21), and the latter by CD 19:1-33a (or XIX.1-33a). There are not a few differences between these two MSS, on which see below, pp. 153-158.

[2] This aspect of the material entails two interrelated points: the fact that the author thought he was living in the period approaching the eschaton or אחרית הימים (cf. CD 6:11), and his own role as proclaimer of God's message for the times. The latter motivation is particularly interesting, if rather elusive, although such an evaluation

involvement was not so evident in quite the same direct way when he was recounting the events of ancient Israel or even the origins of the sect. In the sections we are about to analyse, however, the excessive praise of those whom the author views positively over against the extreme condemnation of his enemies, as well as the urgent tone of the warnings, reveals that the writer thought that much depended on the acceptance of what he was seeking to communicate. No doubt, this is true of the historical sections as well but the importunate note contained in them is less pressing.

Although the material we shall now examine may be described simply as miscellaneous, after the removal of the historical sections considered in the preceding chapter, we may expand on the above general categorization in one respect at this juncture. The sense of immediacy that comes across in CD 2:2-13, 4:12b-5:15a, 6:11b-8:21, and 19:1-20:34 correlates to the sect's self-identity, including how it viewed its relationship to those around it. In the historical parts of the Admonition, this identity is established in a somewhat sober fashion, is presented as continuous with ancient Israel's elect status, and finds expression principally through historical 'proof' of the community's true possession of the covenant. While this theme is not entirely absent from the remainder of CD 1-8 or 19-20, the claim that the sect constitutes the true בעלי ברית is asserted by and large in halakhic terms.[3] These sections of the Admonition maintain that the community's understanding of and obedience to the Torah is correct and superior to that of those outside; this is affirmed both indirectly by criticism of outsiders, as well as by the express promulgation of a particular interpretation of the Law. This legal orientation might suggest the appellation 'halakhic' for the material now under consideration, at least for CD 4:12b-5:15a and a good deal of 6:11b-8:21. However, a related point is

---

of the times, as well as the authoritative role of the author and/or his community in them, was not uncommon in the Second Temple period; cf. Dn, 1 En, and the writings of Paul. On Qumran eschatology, see in the first instance R.T. Beckwith, 'The Significance of the Calendar for Interpreting Essene Chronology and Eschatology', *RQ* 10 (1980), pp. 167-202; P.R. Davies, 'The Teacher of Righteousness and the End of Days', *RQ* 13 (1988), pp. 313-317; Schürer, II, pp. 550-554; A. Steudel, 'אחרית הימים in the Texts from Qumran', *RQ* 16 (1993), pp. 225-244.

3   While not absent, the theme of correct behaviour in the historical sections of the Admonition is expressed in a standard idiom: 'following the stubbornness of one's heart', 'not keeping the commandments of God', etc. In the portions that are the subject of this chapter, the halakhic theme is contemporarized into more specifically legal terms. Even so, the behaviour enjoined or criticized is articulated in a rather generalized manner; see above, p. 68, note 34.

worth noting: the halakhic supremacy of the community is demonstrated by direct appeal to scripture, accompanied by more frequent quotation and explicit interpretation of the bible in CD 4:12b-5:15a, 6:11b-8:21, and 19:1-20:34 than in the historical sections. At the formal level, exegesis now appears more integral to the portions we are about to analyse than was the case for the latter sections. Indeed, the remainder of the Admonition can be characterized by its immediate, practical interest, expressed very largely through the direct quotation and interpretation of scripture.[4]

Against this background, therefore, while 'miscellaneous' and 'halakhic' each represents one facet or another of the material before us, because our overall subject is the usage of scripture, we shall opt for 'midrashic' as an apt description.[5] The desire to be more precise, when the evidence does not allow it, must be resisted. We have already observed that attempts to be more exact almost invariably generate theories of sources and redaction or involve dividing up the document in a manner contrary to what are arguably the contours of the present state of the text. Therefore, although it seemed safe, with certain qualifications, to outline CD 1:1-2:1, 2:14-4:12a, and 5:15b-6:11a as historical, it must be conceded that CD 2:2-13, 4:12b-5:15a, 6:11b-8:21, and 19:1-20:34 fit rather less well into the designation 'midrashic'.[6]

Nonetheless, let us move on to the first of the remaining portions of the Admonition still requiring our attention, namely, CD 2:2-13.

---

[4]   As we saw, the quotations in the historical sections were accompanied by a change in style, so that CD 1:1-2:1; 2:14-4:12a; and 5:15b-6:11a could, in theory, function without them. Unlike the citations in CD 1:13f; 3:21f; 6:3f, those in the midrashic parts of the Admonition are more intertwined with the surrounding material, which frequently consists of overt interpretation of scriptural verses; without them, indeed, the text would often make little sense. However, it should be stressed that these observations relate essentially to the form of CD 1-8 and 19-20 as we now have it. On the level of dependence on scripture, we shall see that there is, in fact, a substantial degree of interconnection between the historical and midrashic sections.

[5]   Another possible title worthy of mention is 'synchronic'. In view of the apt contrast with the historical (i.e., 'diachronic') sections, manifest in the former's narrower time-frame and immediacy, it is with some reluctance that this is not adopted as a fitting heading for CD 2:2-13; 4:12b-5:15a; 6:11b-8:21; and 19:1-20:34.

[6]   For a list of detailed studies of CD 2:2-13; 4:12b-5:15a; 6:11b-8:21; and 19:1-20:34, see Broshi, pp. 65-72.

5.2 Scripture in CD 2:2-13

Commentators have noted the distinctive character of this section of CD, which is rather more deterministic in tone than the material before and after it.[7] It may be compared to 1QS 3:13-4:26.[8]

Despite the rubrics in CD 2:2-3a, and even if בדרכי רשעים is loosely meant as 'how it is with the wicked', what the author proceeds to describe is God's attitude towards evildoers, on the one hand, and towards those who are repentant or righteous, on the other. In looking at CD 1:1-2:1, it was noticed how the writer, after the introductory words of 1:1-2a, moved on to describe the שאירית equally as much as the declared subject, God's ריב with כל בשר. Similarly, at the end of this section, the climax falls on the claim that in every age God always has a group of righteous followers in an otherwise corrupt world; to these he passes on his teaching through his specially anointed servants. Although the language here and elsewhere sounds universal in application, in reality the author is dealing only with Jews, who are either righteous or wicked depending on their relation to the sect; Gentiles are assumed to be evil and lost, unless they convert (i.e., become sectarians).[9] In any case, having mentioned the condition and responsibility of those who repent in 2:5, followed by the decision of those who (rebelliously) turn aside from the (righteous) way in 2:6, the text then attributes the existence of both categories of people to God's design. The latter were not chosen by him from of old (2:7ff); the former have been raised up throughout every generation (2:11ff). In light of these comments, the purpose of the introductory formula is clearly rhetorical, the desired result being to attract attention, and it would

---

7   Davies, p. 76, also notes this but puts it down to form more than content. He maintains that the same basic point is found in both 1:1-2:1 and 2:2-13; these two historical discourses are then the foundation for that in 2:14-4:12a. Although we have not included 2:2-13 among the historical sections, Davies is correct to see a similarity of style and vocabulary so that, of the remaining material in our document, 2:2-13 is the nearest in character to these.

8   D.R. Schwarz, 'To Join Oneself to the House of Judah (Damascus Document IV.11)', *RQ* 10 (1981), pp. 435-446, suggests the less developed predestination in CD 2:2-13, compared to that in 1QS, renders CD chronologically prior to the latter, while Boyce, pp. 67-85, makes much of the similarity with parts of 1QS. CD 2:2-13 may also be compared to 1 Jn and the Didache.

9   Mention of the גר in CD 11:2 and 14:6 may be cases of such conversion.

be precarious to build much on any supposed identification of the באי ברית in CD 2:2.[10]

So far, the distinguishing features of CD 2:2-13 have been noted. Yet, this portion also overlaps with the sections of the document dealt with in the previous chapter in a way that 4:12b-5:15a, 6:11b-8:21 and 19:1-20:34 do not. This is in the form of vocabulary and idiom.[11] Nevertheless, the historical, linear style is much less present, if at all, and there is an absence of personages and supposed dates. At the same time, it is with some hesitation that this part of the Admonition of our text is placed within the present chapter, for it must be admitted that there are no quotations with interpretations in 2:2-13, nor any preoccupation that could be described as halakhic.[12]

It is appropriate to include the text of CD 2:2-13 at this point:

ועתה שמעו אלי כל באי ברית ואגלה אזנכם בדרכי

רשעים   אל אהב דעת חכמה ותושייה הציב לפניו

ערמה ודעת הם ישרתוהו ארך אפים עמו ורוב סליחות

לכפר בעד שבי פשע וכוח וגבורה וחמה גדולה בלהבי אש   5

בי כל מלאכי חבל על סרוי דרך ומתעבי חק לאין שארית

ופליטה למו כי לא בחר אל בהם מקדם עולם ובטרם נוסדו ידע

את מעשיהם ויתעב את דורות מדם ויסתר את פניו מן הארץ

מי עד תומם וידע את שני מעמד ומספר ופרוש קציהם לכל

הוי עולמים ונהיית עד מה יבוא בקציהם לכל שני עולם   10

ובכולם הקים לו קריאי   שם למען התיר פליטה לארץ ולמלא

פני תבל מזרעם   ויודיעם ביד משיחו רוח קדשו וחוזי

אמת ובפרוש שמו שמותיהם ואת אשר שנא התעה

---

10   See above, p. 49, note 1, and cf. J. Murphy-O'Connor, 'An Essene Missionary Document? CD II,14-VI,1', *RB* 77 (1970), pp. 226-229. Also, Rabin, p. 6, maintains that use of בוא here describes a state, not an action, and he points to the Mishnaic Hebrew באי עולם as parallel in nuance. However, while it could be argued that the *hophal* in CD 6:11b, which seems unusual, can be explained by the possibility that בוא in the *qal* was a standard idiom for membership of the community, it is unwise to depend on such evidence, for the only way of attempting to identify the באים in any given passage is through the context.

11   Examples of these are obvious: the initial rubric in CD 2:2-3 (cf. CD 1:1f; 2:14f); סרוי דרך and שארית/פליטה in 2:6,7 (cf. 1:13f and 1:4); פניו...ויסתר in 2:8 (cf. 1:3); קריאי שם in 2:11 (cf. 4:4); פרוש in 2:13 (cf. 4:4), and others.

12   Again, we find difficulty in definitively categorizing our material. This is a less pressing problem for a thematic division into 'paragraphs', however, than for any attempt to divide the Admonition into historical sources.

There are a number of textual matters that require some comment. First of all, we should note that 4QD^a adds ומכול שבילי חט after CD 2:2's בדרכי רשעים. Secondly, in view of the puzzling form בי in CD 2:6, most scholars propose a restoration to ביד.[13] Although it is possible to retain מדם in 2:8, rendering it "on account of blood(-shed/-eating)", scholarly opinion usually prefers emendation to מקדם, given that the same occurs in 2:7, although סדם has also been suggested.[14] Similarly, מי in 2:9 is variously emended to מישראל or omitted.[15] Also, we may take נהיית as נהיות in 2:10, while משיחי reads much better than משיחו in 2:12. The cause of the latter equivocacy is a vagueness in distinction between *waws* and *yods*, a common feature in numerous sectarian DSS, as well as in Hebrew MSS of medieval times. For קריאי שם, present in the intervening line, it is interesting to observe that 4QD^a has קריאים. Finally, there is some ambiguity as to the significance of שמו in 2:13. Most scholars suggest emendation and read "he established their names" or something similar.[16] However, it may well be best to leave the plural form and avoid changing the text; שמו would then have the sectaries as its subject, or else refer to a general "they" as indicative of a passive meaning.

Of greater interest to us is the fact that the difficulties in conjoining CD's historical sections are not replicated to anything like the same degree when relating CD 2:2-13 to the rest of the document. Nonetheless, for theological rather than historical reasons, CD 2:2-13 has often been viewed as stemming from an originally separate source, particularly in association with evaluations of the introductory formulae in CD 1:1f, 2:2f, and 2:14ff.[17] However, against the background of the findings of our previous chapter, we shall

---

[13] Thus, see *DSSE*, p. 98; Knibb, p. 25; Rabin, p. 6. This seems to constitute the simplest proposal, although Qimron in Broshi, p. 13, suggests that בי could represent בו כל or ובכל.

[14] Thus, e.g., Knibb, p. 25, has "on account of the blood", while Davies, p. 237, prefers "from the beginning". For סדם, see Qimron in Broshi, p. 13.

[15] Vermes, p. 159, restored מי to מועד, but in *DSSE*, p. 98, he chooses to omit it, as does Davies, p. 237. Knibb, p. 25, suggests מישראל; Rabin, p. 6f, puts forward both מיעמדם and מישראל as possibilities.

[16] Thus, see Knibb, p. 26. See also Rabin, p. 9; Davies, p. 237. Cf. *DSSE*, p. 98, which omits the whole phrase. Unfortunately, there is no precedent for postulating a *pual*, giving "their names were established". Qimron in Broshi, p. 13, remarks that 4QD^e appears to read [בפרוש שמותי]ן and he suggests an emendation in CD 2:13 to אמתו בפרוש שמותיהם.

[17] See again J. Murphy-O'Connor, 'An Essene Missionary Document? CD II,14-VI,1', *RB* 77 (1970), p. 107f. The line of argument is that 2:2-13 (and 1:1-2:1) envisages a different group of addressees than 2:14ff, and must, therefore, be a separate source stemming from a radically different *Sitz im Leben*.

examine scripture in CD 2:2-13 and discover that, once more, certain prominent biblical passages emerge as influential on CD's phraseology. This aspect of the material is demonstrated in the highlighted text below (p. 110), which we shall now proceed to examine in more detail.[18]

5.2.1 Torah in CD 2:2-13

It can be seen immediately that certain familiar pentateuchal passages reappear. Thus, the description of God as possessing ארך אפים and רוב סליחות is similar to Ex 34:6. After the rebellion narrated in Ex 32 and the consequent destruction of the לחות of the Law, God tells Moses he is to receive new tables. A climax is reached in Ex 34:5ff, when God reveals his glory to Moses as he passes by. Ex 34:6,7a reads:

ויעבר ה׳ על פניו ויקרא ה׳ ה׳ אל רחום וחנון ארך אפים ורב חסד ואמת: ⁷נצר חסד
לאלפים נשא עון ופשע וחטאה...:

Furthermore, this brings to mind Nu 14:18, where the same formula is repeated as Moses pleads with God to be merciful after the people expressed a desire to return to Egypt, a desire kindled by the report of the spies. Strictly speaking, Moses quotes God's own description of himself in this verse, deliberately recalling the incident related in Ex 34.[19] As will become clear below, it seems that the connection between these two contexts in the bible itself was one which our author saw fit to draw upon. Certainly, Nu 14:23 is utilized in CD 1:2, as we observed earlier.[20]

In 2:9, our writer uses the phrase עד תומם.[21] This would seem to be more relevant than might appear at first sight. In CD, the phrase has to do with the final destruction of those who "backslide from the way" and who "abhor the ordinance". It also connects well to Dt 2:14, which reads:

והימים אשר הלכנו מקדש ברנע עד אשר עברנו את נחל זרד שלשים ושמנה שנה עד תם
כל הדור אנשי המלחמה מקרב המחנה כאשר נשבע ה׳ להם:

This describes the generation that rebelled during the desert wanderings, which had to be destroyed before entry into the Land. Dt 2 addresses the

---

18   Again, major influences from the <u>Torah,</u> *Nevi'im*, and **Ketuvim** are <u>underlined,</u> set in *italics* or **bold** type; some words or phrases mix more than one of these.

19   This is shown in Nu 14:17, ...ועתה יגדל נא כח אדני כאשר דברת לאמר.

20   See above, p. 57. We also saw echoes of Nu 15ff in CD 2:14-4:12a; see the highlighted text on p. 75f.

21   For the textual problem in 2:9, מי עד תומם, see above, p. 108.

ועתה שמעו אלי כל באי ברית ואגלה אזנכם בדרכי רשעים   *Is 46:3 51:1,7 55:2*

אל יאהב ואשר שנא התעה ממנו לכל בשר חפץ בם   *Hos 4:1,6*

5   **אל אהבי** חסד ושנאי עולה ורב סליחות לכפר בעד שבי פשע וכוח גבורה   Ex 34:6 Nu 14:18 **Dn 9:9 Neh 9:17**

וחמה גדולה בלהבי אש בם כל מלאכי חבל על סררי דרך ומתעבי חק   *Is 59:20*

לאין שרית ופליטה למו כי לא בחר אל בהם מקדם עולם ובטרם נוסדו ידע   *Mic 3:9* **Ezr 9:14**

את מעשיהם ויתעב את דרות מדם ויסתר את פניו מן הארץ   Ez 39:23 **Ps 106:40**

מן עד תמם ובדע את שני מעמד ומספר ופרוש קציהם לכל   Dt 2:14

10   הוי עולם ונהיות עד מה יבוא בקציהם לכל שני עולם ובכולם   Ex 31:2 35:30 Nu 16:2 *Is 27:6 Ez 14:22*

הקים לו קריאי שם למען התיר פליטה לארץ ולמלא פני תבל מזרעם

ויודיעם ביד משיחו רוח קדשו וחוזי אמת ובפרוש שמו שמותיהם

people about to enter into their promises, after the expurgation of such rebels, and naturally connects to the Nu 13f context just mentioned.[22]

As for the reference to the קריאי שם in 2:11, it is not clear on which, if any, biblical context the author may be drawing. Two possibilities present themselves: either Ex 31:2 and 35:30, on the one hand, or Nu 1:16, 16:2, and 26:9, on the other. The verbal link with the latter cluster of texts is strong and is, therefore, preferred by most scholars. Nu 1:16 says of certain figures among the Israelites:

אלה קריאי העדה נשיאי מטות אבותם ראשי אלפי ישראל הם:

These are leaders and heads of tribes, called to help Moses perform a census. Nu 16:2 contains a similar reference:

ויקמו לפני משה ואנשים מבני ישראל חמשים ומאתים נשיאי עדה קראי מועד אנשי
שם:

This is part of the description of the rebellion against the authority of Moses and Aaron by Korah, Dathan and Abiram; the wider context is Nu 13-16, to which we drew attention above and on a number of previous occasions. Nu 26:9 too uses much the same vocabulary:

ובני אליאב נמואל ודתן ואבירם הוא דתן ואבירם קרואי העדה אשר הצו על משה ועל
אהרן בעדת קרח בהצתם על ה':

This passage concerns a second census and, in passing, reference is made to Dathan, Abiram and Korah, who had rebelled against Moses.[23]

Another possible biblical connection for קריאי שם in CD 2:11 is Ex 31:2 and 35:30. In Ex 31:1f, God tells Moses that he has chosen Bezalel to do special work:

וידבר ה' אל משה לאמר: ²ראה קראתי בשם בצלאל בן אורי בן חור למטה יהודה:

This is part of the final chapter in Ex dealing with instructions for the temple, priesthood and associated items, and Moses informs the people that God קרא...בשם בצלאל, giving him the required artistic skills. From the perspective of our analysis of the Admonition, the interesting point is that Ex 31:2ff and 35:30ff, which contain almost identical wording, form a bracket around the golden calf episode narrated in the intervening material. Thus, Ex 31 is the final piece of instruction on temple and priestly matters but, in Ex 32f, the people are led by Aaron to rebel, and Moses breaks the tables of the covenant. After Moses' supplication and the purging of the rebels, the

---

22   Note CD 20:13-15, which reads, ומיום האסף יורה היחיד עד תם כל אנשי המלחמה
     אשר הלכו עם איש הכזב כשנים ארבעים. This too clearly depends on Dt 2:14, and
     could be taken as corroboratory evidence for another connection here; see below, p.
     166.

23   However, these three characters are still referred to as קריאי עדה (i.e., following MT
     Qere קריאי, rather than the Ketiv קרואי; LXX reads επικλητοι).

covenant is reaffirmed and new tables are written in Ex 33f. Ex 35-40 then sets forth the establishment of the cult according to the details given in the chapters before the rebellion. If we are justified in positing an influence from this context within CD here, the author of our document may have had an interest in the second giving of the Law. In any case, it would appear that, as on other occasions and at the instigation of the biblical text, our writer has connected Nu 13-16 with Ex 31-35. He has used the phrase קריאי שם as an apt appellation for those who remain faithful, despite and after the rebellion and purging of others, drawing on similar phraseology utilized in both biblical contexts.[24]   This phenomenon mirrors what has been noticed above in relation to the ארך אפים idiom, also involving both Ex 34 and Nu 14.

5.2.2 Nevi'im in CD 2:2-13

Turning to the relation between CD 2:2-13 and the Prophets, we find a mixture of familiar and new biblical texts coming to the fore.[25]

CD 2:2f, with a distinctive אלי, contains the same sort of rubrics as in 1:1f and 2:14ff. In addition to Is 51:7, previously noted, see Is 46:3, שמעו אלי בית יעקב וכל שארית בית ישראל, and 55:2f. The latter reads:

...שמעו שמוע אלי ואכלו טוב ותתענג בדשן נפשכם: ³הטו אזנכם ולכו אלי שמעו ותחי
נפשכם ואכרתה לכם ברית עולם חסדי דוד הנאמנים:

The reference to the שארית in Is 46:3 is noteworthy (cf. CD 1:4 and 2:6), while Is 55:2, ואכלו טוב...בדשן, is similar to the promise of CD 1:8. Indeed, the notion of the enjoyment of a fruitful land, in accordance with the covenantal blessings and righteousness, is central both to biblical restoration

---

24   See also CD 4:3-5, which describes the בני צדוק as the קריאי השם העמדים באחרית הימים. Inasmuch as CD at this point is interpreting a citation from Ez 44:15, our author may have seen a typological connection between the exodus/giving of the Law, and the exile.

25   Two groups of biblical context, exhibiting some linguistic connection to CD 2:2-13, should be mentioned at this point but, since they do not link to use of scripture in other portions of the Admonition, will otherwise be left to one side:
For חמה גדולה and להבי אש in CD 2:5, cf. Zec 8:2 and Is 66:15, respectively, dealing with Zion's restoration and prosperity, in contrast to her enemies' destruction;
For עד תומם in 2:9, see Jos 8:24, ויפלו כלם לפי חרב עד תמם. If there were corroborative evidence that this context was on the mind of our author, it would suggest that, in the search for theological insults for its enemies, the sect may have appealed to the notion of the wicked Canaanites in the land, as well as the rebels within Israel (in the form of allusion to Nu 13ff, etc).

ideology and to the Admonition, and also clearly lies behind CD 2:11f, למלא פני תבל מזרעם.[26]

Hos 4:1 was earlier connected with CD 1:1. Hence, God's possession of דעת, referred to in CD 2:3, stating that דעת belongs to God and, by implication, that the sect shares in such knowledge, might be deemed to constitute a link with the earlier employment of the same context.[27]

In 2:5, our writer refers to the שבי פשע. This is reminiscent of another epithet in CD, שבי ישראל. In both cases, CD's words appear to depend on Is 59:20; we have already referred to this passage in the previous chapter.[28]

Given that the Admonition draws on the early chapters of Mic elsewhere, the words מתעבי חק in CD 2:6 are redolent of Mic 3:9. This text holds the rulers, priests and prophets responsible for the punishment and destruction that will come upon Israel due to their corruption. It reads:

שמעו נא זאת ראשי בית יעקב וקציני בית ישראל המתעבים משפט ואת כל הישרה יעקשו:

The presence of שמעו here once again points to it as a connecting word for our author; in other words, he appears to have linked such biblical passages via גזרה שוה.

We have already met Ez 39:23, and related texts from Ez, in association with CD 1:3. Likewise, ויסתר... in CD 2:8 alludes to the same passages. The most natural reference behind the words, as in CD 1:3, is the punishment of the exile, and this is one of the few historical pointers in 2:2-13.

Our author says of God in 2:11 הטיר פליטה, and this brings to mind Ez 14:22. Thus, Ez 14:22,23 reads:

והנה נותרה בה פלטה המוצאים בנים ובנות הנם יוצאים אליכם וראיתם את דרכם ואת עלילותם ונחמתם על הרעה אשר הבאתי על ירושלם את כל אשר הבאתי עליה: ונחמו[23] אתכם כי תראו את דרכם ואת עלילותם וידעתם כי לא חנם עשיתי את כל אשר עשיתי בה נאם אדני ה':

This is an interesting passage, since it parallels the story-line in CD's historical sections. Note in particular the use of נותרה and יוצאים, and the notion that

---

26   Moreover, regarding the notion of a ברית reconstituted after the punishment of the exile accoring to the promises made to David, note the resemblance between ברית עולם חסדי דוד הנאמנים (Is 55:3) and ברית אל נאמנות להם in CD 7:5.

27   In Hos 4:1,6; 6:6, we find lament of the people's lack of דעת and the negative consequences of this.

28   See CD 4:2f and 6:5f for the שבי ישראל היוצאים מארץ יהודה. As noted, Rabin, p. 13, considers both שבי פשע and שבי ישראל to be abbreviations of Is 59:20, שבי פשע ביעקב.

the punishment of the exile was worthwhile, since a new or reconstituted Israel was the end-product.[29]

Finally, let us take note of Is 27:6. This verse reads:

הבאים ישרש יעקב יציץ ופרח ישראל ומלאו פני תבל תנובה:

The 'Isaiah Apocalypse' here describes the promise of restoration for a purged and renewed Israel. Such a passage could easily have been interpreted meaningfully by the sect and, indeed, it seems to lie behind CD 2:11, למלא פני תבל מזרעם. As with CD 1:7f, the idea prevalent here concerns fecundity and blessing for those who are the true inheritors of the covenant. For use of the root שרש, see also CD 1:7.

5.2.3 Ketuvim in CD 2:2-13

When turning to the Writings, we are once more faced with a greater degree of ambiguity, especially concerning the Pss, inasmuch as a number of possible allusions in CD 2:2-13 lack any corroborative evidence elsewhere in the Admonition.[30]

The first main passage of relevance is Dn 9:9. With the standard phrase in CD 2:4, ארך אפים, compare the following:

לאדני אלהינו הרחמים והסלחות כי מרדנו בו:

---

[29] For נותרה, see CD 3:13, אשר נוטרו מהם; for יוצאים, cf. 4:3 and 6:5, both of which have היוצאים מארץ יהודה.

[30] Thus, note the following in this regard:
In connection with CD 2:2, דרכי רשעים, it is easy to imagine that Ps 1:6, כי יודע ה׳ דרך צדיקים ודרך רשעים תאבד, might have been interpreted in sectarian terms by the community, especially given that Ps 1 stands at the head of the Psalter;
With ובטרם נוסדו ידע את מעשיהם in CD 2:7f, cf. Ps 33:15, ascribing to God rule over the destiny of mankind, המבין אל כל מעשיהם...;
For תעב in CD 2:8, with God as subject, cf. Ps 5:7, declaring that God loathes an איש דמים;
With CD 2:12, משיחו רוח קדשו; cf. Ps 105:15, where the Israelites are described as God's anointed, whom no one may harm during the sojourn between Egypt and Canaan;
See also Ps 86:15, part of a prayer for deliverance from enemies, for ארך אפים language, noting v 1 (אביון אני; cf. CD 6:21); v 11 (הורני ה׳ דרכך; cf. CD 1:11 and 6:11); and v 14 (עדת אריצים; cf. CD 1:12). Pss 103:8 and 145:8 contain similar words also, the former as a thanksgiving for recovery from sickness, and the latter praising God's works and goodness;
Finally, for the typical Wisdom language reflected in CD 2:2, cf. Pr 8:12.

Dn 9 may be important in connection with CD 1:3 and, hence, we may tentatively posit another link here. Similarly, it is interesting to compare Neh 9:17, which reads:

וימאנו לשמע ולא זכרו נפלאתיך אשר עשית עמהם ויקשו את ערפם ויתנו ראש לשוב
לעבדתם במרים ואתה אלוה סליחות חנון ורחום ארך אפים ורב וחסד ולא עזבתם :

Both scriptural passages contain confessions and summaries of Israel's past, which contain story-lines similar to those in the historical sections of CD.[31]

We come to another familiar passage from the Writings in considering CD 2:6. Here, the reader is informed that those designated סררי דרך will be left אין שארית ופליטה. This is a reflection of Ezr 9:14, to which we referred in dealing with CD 1:4.[32]

Finally, it is necessary to mention briefly Ps 106:40 in relation to CD 2:8. Because the influence of this Ps is clearly detectable elsewhere in our document, it seems reasonable to postulate another link here.

5.2.4 Summary

The most interesting feature of CD 2:2-13 that has emerged from the above discussion is the connection it seems to have, in common with other portions of our document already examined, to certain parts of the Torah - especially the context around Ex 32ff and Nu 13-16. Regarding the influence of the Prophets, the reappearance of Is 59 and Hos 4 was noteworthy, as were clear connotations of the exile echoed in phrases derived from Is 27, Ez 14 and Ez 39. In dealing with the Ketuvim in this section, we returned to four central passages, namely, Dn 9, Ezr 9, Neh 9, and Ps 106.

The difficulty in positing a suitable categorization for CD 2:2-13 in relation to the rest of the Admonition, due in part to its shortness and because it overlaps in character with the historical sections, caused us to hesitate over the appropriateness of its inclusion in this chapter. However, these doubts are not sufficiently strong for us to exclude CD 2:2-13 from the present chapter, especially in view of the fact that 4:12b-5:15a, 6:11a-8:21, and 19:1-20:33 are similarly difficult to quantify in view of the diverse material

---

[31] In particular, we may recollect that Dn 9:7 reads במעלם אשר מעלו בך, which is a phrase very similar to CD 1:3, במועלם אשר עזבוהו. Moreover, in Dn 9:20-27 Gabriel appears to Daniel to explain the meaning of Jeremiah's "70 years"; cf. "390 years" (i.e., 7x70 years) in CD 1:5f. As for Neh, see especially, 9:29, אשר יעשה אדם וחיה בהם; this is one of several texts echoed in CD 3:15f.

[32] See above, p. 64.

contained within them. In any case, it is beginning to look increasingly likely that the whole of the Admonition hangs together, at least at the level of dependency on scripture, confirming the validity of our own study and giving credence to points made in the introductory chapters.

5.3 Scripture in CD 4:12b-5:15a

We turn now to one of the most interesting passages in the Admonition, for CD 4:12b-5:15a concerns itself with Judaism outside the sect בכל השנים האלה (4:12b), namely, during "the number of those years" (4:10). The preceding section, CD 2:14-4:12a, described the ruin of the mass of Israel and the community as its replacement, and the author now attacks the Judaism that remains outwith his group, showing that it is misguided and under Satan's control.

He achieves this in a two-fold manner. First of all, in CD 4:12b-19a, a statement is made to the effect that בליעל is in control of non-sectarian Jewry during the time before and approaching the eschaton.[33] Secondly, this is substantiated in 4:19b-5:15a by the citation and interpretation of Is 24:17 in terms of the שלושת מצודות בליעל, on which a certain Levi, the son of Jacob, also spoke or wrote.[34] It is at this point that we come across the only instance of Pesher exegesis in the Qumran Rules, so that the "nets" are identified: fornication, wealth, and defilement of the sanctuary.[35] CD 4:19b-

---

[33] In other words, non-sectarian Judaism is in the hands of the devil during the time of the author and his community. Whether the eschaton or אחרית הימים should be viewed as the final portion of the current age or as the beginning of the next or as a special, in-between-time is an interesting question but not of great import for our own analysis. See above, p. 103, note 2.

[34] It is noteworthy, in passing, that the Isaian passage has already been taken up in Jer 48:43,44 and in Lam 3:47. Unfortunately, the identity of לוי בן יעקב and his writing is not clear; some text parallel, or related, to TestXII, or, more particularly, TLev, is most likely. Regarding the latter, see J.C. Greenfield, 'The Words of Levi Son of Jacob in Damascus Document VI, 15-19', *RQ* 13 (1988), pp. 319-322.

[35] Following *DSSE*, pp. 69-186, the Qumran Rules may be taken to include 1QS/4QS, 1QSa, CD/4QD, 1/4QM, 11QT, 4QMMT, 4Q181, 4Q274, 4Q286-7, and 4Q280, although the precise characterization of individual works or groups of similar works may change as texts released in recent years are digested by scholars. In any case, Pesher terminology in usually employed in the so-called Pesharim, especially the most extensive of them, 1QpHab. As mentioned before, however, a text or part of a text without this nomenclature may evince similar characteristics and can be

5:15a attempts to apply this understanding of Is 24:17 to the contemporary situation. Various persons and groups are accused both of זנות and of defilement of the temple and their own spirits. However, as numerous commentators have pointed out, it is difficult, if not impossible, to match up coherently the "three nets" in 4:12b-19a with the corresponding sins reported in 4:19ff. This difficulty has resulted in theories of redaction in some scholarly circles. Thus, Knibb, enumerating four different accusations (polygamy, defilement of the sanctuary, niece-marriage, and rendering unclean one's holy spirit), states:

> "...[the] structure of this material is not entirely straightforward, but it seems most probable that the first and third of these accusations are presented as examples of 'fornication', the first of the nets of Belial...The second accusation (making the sanctuary unclean, the third of the nets of Belial) breaks the connection between the two examples of fornication; it is also much shorter than these and makes no reference to the Old Testament. For these reasons it is possible that this accusation was inserted at a second stage, or that it has been misplaced from after v.11a".[36]

The two main problems, therefore, in dealing with this portion of the Admonition are the relation of the "three nets" in 4:12ff to the specific accusations in 4:19ff, on the one hand, and the identity of the character called צו and of those dubbed בוני החיץ, on the other. Before going any further, however, it will be helpful to include the text of CD 4:12b-5:15a as follows:

ובכל השנים האלה יהיה

בליעל משולח בישראל כאשר דבר אל ביד ישעיה הנביא בן

אמוץ לאמר פחד ופחת ופח עליה יושב הארץ   פשרו

שלושת מצודות בליעל אשר אמר עליהם לוי בן יעקב   15

אשר הוא תפש בהם בישראל ויתנם פניהם לשלושת מיני

הצדק הראשונה היא הזנות השנית ההין   השלישית

טמא המקדש העולה מזה יתפש בזה והניצל מזה יתפש

בזה   בוני החיץ אשר הלכו אחרי צו הצו הוא מטיף

אשר אמר הטף יטיפון הם ניתפשים בשתים בזנות לקחת   20

שתי נשים בחייהם ויסוד הבריאה זכר ונקבה ברא אותם

ובאי התבה שנים שנים באו אל התבה   ועל הנשיא כתוב   1

לא ירבה לו נשים ודויד לא קרא בספר התורה החתום אשר

היה בארון כי לא נ∌ X נ∌ נפתח בישראל מיום מות אלעזר

ויהושע ויושע והזקנים אשר עבדו את העשתרת ויטמון

נגלה עד עמוד צדוק ויעלו מעשי דויד מלבד דם אוריה   5

---

designated pesher-like; several parts of CD fall into this category, as we saw above, p. 20f and p. 45f.

36   Knibb, p. 41.

ויעזבם לו אל וגם מטמאים הם את המקדש אשר אין הם

מבדיל כתורה ושוכבים עם הרואה את דם זובה ולוקחים

איש את בת אחיה׳ם ואת בת אחותו   ומשה אמר אל

אחות אמך לא תקרב שאר אמך היא ומשפט העריות לזכרים

הוא כתוב וכהם הנשים ואם תגלה בת האה את ערות אחי   10

אביה והיא שאר   וגם את רוח קדשיהם טמאו ובלשון

גדופים פתחו פה על חוקי ברית אל לאמר לא נכונו ותועבה

הם מדברים בם כלם קדחי אש ומעברי זיכות קורי

עכביש קוריהם וביצי צפעונים ביציהם הקרוב אליהם

לא יקנה כהר ביתו יאשם כי אם נלחץ   15

There are a number of textual and grammatical difficulties here, which deserve brief comment. בהם in 4:16 clearly refers to the מצודות just mentioned, though the latter noun is feminine. Several translations of ויתנם פניהם לשלושת מיני הצדק have been proposed (4:16,17), but the most satisfactory is that of Davies or Knibb; the former reads: "...and presents them in the guise of three kinds of righteousness".[37] In 4:17, the by-now familiar confusion between *waw* and *yod* means that we can safely assume that ההון was intended, even though the word does appear in the text as ההין. In contrast, although it has been suggested that שוא ought to be read in 4:19, following LXX of Hos 5:1 (which translates its *Vorlage* as ματαιων), it seems wise to leave צו as it stands, given the distinct biblical precedent in the Hebrew of Hos 5:11, הלך אחרי צו, which was undoubtedly an important biblical verse for our author.[38] Whether we accept the reading in 5:7, מבדיל, or assume a mistake has occurred and emend to the plural, the meaning is clear. A further question concerns how best to understand and relate the verbs ויעלו...ויעזבם in 5:5,6; although certainty is not possible, the general sense is reasonably perceptible.[39] Finally, as is evident from 6QD, הקרוב

---

[37]   Davies, p. 243. Knibb, p. 38, translates: "...makes them appear to them as three kinds of righteousness", and Rabin, p 16, is similar; *DSSE*, p. 100, has "setting them up as three kinds of righteousness". The differences between these renderings are minimal, centring on whether to read לפניהם instead of פניהם, but S. Schechter, *Documents of Jewish Sectaries: Fragments of a Zadokite Work*, Cambridge (1970), p. 67, "and directed their faces to the three kinds of righteousness", is to be rejected.

[38]   See Rabin, p. 17, and below, p. 122, on Ex 32:25f. As for Hos 5:11, it reappears as influential in CD 8:3.

[39]   Rabin, p. 18, translates: "the deeds of David were reckoned <as inadvertent sins>...and God allowed them to him". Davies, p. 245, has: "the deeds of David were overlooked...and God allowed them to him". Knibb, p. 39, similarly reads: "the deeds of David were cancelled...and God allowed them to him". *DSSE* , p. 100,

(5:14) is a mistake for הקרב, and we shall follow most scholars in interpreting
כהרבותו (5:15) as כהר ביתו.[40]

There are three other points of interest, worth mentioning at this juncture,
which are of somewhat greater importance. CD 4:15f refers to לוי בן יעקב; it
is not clear who this is nor which oral or textual source is being referred to.
Most scholars suggest a work similar to or connected with TLev.[41] In like
manner, it is not obvious to what exactly the author is referring in 5:2;
probably, the ספר התורה החתום is either the Pentateuch, which was thought to
have been lost for a period of time, or else another, possibly sectarian,
writing.[42] Thirdly, and despite the different significance given to the
defilement language in 5:11ff, it seems clear that the טמא המקדש described in
5:6ff is almost certainly to be understood literally, that is, as real defilement of
the building in Jerusalem, not as some spiritual or metaphorical pollution of
the sect, because the criticism is levelled against outsiders. [43]

Let us now return to the two main complications involved in the passage:
how CD 4:12b-19a and 4:19b-5:15a interrelate, and the difficulties in
identifying the persons mentioned. The first concerns the apparent mismatch
between the "three nets" enumerated in 4:12b-19a (טמא המקדש, הון, זנות)
and the specific accusations levelled against the "builders of the wall" in
4:19b-5:15a.[44] Having said of the latter in 4:19f that הם ניתפשים בשתים, the
sins then attributed to them are:

---

prefers a more literal translation: "the deeds of David rose up...and God left them to
him".

[40] Thus, for the latter, see Knibb, p. 39, "the more he does so..."; Davies, p. 245, "The
more he does it..."; *DSSE*, p. 101, "the more he does so...". For הקרב, see DJD, III,
p. 129.

[41] See again J.C. Greenfield, 'The Words of Levi Son of Jacob in Damascus Document
IV,15-19', *RQ* 13 (1988), pp. 319-322.

[42] See J.C. VanderKam, 'Zadok and the Spr Htwrh Hhtwm in Dam. Doc. V, 2-5', *RQ*
11 (1982), pp. 561-70; with this, cf. B.Z. Wacholder, 'The <<Sealed>> Torah
versus the <<Revealed>> Torah: An Exegesis of Damascus Document V, 1-6 and
Jeremiah 32, 10-14', *RQ* 12 (1986), pp. 351-68.

[43] Cf. H. Kosmala, 'The Three Nets of Belial. A Study in the terminology of Qumran
and the New Testament', *ASTI* 4, (1965), p. 103, who argues that, because the
Jerusalem temple was of little import for the sect, the uncleanness in view was
defilement of the community itself as a spiritualized מקדש.

[44] Note that R.H. Eisenman, 'The Historical Provenance of the Three Nets of Belial:
Allusion in the Zadokite Document and Bella/Bela' in the Temple Scrolls', *FO* 25
(1988), pp. 51-66, has argued rather unconvincingly that the three sins enumerated
in CD 4:12b-19a fit the reign of Herod the Great, rather than the period of the

1. taking two wives בחייהם;
2. defiling the sanctuary by not separating according to the Torah, sleeping with menstruants and marrying nieces;
3. defiling their own holy spirit by uttering blasphemies against the commands and speaking abomination.

Not only are we left wondering how to relate the accusations to the "three nets", but also how the words בשתים בזנות fit in with what follows. There are two basic ways of trying to solve the latter dilemma. One sees בשתים בזנות as a two-fold snaring in the net of זנות. The first of these is by marriage to two women בחייהם (4:20-7:5); the second is marriage to a niece (5:7-11).[45] 5:6b-7a, bringing in the prohibition of lying with הרואה את דם זובה, must then be secondary.[46] The other way of approaching the problem is to place a colon, as it were, after בשתים (with מצודות thereafter understood). Then, the בוני החיץ are caught in two of the three nets of the devil. The first is זנות (4:20-5:6), and the second is טמא המקדש (5:6-11). However, the latter has to be divided into two sub-categories: lying with a menstruant (5:6-7); union with a niece (5:7-11). With this solution, 5:11b-15a (...וגם את רוח קדשיהם טמאו) must be treated either as secondary or as beginning another section.[47]

Neither of these theories can encompass every detail of the text but the second way of taking the relation of 4:12b-19a to 4:19b-5:11(15a) ties in better with our listing of the accusations above than does the first proposal. However, it pays insufficient attention to 5:11ff, for it is not appropriate simply to relegate it to the level of a secondary addition.[48] Nor is it

---

Maccabean uprising and its aftermath, and that CD should, therefore, be classed as Herodian in date.

[45] There has been much scholarly disagreement as to the significance of the masculine suffix on בחייהם. For a recent discussion, with further bibliographical data, see J. Kampen, 'A Fresh Look at the Masculine Plural Suffix in CD IV,21', *RQ* 16 (1993), pp. 91-97.

[46] This explanation was proposed by Rabin, pp. 17-19, and J. Murphy-O'Connor, 'An Essene Missionary Document? CD II,14-VI,1', *RB* 77 (1970), pp. 220-221.

[47] Boyce, p. 171ff, takes the latter option.

[48] The same can be said of the proposition that CD 4:12b-19a itself is an interpolation. If these lines were added later, it was presumably to aid the reader in understanding the text, so that the suggestion that our difficulties in grasping the meaning of 4:12b-5:15a can be put down to such an addition clarifies little. Thus, it is not helpful to propose that, 4:12b-19a having perhaps once been separate, "...if one sees the abrupt introduction of 'the builders of the wall' as beginning a new section, there is less need to equate *bstym* with two of the three nets" (Boyce, p. 158).

satisfactory, if our interest is in CD as now available, to designate 5:11ff as the start of a new section, unrelated to what precedes. The present arrangement of the material, with its listing of the faults of those under attack, must include 5:11-15a, because, if זנות is mentioned as the first sin of the "builders of the wall", then ...גם in both 5:6 and 5:11 must be a continuation of their denunciation.

If this seems awkward, our expectations of what was acceptable as literary consistency at this time may need to be modified.[49] It is of interest here to take note of the not infrequent 'numerical proverb', found both in various biblical and other Second Temple writings. In particular, note the apparently confused Ecclus 23:16,17 which states:

16 Δυο ειδη πληθυνουσιν αμαρτιας,
   και το τριτον επαξει οργην·
17 ψυξη θερμη ως πυρ καιομενον,
   ου μη σβεσθη εως αν καταποθη·
   ανθρωπος πορνος εν σωματι σαρκος αυτου,
   ου μη παυσηται εως αν εκκαυση πυρ·
   ανθρωπω πορνω πας αρτος ηδυς,
   ου μη κοπαση εως αν τελευτηση.

From verse 16, the reader expects a clear listing of three categories of person.[50] However, he or she has to make do with learning about the "fornicator", the first of the three, because the writer becomes preoccupied with his description of this kind of sinner. As a result, it is difficult to distinguish an end to the section or 'paragraph' starting at 23:16f.[51]

The other difficulty confronting us in seeking to understand CD 4:12b-5:15a is the identity both of the one described as צו and of the בוני החייץ, who are presumably to be taken as his followers. These "builders of the wall" have been identified by some as the Pharisees, since their fault lies in their status as false prophets.[52] One problem with this suggestion, however, is the

---

49   See above, pp. 43-48.
50   An example is found in Ecclus 25:2, which reads:
      "I hate three kinds of people,
      and I loathe their manner of life:
      a pauper who boasts, a rich person who lies,
      and an old fool who commits adultery".
51   Unfortunately, there is no Hebrew for Ecclus 23:16f from Masada or the Cairo Genizah. The vocabulary used for the Greek wording πορνος and εν σωματι σαρκος αυτου would have been of interest. Other examples of the 'numerical proverb' include: Is 17:6; Am 1:3,6,9,11,13; Mic 5:4; Pr 6:16ff; 30:15-33; Job 5:19; 40:5; Eccl 11:2; Ecclus 25:7; 26:5-7; 50:25.
52   Thus, Schechter, p. 68; Charles, p. 810.

description of the current situation, as the author sees it, in 4:12f, יהיה...
בליעל משולח בישראל, since this implies that it is not simply one party within
the Judaism external to the sect that is in error, although this objection may
be over-precise. Another possibility is to identify the צו with the איש הלצון of
CD 1:14, because both contexts utilize the epithet מטיף. He may then be
equated with one of the Maccabee brothers, so that the בוני החיץ are then
literally "builders" of Jerusalem in the mid-second century BCE, working
under his command. Numerous other theories of identification have, of
course, been put forward.[53] It may be unwise, however, to be too keen to
identify terms for groups or individuals, for, in addition to the reasonable
assumption that the situation informing CD 1-8 and 19-20 was more rather
than less complicated, the fact that most of the epithets applied to various
persons or groups involve a use or even an interpretation of scripture is
likewise an argument for caution.[54]

Therefore, rather than posit some new identification for the characters
involved or reaffirm an already-existing theory, along with any concomitant
Sitz or *Sitze im Leben* for this portion of the Admonition, the layout below
(pp. 123-4) may add a different dimension to our understanding of CD 4:12b-
5:15a.[55] Accordingly, let us proceed to a detailed examination of this
arrangement.

5.3.1 Torah in CD 4:12b-5:15a

As the arrangement below demonstrates, there are a number of passages from
the Torah that seem relevant for our analysis of CD 4:12b-5:15a.[56] In CD

---

[53]   Knibb, p. 42, e.g., proposes that the epithet בוני החיץ applies to "Jewish society in
general", and that the words concerning צו, which redirect the accusations more
specifically, are secondary.

[54]   The following connections between CD's negative sobriquets and the bible have
been or will be noted: CD 1:18 (דרשו בחלקות ויבחרו במהתלות) and Is 30:10 (דברו
אל תטפו יטיפון) and Mic 2:6 (הטיף יטיפון); CD 4:20 (לנו חלקות חזו מהתלות); CD
6:1 (וינבאו שקר) and Jer 23:25 (שקר...הנבאים). The most important positive one is
מורה צדק in CD 1:11, derived from Hos 10:12 in conjunction with Is 30:20.

[55]   In the highlighted text, we have omitted echoes of Lv 18:18; 21:7; and 15:19, since,
although influential, the extent of the phraseology concerned, as well as its
imprecision, precludes accurate representation. Note that CD's use of Dt 31:26 is
probably more than accidental due to other clear pointers towards utilization of the
story-line in the final chapters of Dt within the Admonition.

[56]   For Dt 10:2, see below, note 64.

וכל המשל בם כי כל אשר באו בברית לבלתי סור מחקי התורה

	אלה יבראל לחטאם ביראתם בגואל לאאה לה בעליבל	*Is 24:17*
15	אשר אמר ישעיה בן אמור נביא אמר אליך פחד ופחת ופח עליך יושב הארץ	*Ez 12:13*
	אשר הוא מצודות בליעל אשר דבר עליהם לוי בן יעקב אשר הוא מושל בם	*Ez 14:5*
	המה יצודו בהם להתפש בהם בשלושת מצודות בליעל אשר אמר עליהם לוי בן יעקב	*Ez 5:11 23:38 44:7 Is 24:18*
	כי מקדם הוא והשלישית הממון הראשונה היא הזנות השנית ההון השלישית טמא המקדש	*Ex 32:25 Ez 13:10 Hos 5:11*
20	העולה מזה יתפש בזה הניצל מזה יתפש בזה בוני החיץ אשר הלכו אחרי צו הצו הוא מטיף אשר אמר	*Mic 2:6*
	הטף יטיפון הם ניצודים בשתים בזנות לקחת שתי נשים בחייהם ויסוד הבריאה זכר ונקבה ברא אותם	*Gn 1:27*
1	ובאי התבה שנים שנים באו אל התבה ועל הנשיא כתוב לא ירבה לו נשים ודויד לא קרא בספר התורה החתום אשר	*Gn 7:9*
		Dt 17:17
		Dt 10:2 31:26 Ju 2:7

Quotation and Allusion in CD 4:12b-5:3

2 Sa 12:13 1 Ki 15:5

Lv 18:13

Is 50:11 59:5

5

וגלה עד עמוד צדוק ויעלו מעשי דויד מלבד דם אוריה ויעזבם לו אל

וגם מטמאים הם את המקדש אשר אין הם מבדילים כתורה ומטמאים גם את

מקדשם ושוכבים עם הרואה את דם זובה ולוקחים איש את בת

10

אחיהו ואת בת אחותו ומשה אמר אל אחות אמך לא תקרב שאר אמך

היא ומשפט העריות לזכרים הוא כתוב וכהם הנשים ואם תגלה בת האח את ערות אחי

אביה והיא שאר

וגם את רוח קדשיהם טמאו ובלשון

גדופים פתחו פה על חוקי ברית אל לאמר לא נכונו ותועבה הם מדברים בם

15

כלם קדחי אש ומבערי זיקות קורי עכביש קוריהם וביצי

צפעונים ביציהם הקרוב אליהם לא ינקה

Quotation and Allusion in CD 5:4-15a

4:19, our author refers to the "builders of the wall" who have gone אחרי צו. Upon reflection, the latter may be connected to Ex 32:25f, part of the story about the golden calf:

וירא משה את העם כי פרע הוא כי פרעה אהרן לשמצה בקמיהם: ²⁶ויעמד משה בשער המחנה ויאמר מי לה׳ אלי ויאספו אליו כל בני לוי:

This is Moses' response to Aaron's recounting of the incident, and some of the ancient versions understood לשמצה as לשם צאה. If so, this may have been connected to Hos 5:11 in CD 4:19 (for which, see below) by way of another text in the scriptures which was important for CD, namely, Is 28, which contains occurrences of both צאה and צו.[57]

In CD 4:21 and 5:1 we find two virtual quotations from Gn, namely, Gn 1:27 and 7:9. The first refers to God's creation of humankind as both זכר ונקבה. The second describes the animals entering Noah's ark before the Flood:

שנים שנים באו אל נח אל התבה זכר ונקבה כאשר צוה אלהים את נח:

Both are straightforwardly used by our author; a connection may have been made between them due to the presence of זכר ונקבה in each.[58]

Dt 17:17 is used to justify further the point being argued on marriage by appealing to God's command concerning the king of Israel:

ולא ירבה לו נשים ולא יסור לבבו וכסף וזהב לא ירבה לו מאד:

The employment of this text in CD 5:2 seems clear-cut, although there are problems involved in relation to the parallel passage in 11QT 57:17b-19a.[59]

Scholars have disagreed as to the precise meaning of the reference in 5:3 to the ספר התורה החתום.[60] Assuming that, in fact, it refers to the Pentateuch,

---

[57] See Rabin, p. 17f, who points out that Aq, Syr, and some of the Targums took לשמצה in Ex 32:25 as לשם צאה. Even Targum Onkelos has שום ביש. Moreover, Is 28:10,13 refer to צו, while 28:8 mentions צאה; of course, 28:14 refers to the אנשי לצון, as we saw in association with CD 1:14. Given their complexity, it seems more than likely that these interconnections are deliberate rather than coincidental. Note too, out of interest, W.L. Holladay (ed.), *A Concise Hebrew and Aramaic Lexicon of the Old Testament*, Grand Rapids-Leiden (1988), p. 304 (entry צו), "syllable mimicking prophetic speech...".

[58] If so, we may suspect another instance of גזרה שוה.

[59] Whether the principle in CD 4:20ff is monogamy at any one time, or a single, life-long partner is not relevant to our present task. For discussions of this issue, see, e.g., G. Vermes, 'Sectarian Matrimonial Halakhah in the Damascus Rule', *JJS* 25 (1974), pp. 197-202, and P.R. Davies, *Behind the Essenes: History and Ideology in the Dead Sea Scrolls*, Atlanta (1987), pp. 73-85. It should be noted that, in view of the form בהם in relation to the מצודות, it may not be wise to hang a great deal on the masculine ending of בחייהם in CD 4:21.

a passage which seems relevant is Dt 31:26. Here, Moses commands the Levites in the following manner:

לקח את ספר התורה הזה ושמתם אתו מצד ארון ברית ה׳ אלהיכם והיה שם בך לעד:

Moreover, VanderKam has argued convincingly about the meaning of CD 5:1b-5a. He shows that "Zadok" is the priest of that name in the time of David.[61] Further, the mention of the נגלה being hidden עד עמד צדוק[62] refers to the fact that it was Zadok, upon his taking charge of the sanctuary when the ark was returned to Jerusalem, who put the Law into effect; see 1 Chr 16:39-40.[63] From this, it appears that part of the basis of this story is a reading of Dt 31:26, ספר התורה...מצד ארון, as though it signified the placing of the Law inside the ark rather than beside it, bringing that verse into line with other biblical texts.[64]

As mentioned earlier, there are a number of general allusions to Lv in this portion of CD. Thus, "taking two wives..." in 4:20ff, whatever its precise interpretation, reflects the kind of regulations found in Lv 18:18 and 21:7; these texts express the ethics of the Holiness Code, the former for any Israelite and the latter for priests, and they require no further comment. Similarly, for הראוה את דם זובה, see Lv 15:19, and for אחות אמך לא תקרב, see Lv 18:13.

---

60   Thus, cf. J.C. VanderKam, 'Zadok and the Spr Htwrh Hhtwm in Dam. Doc. V, 2-5', *RQ* 11 (1982), pp. 561-70, with B.Z. Wacholder, 'The <<Sealed>> Torah versus the <<Revealed>> Torah: an exegesis of Damascus Document V, 1-6 and Jeremiah 32, 10-14', *RQ* 12 (1986), pp. 351-68.

61   Note, however, 2 Ki 22:8 and the discovery of the ספר התורה in the days of Hilkiah. Rabin, p. 18, supposes this to be the incident referred to in CD 5:5, and suggests the emendation of צדוק to בן צדוק, Hilkiah being a grandson of Zadok. However, this alteration of the text is unwarranted.

62   It is best to take ויטמון נגלה עד עמוד as "the Nigleh (=the Torah) was hidden until the coming of Zadok". This follows L. Schiffman, *The Halakhah at Qumran*, Leiden (1975), p. 30, with the benefit that emendations are thereby avoided. Cf. Rabin, p. 18; Davies, p. 245; Vermes, p. 86; Knibb, p. 39.

63   See again J.C. VanderKam, 'Zadok and the Spr Htwrh Hhtwm in Dam. Doc. V,2-5', *RQ* 11 (1982), pp. 561-570.

64   For other references to placing the Law in the ark, see Ex 25:16 and 40:20, using the expression אל אהרן. Dt 10:2, ושמתם בארן, however, is more interesting, since it connects to other dependencies on Dt 9 in CD, inasmuch as Dt 10:1ff retells the second giving of the Law after the rebellion recounted in the previous chapter and, for this reason, Dt 10:2 is included in the highlighted text on p. 123 above.

5.3.2 Nevi'im in CD 4:12b-5:15a

Concerning employment of the Prophets in CD 4:12b-5:15a, it is appropriate to refer to a variety of texts from the second division of the bible. Some of these show clear linguistic usage, interpretation or quotation; others merely provide a general background for our writer.[65]

Is 24:17 is quoted in CD 4:14 in order to demonstrate, via the interpretation of לוי בן יעקב, the fact that Belial is let loose against Israel during the period before the eschaton. Clearly, there is considerable 'licence' involved here. From the perspective of bible usage in the Admonition, it is interesting to note that העולה מזה יתפש בזה... in CD 4:18f is based on Is 24:18, the subsequent verse.[66] Moreover, the language of Is 24:5,6 is reflected in CD 1:20.[67]

There are a number of passages from Ez that are relevant for CD 4:16-19. The verb תפש and the idiom בנה חיץ reflect Ez 14:5 and 13:10, respectively (see CD 4:16 and 4:19). The latter of these two scriptural passages, might not immediately appear pertinent but the use of טוח with תפל in both Ez 13:10,15 and CD 8:1,2 shows otherwise. Regarding Ez 14:5, למען תפש את בית ישראל בלבם, which is impersonal, it could have been interpreted as referring to בליעל without great difficulty, since the subject (who, in the book of Ez, is probably God) is not actually specified.[68] These biblical contexts

---

[65]   The following will be mentioned at this juncture but otherwise left without comment:

For David's misdemeanour, implicitly mentioned in CD 5:2, see 2 Sa 5:13, ויקח דוד...פלגשים ונשים, simply describing his multiplication of wives;

Assuming the Zadok of CD 5:5 to be the priest after the same name in the days of king David, note 2 Sa 8:17 for his first mention in the scriptures.

[66]   Note that Is 24:17f is reproduced almost verbatim in Jer 48:44.

[67]   The critical assumptions and conclusions behind the designation 'Isaiah Apocalypse' are not relevant for our period but there is no reason why Jews then should not have been aware of the characteristics of these chapters that led later scholars to these theories.

[68]   It is not clear whether Ez 14:5 is positive or negative, although most versions take God as the subject. Cf. NRSV, "that I may take hold of the hearts...", with JPSA, "Thus I will hold the House of Israel to account..", and with REB, "my answer will grip the hearts of the Israelites..." However, the negative is to be preferred, as far as understanding CD is concerned, in view of Ez 12:13 and 17:20. In both of these texts, תפש is used with מצודה (cf. CD 4:15's "three nets") in reference to God removing his people into exile; it would not be without parallel for this activity then to be attributed to Satan by the author of our text (cf. 2 Sam 24:1 and 1 Chr 21:1!). In view of its proximity to Ex 13f, therefore, Ez 12:13 has been included within the

also evince a number of other interesting, if minor, interconnections with our document.[69]

When our author refers to 'defilement of the sanctuary' in 4:18, there are three other texts from Ez that seem relevant. God's criticism in Ez 5:11, את מקדשי טמאת, concerns his anger at the pollution of the temple and the resulting punishment; in view of other connections we have observed between the early chapters of Ez and the Admonition, we may now posit a link between this verse and CD 4:18. Similarly, Ez 23:38, a passage we shall return to in dealing with CD 19:33b-20:34, warns as follows:

עוד זאת עשו לי טמאו את מקדשי ביום ההוא ואת שבתותי חללו:

Such spiritual adultery on the part of Samaria and Judah will not go unchastened. Note too Ez 44:6,7 which is part of the section in Ez on the new pattern for the temple:

ואמרת אל מרי אל בית ישראל כה אמר אדני ה' רב לכם מכל תועבותיכם בית ישראל:
בהביאכם בני נכר ערלי לב וערלי בשר להיות במקדשי לחללו את ביתי בהקריבכם את[7]
לחמי חלב ודם ויפרו את בריתי אל כל תועבותיכם:

Possible allusion to this text is interesting, because Ez 44:15 is quoted in CD 3:21-4:2. Indeed, both verses 7 and 15 refer to the offering of חלב ודם, and our writer may have connected them via גזרה שוה.

In CD 4:19,10 our writer states: בוני החיץ אשר הלכו אחרי צו הצו הוא מטיף אשר אמר הטף יטיפון הם ניתפשים בשתים. The best way of understanding these words can be expressed in the following translation:

> "As for the builders of the wall who went after צו (צו is a Spouter, of whom it is said, 'They shall certainly spout'), they are caught in two:".

Two passages of scripture are involved here, namely, Hos 5:10,11 and Mic 2:6. Any uncertainty that the latter passage, אל תטפו יטיפון לא יטפו לאלה לא יסג כלמות, exerted some influence upon CD at this point is removed by the clear allusion to Mic 2:11 in CD 8:13. Regarding Hos 5:10,11 - which reappears very strongly in CD 8:3 - these biblical verses read:

היו שרי יהודה כמסיגי גבול עליהם אשפוך כמים עברתי: [11]עשוק אפרים רצוץ משפט
כי הואיל הלך אחרי צו:

---

highlighted text on p. 123. There are some other interesting parallels between Ez 12 and CD's story-line: Ez 12:11 has שבי; 12:16, והותרתי מהם אנשי מספר; and 12:23ff describes the "days" as "at hand", as also the דבר כל חזון. Out of interest, Ez 17 uses הפר and ברית (which we have met in CD 1:20), as well as the notion of being taken בבלה.

69   Thus, in Ez 13, note כזב (v 8), and reference to an exclusion of names from a כתב, as well as the forfeiting of the right to enter the land (v 9); cf. CD 1:15 and 2:13. Ez 14 uses תעה (v 11), and contains a brief promise of restoration after purging (v 22, נותרה בה פלטה); cf. especially CD 3:13.

Both scriptural contexts under consideration here describe the negative state of Israel or Judah, disobedient and defiled, and their resultant predicament of approaching or actual woe.

In CD 5:2, the reason given for David's apparent disobedience to the law against multiplication of wives is his ignorance.[70] This in turn was due to the fact that the Law was hidden for a period of time; it was not available מיום מות אלעזר ויהושע והזקנים.[71] This 'information' seems to have been gleaned from a combination of Jos 24:29 (describing Joshua's demise), Jos 24:33 (where it is said that Eleazar too died), and the fuller account in Ju 2:7-10. The latter passage describes the mortal and spiritual decline that took place after the death of Joshua and the elders:

ויעבדו העם את ה׳ כל ימי יהושע וכל ימי הזקנים אשר האריכו ימים אחרי יהושוע אשר
ראו את כל מעשה ה׳ הגדול אשר עשה לישראל: ⁸וימת יהושע בן נון עבד ה׳ בן מאה
ועשר שנים: ⁹ויקברו אותו בגבול נחלתו... ¹⁰וגם כל הדור ההוא נאספו אל אבותיו
ויקם דור אחר אחריהם אשר לא ידעו את ה׳ וגם את המעשה אשר עשה לישראל:

We can see how a combination of texts has contributed to the story as briefly recorded in CD at this point. In other words, although the deaths of Joshua and Eleazar are not especially connected in Jos 24, their proximity in that context, as well as the importance of Eleazar as an ancestor of Zadok and the tone of Ju 2:7-10, appears to have prompted our author to bring them together.

Turning to the description of David in CD 5:5, ויעלו מעשי דויד מלבד דם אוריה, it should be pointed out that our author's choice of words seems to have been shaped by both 2 Sam 12:13, where Nathan states גם ה׳ העביר חטאתך לא תמות, and 1 Ki 15:5, summarizing David's life as righteous רק בדבר אוריה החתי.

We come across a further interesting combination of texts in 5:13f. Our writer portrays his enemies in the following manner: קדחי אש ומבערי זיקות קורי עכביש קוריהם וביצי צפעונים ביציהם. This depiction combines words from both Is 50:11 and 59:5. The latter reads:

ביצי צפעוני בקעו וקורי עכביש יארגו האכל מביציהם ימות והזורה תבקע אפעה:

Obviously, the author of the Admonition is virtually citing Is 59:5 in CD 5:13f, and we have already noted the importance of Is 59 for CD, especially in 1:8,9 and in relation to the overall story-line contained in the historical sections. Turning to Is 50:11, this passage states:

---

70   See, e.g., 2 Sam 5:13, which states: ויקח דוד עוד פלגשים ונשים. Such an explicit text must be harmonized, because it is so blatantly in contravention of Dt 17:17 and cannot, therefore, be ignored.

71   In Ms A, an additional ויושיע is present.

הן כלכם קדחי אש מאזרי זיקות לכו באור אשכם ובזיקות בערתם מידי היתה זאת לכם
למעצבה תשכבון:

These words immediately precede Is 51:1,7 which, as we have seen, inform
the language of CD 1:1, 2:2, and 2:14.[72]

5.3.3 Ketuvim in CD 4:12b-5:15a

There appears to be no substantial employment of the Writings in CD 4:12b-
5:15a. Although at first sight promising, it is difficult to make much of either
Ps 18:5 in relation to בליעל, or Pr 17:11 vis à vis משולח in CD 4:13, although
the wickedness of Israel calling forth the devil as its consequence could easily
be read into the latter of these two biblical texts.[73] Of similarly minimal
significance is the fact that Lam 3:47 partially repeats the wording of Is
24:17, which is also, as noted, cited in Jer 48:43f.

5.3.4 Summary

CD 4:12b-5:15a is the first extended passage to be examined within those we
have designated 'midrashic'. Indeed, it can be seen that, overall, the subject-
matter and style merit that categorization, although 'halakhic' and 'synchronic'
would also represent genuine aspects of the material.

Our consideration of the relationship between the citation of Is 24:17 with
its interpretation in 4:12b-19a and the elaboration of the sins of those under
attack in CD 4:19b-5:15a was not intended to give definitive solutions to
many of the ambiguities involved. Nonetheless, we affirmed that the passage
as a whole hangs together and is 'readable', if we allow a certain fluidity; in
this judgement, we differed from the evaluation reached by some other
scholars. As for the identity of צו and the בוני החיץ, whilst refraining from
positing concrete persons or groups, we noted that these epithets, as others in
CD 1-8 and 19-20, are based upon a usage of the scriptures. This factor,
rather than their precise identification, is our chief interest.

---

[72] See below, p. 150, for שבי ישראל in CD 8:16.

[73] Concerning Belial in Ps 18:5, most versions translate like NRSV, "the torrents of
perdition assailed me", or REB, "the destructive torrents overtook me". Cf. JPSA,
"torrents of Belial terrified me". LXX takes בליעל as ανομια. Other occurrences of
בליעל in the scriptures can be found at Job 34:18 and Nah 2:1, neither of which
appears to have been drawn upon elsewhere in the Admonition.

Regarding dependence on the Torah, and apart from the fact that the change in subject matter almost necessitates allusion to new scriptural contexts, the reappearance of certain passages was noticeable: Ex 32, parts of the Holiness Code, and Dt 31. Further, appeal to Gn 6,7 confirms our earlier suggestion that that context was viewed as analogous to the numerous other rebellions reported in the Pentateuch and drawn upon by CD, as was proposed when we considered the possibility of allusion to Gn 6:16 and 7:22 in CD 2:20.[74] Influence from prophetic texts also involved familiar sections from Is, Ez, Hos, and Mic, as well as new ones from these and other biblical books. Although the Writings probably hold no sway over CD 4:12b-5:15a, mention of the work of one לוי בן יעקב brought in a new factor, in that our author considered certain traditions attributable to him as authoritative.

Most interestingly, and despite placing the material within CD 1-8 and 19-20 into historical and midrashic categories, our consideration of CD 4:12b-5:15a points to a substantial common dependency upon scripture in both. This was the case for influence from the Torah and Nevi'im, and we shall see below that the same applies to the Writings. Even allowing for considerable subjective misconstruction on our part, this common preoccupation with many of the same biblical texts cumulatively supports our insistence that an attempt must be made to treat the Admonition as a whole document in its own right.

Finally, noting Jos 24:29, 24:33, and Ju 2:7-10 behind CD 5:2, it is worth considering that a certain use of the scriptures here may have led to what can be called the 'creation of history'. Several passages, already related in their scriptural settings, have been further combined and interpreted so as to produce additional historical details, albeit of a minor nature in this instance. We have already noted other probable examples of this phenomenon elsewhere in the document.[75]

5.4 Scripture in CD 6:11b-8:21

The remainder of the Admonition according to Ms A must now be examined and, presently, we shall view Ms B, which runs parallel to it from 7:5b onwards. If scholars have handled the portions within CD 1:1-6:11a in markedly different ways, an even greater variety in approach is evident with

---

[74]   See above, p. 74.
[75]   See above, p. 102.

regard to CD 6:11b-8:21.[76] The competing MS evidence, as well as the text's rambling and, at times, apparently disjointed nature, has led to diverse hypotheses concerning its composition and interpretation. As might be expected, theories of redaction have been propounded to explain the interrelation of CD 7:5b-8:19 and 19:1-33a, and these shall be considered briefly later. In line with our analysis so far, however, it is worth making every effort to 'read' CD 6:11b-8:21 in its present form before resorting to speculation about the use of sources or appealing to theories of redaction.

Thus far, it has seemed reasonable to place 'paragraph' breaks at CD 2:2, 2:14, 4:12, and 5:15. If we search for similar pauses in the material now under consideration, two are noticeable: 6:11a/11b and 7:9a/9b. Both commence in a similar vein, namely, with וכל המואסים... and וכל אשר הובאו..., respectively. CD 6:11b-7:9a, enlarging on 6:10,11a, claims that the sect's halakhah should be followed during the קץ הרשע (6:14). A brief list of some of what the sect found important in this regard follows, concluding with a promise of eternal life in CD 7:6 for those who fulfil these injunctions. CD 7:6b-8 contains an aside about those who live in מחנות.

The writer moves on to consider the מואסים in CD 7:9ff, and this contrasts with the preceding positive material. 7:9b-8:2a pronounces a warning against any who reject God's ways, exemplified in the case of those "delivered up to the sword" (7:13; 8:1), in contrast to the מחזיקים who "escaped to the land of the north" (7:14). The fate of the former awaits those counted as analogous to them in the author's own day, including those from within the community who apostasize.[77] 8:2b-19 continues the warning theme, referring to God's judgement at the eschaton. Thus, 8:2b-13 criticizes those who appear to be recent or contemporary Jewish leaders, whilst God's blessing is promised to the שבי ישראל in 8:14-18a. However, 8:18b-19 is directed against those within the sect who desert the מצות אל.

Despite the obvious difficulty in trying to read CD 7:9b-8:21 in a flowing manner, it is best to keep 8:2b-21 with 7:9b-8:2a for the purpose of understanding the text in its present form.[78] Before discussing some of the

---

[76] Note, however, that CD 8:20,21a is so brief and obscure as to defy meaningful evaluation.

[77] There are marked differences between Mss A and B in CD 7:9b-8:2a and 19:5b-14, respectively. This chiefly concerns the biblical texts chosen for proof and illustration. Ms A uses Is 7:17; Am 5:27a; and Nu 24:17, whereas Ms B employs Zec 13:7 and Ez 9:4.

[78] The differences between the two witnesses are particularly complex regarding 8:2b-19 and 19:14b-33. Murphy-O'Connor has suggested that Ms B's variations in this part of the overlapping material are due to a tendency on the part of the writer to see

specific problems involved in reading the passage, however, let us include the text of CD 6:11b-8:21 at this juncture:

וכל אשר הובאו בברית

לבלתי בוא אל המקדש להאיר מזבחי חנם ויהיו מסגירי
הדלת אשר אמר אל מי בכם יסגור דלתי   ולא תאירו מזבחי
חנם אם לא ישמרו לעשות כפרוש התורה לקץ הרשע ולהבדל
מבני השחת ולהנזר מהון הרשעה הטמא בנדר ובחרם   15
ובהון המקדש ולגזול את עניי עמו להיות אלמנ[ו]ת שללם
ואת יתומים ירצחו ולהבדיל בין הטמא לטהור ולהודיע בין
הקודש לחול ולשמור את יום השבת כפרושה ואת המועדות
ואת יום התענית כמצאת באי הברית החדשה בארץ דמשק
להרים את הקדשים כפירושיהם לאהוב איש את אחיהו   20
כמהו ולהחזיק ביד עני ואביון וגר   ולדרוש איש את שלום

אחיהו ולא ימעל איש בשאר בשרו להזיר מן הזונות   1
כמשפט להוכיח איש את אחיהו כמצוה ולא לנטור
מיום ליום ולהבדל מכל הטמאות כמשפטם ולא ישקץ
איש את רוח קדשיו כאשר הבדיל אל להם כל המתהלכים
באלה בתמים קדש על פי כל יסורו ברית אל נאמנות להם   5
לחיותם אלף דור   ואם מחנות ישבו כסדך הארץ ולקחו
נשים והולידו בנים והתהלכו על פי התורה   וכמשפט
היסורים כסרך התורה כאשר אמר בין איש לאשתו ובין אב
לבנו וכל המואסים בפקד אל את הארץ להשיב גמול רשעים
עליהם בבוא הדבר אשר כתוב בדברי ישעיה בן אמוץ הנביא   10
אשר אמר יבוא עליך ועל עמך ועל בית אביך ימים אשר
באו מיום סור אפרים מעל יהודה בהפרד שני בתי ישראל
שר אפרים מעל יהודה וכל הנסוגים ה'סגרו לחרב והמחזיקים
נמלטו לארץ צפון   כאשר אמר והגליתי את סכות מלככם
ואת כיון צלמיכם מאהלי דמשק   ספרי התורה הם סוכת   15
המלך   כאשר אמר והקימותי את סוכת דוד הנפלת   המלך
הוא הקהל וכיניי הצלמים וכיון הצלמים הם ספרי הנביאים
אשר בזה ישראל את דבריהם   והכוכב הוא דורש התורה
הבא דמשק כאשר כתוב דרך כוכב מיעקב וקם שבט
מישראל השבט הוא נשיא כל העדה ובעמדו יקרקר   20
את כל בני שת   אלה מלטו בקק הפקודה הראשון

והנסוגים הסגירו לחרב וכן משפט כל באי בריתו אשר   1
לא יחזיקו באלה לפוקדם לכלה ביד בליעל הוא היום

---

an increased connection between the sect's deserters and external rulers; see J. Murphy-O'Connor, 'The Critique of the Princes of Judah (CD 8,8-19)', *RB* 79 (1972), pp. 200-216.

אשר יפקד אל היו שרי יהודה אשר תשפוך עליהם העברה

כי יחלו למרפא וידקמום כל מורדים מאשר לא סרו מדרך

בוגדים ויתגוללו בדרכי זונות ובהון רשעה ונקום וניטור   5

איש לאחיו ושנוא איש את רעהו ויתעלמו איש בשאר בשרו

ויגשו לזמה ויתגברו להון ולבצע ויעשו איש הישר בעיניו

ויבחרו איש בשרירות לבו ולא נזרו מעם ויפרעו ביד רמה

ללכת בדרך רשעים אשר אמר אל עליהם חמת תנינים יינם

וראש פתנים אכזר   התנינים הם מלכי העמים   ויינם הוא   10

דרכיהם וראש הפתנים הוא ראש מלכי יון הבא לעשות

בהם נקמה ובכל אלה לא הבינו בוני החיץ וטחי התפל כי

שוקל רוח ומטיף כזב הטיף להם אשר חרה אף אל בכל עדתו

ואשר אמר משה לא בצדקתך ובישר לבבך אתה בא לרשת

את הגוים האלה כי מאהבתו את אבותך ומשמרו את השבועה   15

וכן המשפט לשבי ישראל סרו מדרך העם באהבת אל את

הראשנים אשר היעירו אחריו אהב את הבאים אחריהם כי להם

ברית האבות   ובשונאי את בוני החיץ חרה אפו   וכמשפט

הזה לכל המואס במצות אל   ויעזבם ויפנו בשרירות לבם

הוא הדבר אשר אמר ירמיהו לברוך בן נרייה   ואלישע   20

לגחזי נערו   כל האנשים אשר באו בברית החדשה בארץ דמשק

A number of points concerning the detail of the text here deserve comment.[79]
The most important is how to take לבלתי and the surrounding words in 6:12f
and, not surprisingly, scholars have suggested interpolations and consequent
emendations due to the difficulties involved in grasping the flow of CD in
these lines.[80] Also of significance is the sense of שר in 7:13 and of הועירו in
8:17. Some take the former as "ruled" from שרר, while others prefer a
variation on סר from סרר. The latter may be preferable, given the presence of
סרר/סור vocabulary elsewhere, particularly in CD 1:1-2:1.[81]   Less

---

[79]   For the form הובאו in CD 6:11b, for which 4QD^a appears to read הובא, see above,
p. 107, note 10.

[80]   Boyce, pp. 199-205, e.g., follows Davies, p. 139, in positing the following original
form to the text of CD 6:12ff:

וכל אשר הובאו בברית

לבלתי בוא אל המקדש להאיר מזבחו חנם

אם לא ישמרו לעשות כפרוש התורה לקץ הרשע

להבדיל...

Boyce argues that the מקדש here is meant metaphorically and spiritually as the sect
but this is surely not the case, at least as far as the final form of the Admonition is
concerned, especially in view of 1:3 and 6:11b-12.

[81]   Cf. Davies, p. 251, "Ephraim ruled over Judah", with Knibb, p. 56,
"Ephraim...broke away from Judah".

controversially, the reading העידו in 19:30 is usually chosen in preference to the הועירו of 8:17, although Davies has opted for an emendation to הלכו.[82] A relatively simple solution to the awkward reading ובשונאי את בוני החיץ in 8:18, especially in view of other instances of confusion between *yod* and *waw* in the Admonition, is to assume that ובשונאו was intended at this point, as suggested by Qimron.[83]

Several other points are of less import. Thus, זונות in 7:1 and 8:5 could be emended to זנות, which is present, for example, in CD 4:17, but this is not a necessity. More straightforwardly, Qimron's proposed reading of נאמנת for נאמנות in CD 7:5 is commonsensical, as also is the suggestion that כסרך in 7:6 be taken as כסרך. Further, לא has simply dropped out of the quotation from Is 7:17 in CD 7:11 after אשר.[84] Whilst the form הסגירו in 8:1 does not strictly make sense, the context shows that the meaning is obviously passive. Finally, וידפמום is emended to וידבק מום by virtually all scholars, although Qimron has proposed the reading [וירקמום] מוררים, "and wounds ornamented them".[85]

We suggested above that it is not impossible to view 6:11b-7:9a as a 'paragraph'. Yet, other divisions have been put forward. Stegemann proposed that 6:11-7:4 is best viewed as a *Gemeinderegel*, followed by a blessing in 7:4-6b and a curse in 7:9b-13b, with an interpolatory interruption in between.[86] Murphy-O'Connor treats 6:11-8:1 as a 'Memorandum' with additions in 7:6b-8 and 7:13c-8:1.[87] Davies agrees with the designation 'Memorandum', but ends his section at 7:10a.[88] However, all these suggestions, which may have some relevance to earlier forms of the text, confuse previous hypothetical editions of CD 1-8 with the Admonition as it now stands. As far as the latter is concerned, it is best to follow our own division. Indeed, within CD 6:11b-8:21, ...וכל אשר הובאו and ...וכל המואסים function in a fashion analogous to the constraining repetition within CD 4:12b-5:15a of ...גם in 5:6 and 5:11 after זנות in 4:16.

---

82 Davies, p. 255.
83 Qimron in Broshi, p. 25.
84 Is 7:17 is also cited in CD 14:1.
85 See Qimron in Broshi, p. 25, resting this suggestion on the occurrence of the word מוררים in 4QD[a] for CD 8:4's מורדים. Qimron also notes several other divergences of a minor nature between CD and 4QD[a] which need not detain us.
86 H. Stegemann, *Die Entstehung der Qumrangemeinde*, Bonn (1971), p. 165f.
87 J. Murphy-O'Connor, 'A Literary Analysis of Damascus Document VI,2-VIII,3', *RB* 78 (1971), p. 211.
88 Davies, p. 142.

CD 6:11b-7:9a contains two quotations, namely, Mal 1:10 and Nu 30:17 in CD 6:13ff and 7:8f, respectively. It also has a distinctively halakhic character, reflects biblical language chiefly from Lv, and is arranged as a 'list' of what is important about a person's behaviour. The list covers three areas: commands regarding separation, cultic instructions, and rules concerning conduct and relations with neighbours; all three are, however, intertwined, and do not follow consecutively. Into the first category fall the following:[89]

1. להבדל מבני השחת (6:14f)
2. להנזר מהון הרשעה הטמא (6:15)
3. להזיר מן הזונות (7:1)
4. להבדל מכל הטמאות (7:3)
5. ולא ישקץ איש את רוח קדשיו (7:3f).

Cultic regulations are as follows:

6. להבדיל בין הטמא לתהור (6:17)
7. להודיע בין הקודש לחול (6:17f)
8. לשמור את יום השבת...המועדות...ואת יום התענית (6:18f)
9. להרים את הקדשים כפירושיהם (6:20).

On social intercourse with neighbours, we find these directives:

10. לאהוב איש את אחיהו...ולדרוש איש את שלום אחיהו (6:20ff)
11. אלמנות...יתומים...ולהחזיק ביד עני אביון וגר (6:16f,21)
12. ולא ימעל איש בשאר בשרו (7:1)
13. להוכיח איש את אחיהו כמצוה (7:2)
14. ולא לנטור מיום ליום (7:2,3).

Clearly, this catalogue is not definitive, and variations are possible. Thus, items 4 and 5 above may belong together, as might 6 and 7 also. Moreover, the three categories of injunction overlap, and the precise significance of those designated 'cultic' is not obvious; only להרים את הקדשהם כפירושיהם would imply involvement in the temple service, although not definitely.[90]

---

[89] The following enumeration is based on Schwarz, p. 32ff. A good deal of the language reflects material from the bible, especially Lv; see below, note 94.

[90] Boyce, p. 204, lists twelve precepts with parallels, as he sees them, in CD 9-16, the biblical Decalogue, and the Holiness Code, respectively:

Precept 1	לעשות כפרוש התורה	CD 13:5-6;16:7-8		
Precept 2	להבדיל מבני השחת	CD 13:14	1st	
Precept 3	ולהנזר מהון...	CD 16:13-16	2nd	
Precept 4	ולהנזר...ולהודיע	CD 12:19-20		
Precept 5	ולשמור...השבת...	CD 10:4-11:18		Lv 10:10
Precept 6	להרים את הקדשים	(4QD's laws)		Lv 22:2
Precept 7	לאהוב איש את אחיהו		5th	Lv 19:18
Precept 8	ולהחזיק ביד עני...	CD 14:4-6,13-15	6th	Lv 19:9f, 33f

In any case, notwithstanding the problem over לבלתי in 6:12 and the flow of meaning at that point, CD 6:11b-7:9a holds together. Having stated who is under discussion in 6:11ff (i.e., those "brought into the covenant") with the help of a paraphrase and citation of Mal 1:10, the author provides a framework for their behaviour in his list of injunctions. This description of appropriate conduct employs biblical language which, while certainly present, is general. Further, when we come to those who dwell in מחנות, in 7:6b-9a, there are no insuperable problems in reading the text. Of course, these lines may have existed separately and/or been added to a later edition of CD 1-8. If so, however, it was because the words were fitting to the topic under discussion - the conduct enjoined applies also to those members of the sect living in camps. The essential unity of the final form of our current text is further exemplified in the emended quotation at the end of this sub-section, balancing that in 6:13f, although understanding its precise exegetical significance is another matter.

CD 7:9b-8:21, the final large block of material in Ms A, is more difficult to follow. The subject changes at various points, yet it is not easy to tell precisely where one topic ends and another begins. The only obvious conclusion we may draw from this is that the author has created a text which to us appears disorderly.[91] That being the case, it is necessary to attempt to understand CD 7:9b-8:21 as best we can. CD 7:9ff turns to the opponents of those addressed in 6:11b-7:9a, namely, the מואסים. 7:13b-21 contains an important parenthesis, reaffirming the status of the מחזיקים, but the text returns to God's enemies in 8:1. However, in 8:3 they are termed the שרי יהודה, and it is not clear whether those so designated are the same as the מואסים of 7:9b. It is usually thought they are not and, indeed, that the שרי יהודה are recent or contemporary religious or civil leaders in Jerusalem.[92]

Precept 9	ולדרוש...שלום	CD 9:2-8	7th	Lv 19:17
Precept 10	להזיר מן הזונות		8th	Lv 18:6-23
Precept 11	להוכיח איש את אחיהו	CD 9:2-8	9th	Lv 19:17-18
Precept 12	ולהבדל מכל הטמאות	CD 12:11-18		Lv 20:25

This is helpful. It is not possible, however, to give a definitive enumeration to the injunctions in 6:11b-7:9a, so that, whilst the parallels with CD 9-16 and Lv are worth noting, the incomplete correlation with the Decalogue is of unclear significance. This goes against Boyce's theory that the sect had its own (Do)decalogue, parallel to the biblical one, as 11QT was analogous to the Pentateuch. Cf. further Knibb, p. 51, who arranges his text into 11 instructions.

91   See above, note 48.

92   See especially J. Murphy-O'Connor, 'The Critique of the Princes of Judah (CD VIII,8-19)', *RB* 79 (1972), pp. 200-216. The question of the synonymy or otherwise

The description of them continues up to 8:13, employing a considerable amount of overt scriptural interpretation, as well as a negative portrayal in language familiar from CD 2:14-4:12a and from the immediately preceding lines in CD 6:11b-7:9a. After a brief reminder in 8:14,15 that the sect exists out of God's grace and intention, not due to its own merit, the ultimate fate of those who desert the community is referred to in 8:16-19. Unfortunately, it is difficult to make much of 8:20,21a, as observed earlier, due to the obscure brevity of these lines, but 8:21b returns rather fleetingly to the subject of the members of the sect, and then Ms A breaks off. As will be clear already, it is in CD 7:9b-8:21 that nearly all of the divergences with Ms B occur. Many of them are minor or accidental, or bear little on the overall meaning of the text. The main exception is the Am-Nu Midrash in 7:10b-8:1a, over against the Zec-Ez Midrash in 19:7b-13 of Ms B.

We shall now consider the use of scripture in CD 6:11b-8:21. In order to stay within the bounds of manageable blocks of material, we shall firstly view 6:11b-7:9a and then move on to 7:9b-8:21.[93] Before this, the text of CD 6:11b-8:21 is set out below (pp. 139-141), with quotations and allusions highlighted in the usual manner.

5.4.1 Torah in CD 6:11b-7:9a

Language from the Torah suffuses much of CD 6:11b-7:9a. Some parallels are due largely to a common subject, which necessitates usage of certain words and phrases. This applies chiefly to idiom concerning behaviour found in the list of injunctions in CD 6:14-7:3 (as well as the presence of the same, negatively expressed, in 7:9b-8:21). Whilst this might, at first sight, be thought of as a mere imitative repetition of biblical phraseology and almost inevitable when discussing conduct according to God's will, the fact that the language of Lv 17-25 predominates is noteworthy. Although mention of halakhic matters may require a set idiom, it is also the case that, for the community behind CD, the very notion of appropriate behaviour would

---

of the מואסים and the שרי יהודה is, perhaps, made less pressing when it is realized that the Admonition divides all humanity into sectarians and non-sectarians in any case. We may hypothesize, therefore, that, for them, the מואסים merged into the שרים.

93   This is purely for the sake of convenience, although a 'pause' does appear to exist at CD 7:9a/b between the two halves of the material in 6:11b-8:21. The same was found to be the case regarding CD 2:14-3:12a in relation to 3:12b-4:12a, although no division was made in the arrangement of our analysis.

וכל אשר הובאו בברית

לבלתי בוא אל המקדש להאיר מזבחו חנם ויהיו	
מסגירי הדלת אשר אמר מי גם בכם ויסגר דלתי ולא תאירו מזבחי חנם	*Mal 1:10*
אם לא ישמרו לעשות כפרוש התורה לקץ הרשע ולהבדיל	*Dt 12:1*
מבני השחת ולהנזר מן ההון הטמא הרשע בנדר ובחרם ובהון	
המקדש ולגזל את עניי עמו להיות אלמנות שללם ואת יתומים *יבוזו*	*Is 10:2 **Ps 94:6***
ולהב[ד]יל בין הטמא לטהור ולהודיע בין הקדש לחל ולשמור	*Ez 22:26 44:23*
את יום השבת כפרושה ואת המועדות ואת יום התענית כמצאת	
באי הברית החדשה בארץ דמשק להרים את הקדשים כפירושיהם	*Jer 31:31 **Ezr 9:5***
לאהוב איש את אחיהו כמהו ולהחזיק ביד עני ואביון וגר	*Lv 19:18 Nu 15:19 18:19*
ולדרוש איש את שלום אחיהו ולא ימעל איש בשאר בשרו	*Jer 29:7*
להזיר מן הזונות כמשפט להוכיח איש את אחיהו כמצוה ולא	
יטור מיום ליום ולהבדל מכל הטמאות כמשפטם ולא ישקץ איש את	*Lv 19:17f*
רוח קדשו כאשר הבדיל אל להם כל המחזיקים במשפטים	
האלה לצאת ולבוא על פי התורה ושמעו לקול מורה ויתודו	*Is 55:3*
לפני אל חטאנו רשענו גם אנחנו גם אבותינו בלכתנו קרי	*Nu 13:19 Dt 7:9 Jer 29:6*

15	
20	
1	
5	

Quotation and Allusion in CD 6:11b-7:7

Quotation and Allusion in CD 7:8-8:4

#		Scripture
	הנופלים אשר סרו מן הדרך ויתעבו את החוק חבל אשר אמר אין בהם	
	זכות כי באלה השיג גבול אשר גבלו הראשנים בנחלתם למען	
5	הדבק בהם את האלות בריתו להסגירם לחרב נקמת נקם ברית יען אשר	<u>Dt 12:8</u>
	דרשו בחלקות ויבחרו בתעתעות ויצפו לפרצות ויבחרו בטוב הגרון	
	ויצדיקו רשע וירשיעו צדיק ויעבירו ברית ויפרו חוק ויגודו על נפש צדיק	<u>Dt 32:33</u>
10	ובכל הולכי תמים תעבה נפשם וירדפום לחרב ויגילו למריבת עם ויחר	
	אף אל בעדתם להשם את כל המונם ומעשיהם לנדה לפניהם	
	כי גוי אבד עצות המה מאשר אין בהם בינה כי מקדם עמד משה ואהרן	<u>Dt 32:28</u> *Ez 13:10*
	ביד שר האורים ויקם בליעל את יחנה ואת אחיהו במזמתו בהושע ישראל	*Mic 2:11*
15	את הראשונה וגם בקץ חרבן הארץ עמדו מסיגי הגבול ויתעו את ישראל	<u>Dt 9:5</u>
	ותישם הארץ כי דברו סרה על מצות אל ביד משה וגם	<u>Dt 7:8</u>
	במשיחו הקדש וינבאו שקר להשיב את ישראל מאחר אל	*Is 59:20*
20	ויזכר אל ברית ראשנים ויקם ממהרן נבון וממשה חכם	*Jer 31:31*

Quotation and Allusion in CD 8:5-21

inevitably imply a nexus of scriptural connotations. We are correct, therefore, to treat echoes of Lv 17-25 within CD 6:11b-7:9a as significant, especially if, as seems likely, the employment of these scriptural chapters is the equivalent in the midrashic sections of the use of Lv 26 in the historical portions of the document.

Most of this sort of borrowing of biblical language, however, is in terms of general vocabulary, clear in its broad reference but isolated and lifted from its specific scriptural context.[94] This leaves room for the particular expression of the same basic principles according to the detail of the sect's halakhah in CD 9-16 or in other legal texts.

Beyond such generalized employment of the scriptures, a number of stronger links with the bible are also noteworthy. First of all, the use of שמר with the infinitive of עשה, as in CD 6:14, can be found in Dt 12:1. This may not be too significant, although other contacts between CD and Dt 12 have been observed. In particular, we noted, in association with CD 3:6, that Dt 12 emphasizes that a single sanctuary and abandonment of the practice of eating blood are essential for a long life in the land.[95]

Turning to CD 6:20, להרים את הקדשים, we are reminded of Nu 15:19 and 18:19, both of which refer to the consecrated portions of the sacrifices, the tithes and wave offerings that belong to the priests. We have already observed that this overall context within Nu was certainly on the mind of our author.

In relation to CD 6:20 and 7:2, the verbs אהב, נדח and נטר are found in the well-known passage of Lv 19:17,18. These verses read:

---

[94]   For this reason, it is difficult to represent such bible usage in the highlighted text above. Nevertheless, we may note the following:

נזר (CD 6:15) is found in Lv 22:2 and Nu 6:2ff, the former concerning priests' separation from the קדשים when unclean, and the latter the Nazirite; הבדיל in Lv 10:10; 11:47 and in CD 6:17 expresses the need to separate from uncleanness in terms of food, leprosy, discharges, etc; the root תען (CD 6:19) is employed in Lv 16:29 of the Day of Atonement; Lv 22:15 concerns the offering (הרים) of the priests' קדשים (cf. CD 6:20); Lv 19:10 contains the command to leave enough corn in the field for the poor (cf. CD 6:21).

Such examples show that CD has redirected biblical idiom towards what the author considered important. The same holds for allusions to Lv in CD 7:1-3, which are also of a general nature. Thus, Lv 18:6 and 25:49 use שאר בשרו, as does CD 7:1, the former concerning sexual morality and the latter kinsman-redemption. Also, Lv 21:7 states that a priest should marry no זנה, חללה or גרושה (cf. CD 7:1); the root שקץ (cf. CD 7:3) is employed in Lv 11:43; 20:25 in reference to defilement caused by unclean food.

[95]   See above, p. 74.

לא תשנא את אחיך בלבבך הוכח תוכיח את עמיתך ולא תשא עליו חטא: ¹⁸לא תקם
ולא תטר את בני עמך ואהבת לרעך כמוך אני ה׳:

The language in verse 18 is repeated in CD 8:5f, except negatively of those
who flout this injunction.

The words אלף דור in CD 7:6 connote Dt 7:9, which reads:

וידעת כי ה׳ אלהיך הוא האלהים האל הנאמן שמר הברית והחסד לאהביו ולשמרי
מצותו לאלף דור:

While the meaning of אלף דור within this passage in its earliest context in
ancient Israel may have been something quite different, our author seems to
take it to signifiy that, if the community is obedient to its side of the covenant
relationship, then God, for his part, promises eternal life.   In any case, the
presence of an allusion to Dt 7:9 here is rendered more likely by the virtual
citation of Dt 7:8 in CD 8:15.

The precise significance of the מחנות mentioned in CD 7:6b-9a has been a
subject of scholarly debate since the discovery of the DSS, with copies of CD
among them.[96] It is noteworthy that we find references to the מחנה or מחנות
in Nu 2:17, 2:32, 10:5,6,25, and 13:19.   These passages concern the
organization of Israel into camps along tribal lines, and the appropriate
coordination of them during the wanderings in the wilderness and the
occupation of the land.   The last context may well constitute another
connection to Nu 13ff, given the numerous other links that scriptural context
has with the Admonition. [97]

CD 6:11b-7:9a ends with a quotation from Nu 30:17. However, the text
is different from that evidenced in the MT and ancient versions. The former
reads:

אלה החקים אשר צוה ה׳ את משה בין איש לאשתו בין אב לבתו בנעריה בית אביה:

LXX and Targum Onkelos reflect the same text.   For lack of a better
explanation, we may conjecture that the citation from Nu 30:17 in CD 7:8,9
has been adapted deliberately in the light of Mal 3:24.[98]

---

[96] See, e.g., *DSSE*, p. 9, advocating the view that those who dwelled in מחנות were
"adherents of the Sect [who] lived an urban or village life side by side, yet apart
from, their fellow Jews and Gentile neighbours".   However, throughout our study,
we have deliberately sought to lay to one side as much as possible such historical or
identificatory matters.

[97] Other occurrences of מחנה can be found in Ex 16:13 and Dt 23:10. 1QM takes up
this imagery to describe the final battle at the eschaton, with the sect playing a vital
role.

[98] Mal 3:24 reads, והשיב לב אבות על בנים ולב בנים על אבותם פן אבוא והכיתי את הארץ
חרם; see immediately below on Mal 1:10 in CD 6:13f.   Further, although the
significance to be given to it is indeterminable, it is worth noting that Nu 30 relates
to the preceding historical cycles of rebellion within Nu in a way similar to the

Apart from the final quotation of Nu 30:17, we can see that, as far as the use of the Torah in CD 6:11b-7:9a is concerned, we have to do with a general borrowing of language and idiom. The texts are apt and appropriated fairly straightforwardly, although the phraseology is broadened out to create wider terms of reference within CD itself. This means that our author sounds authoritative, whilst leaving to himself and/or the sect the precise definition of what each individual exhortation signifies. Presumably, this was done in CD 9-16 and/or in other texts (e.g., 11QT, 4QMMT).

5.4.2 Nevi'im in CD 6:11b-7:9a

The first relevant text to be mentioned in connection with the use of the Prophets in CD 6:11b-7:9a is the quotation of Mal 1:10 in CD 6:13,14.[99] However, our document is somewhat unclear as to the precise extent and form of this citation, and this has led to suggestions of emendation by not a few scholars.[100] The MT of Mal 1:9,10 reads:

10 מי גם ועתה חלו נא פני אל ויחננו מידכם היתה זאת הישא מכם פנים אמר ה' צבאות:
בכם ויסגר דלתים ולא תאירו מזבחי חנם אין לי חפץ בכם אמר ה' צבאות ומנחה לא
ארצה מידכם:

Patently, this is the text in mind, even though it is merely paraphrased in 6:12b-13a (להאיר מזבחו חנם ויהיו מסגירי הדלת) before the acknowledged quotation in 6:13b-14a, introduced by אשר אמר. That the latter does not conform to the MT is not elucidated by the versions, except to show that there is some fluidity at this point in the text of Mal.[101] Nonetheless, aside

---

relationship between Lv 27 and the preceding Lv 26. Moreover, both Nu 30 and Lv 27 contain legal material on vows.

99   Of unclear significance or none, note the following:

First, CD 6:21's להחזיק ביד עני ואביון וגר compares to Ez 16:49, where Sodom's chief iniquity is disregard for the אביון or גר. If we possessed corroboratory evidence showing that this passage was on the author's mind, we might hypothesize that CD compares the sect's enemies with the inhabitants of Sodom, as well as with the rebellious Israelites in Nu and, perhaps, the evil pre-Israelite Canaanites (see above, p. 112, note 25);

Secondly, Is 55:3 provides a possible parallel for CD 7:5, especially given that we considered Is 55:2 above, p. 112, in relation to CD 2:2.

100   E.g., see above, p. 134, note 80.

101   Thus, LXX of Mal 1:9,10 reads:

9και νυν εξιλασκεσθε το προσωπον του θεου υμων και δεηθητε αυτου·
εν χερσιν υμων γεγονεν ταυτα· ει λημψομαι εξ υμων προσωπα υμων;
λεγει κυριος παντοκρατωρ. 10διοτι και εν υμιν συγκλεισθησονται

from the textual uncertainty, there are some points of contact between Mal and the Admonition which are worthy of note. Mal overall is a critique of the priests in Jerusalem, complaining that, although God's special covenant is with them, they have been unfaithful, polluted his sanctuary and married foreign women. Instead, from the priesthood should come דעת and תורה, as well as kindness towards the אלמנה, יתום and the גר. More noticeably, in Mal 3:16 and 3:18 we find two texts quoted elsewhere in CD, the former in 20:19 and the latter in 20:21.

The language in CD 6:16 appears to be a combination of Is 10:2 with Ps 94:6. Is 10:1-4 reads:

הוי החקקים חקקי און ומכתבים עמל כתבו: ²להטות מדין דלים ולגזל משפט עניי עמי
להיות אלמנות שללם ואת יתומים יבזו: ³ומה תעשו ליום פקדה ולשואה ממרחק תבוא
על מי תנוסו לעזרה...: ⁴...בכל זאת לא שב אפו ועוד ידו נטויה:

Ps 94:6 contains the words:

אלמנה וגר יהרגו ויתומים ירצחו:

Ps 94 has been referred to in association with 1:1-2:1, and this section of CD evidences a further connection in the occurrence of שחת in both Ps 94:13 and CD 6:15 as a designation for the final abode of the wicked.

When our author says in 6:17 that it is necessary להבדיל בין הטמא לטהור, we are reminded of Ez 22:26 and 44:23. The wider contexts of these have been dealt with above, in association with CD 1:3 and 3:21ff.[102] The first passage is about the lack of concern on the part of the priests to 'distinguish' appropriately (as well as about their opposition to the Law and disregard for the Sabbath). Ez 44:23 concerns one of the functions of the "Levitical priests, the sons of Zadok":

ואת עמי יורו בין קדש לחל ובין טמא לטהור יודעם:

This is a continuation of the same unit that began in Ez 44:15, concerning the כהנים, לוים and the בני צדוק, and which was cited in CD 3:21f.[103]

An interesting parallel to that which is found in CD 6:21 and 7:6f is Jer 29:4-7. This passage advises the exiles of Judah in the following manner:

θυραι, και ουκ αναψετε το θυσιαστηριον μου δωρεαν· ουκ εστιν μου θελημα εν υμιν, λεγει κυριος παντοκρατωρ, και θυσιαν ου προσδεξομαι εκ των χειρων υμων.

102   See above, p. 60, for Ez 20, and p. 83f, for Ez 44.

103   See CD 3:21ff, where Ez 44:15 is cited. The context may have been connected by the author of CD to the ברית חדשה of Jer 31:31, which is echoed in CD 6:19, in view of Ez 44:7, which states:

בהביאכם בני נכר ערלי לב וערלי בשר להיות במקדשי לחללו את ביתי בהקריבכם את
לחמי חלב ודם ויפרו את בריתי אל כל תועבותיכם:

כה אמר ה׳ צבאות אלהי ישראל לכל הגולה אשר הגליתי מירושלם בבלה: ⁵בנו בתים
ושבו ונטעו גנות ואכלו את פרין: ⁶קחו נשים והולידו בנים ובנות וקחו לבניכם נשים
ואת בנותיכם תנו לאנשים ותלדנה בנים ובנות ורבו שם ואל תמעטו: ⁷ודרשו את שלום
העיר אשר הגליתי אתכם שמה והתפללו בעדה אל ה׳ כי בשלומה יהיה לכם שלום:

In context, these verses from Jer refer to appropriate behaviour in exile in
Babylon, and CD would appear to be dependent on them at this point. If so,
then the מחנות are described in exilic terms.[104]

5.4.3 Ketuvim in CD 6:11b-7:9a

Let us now turn to the Writings in this section of CD, although a number of
passages, which seem promising at first sight, do not help us in our task.[105]

A text from the Pss of significance is Ps 94:6, to which we referred earlier
in association with CD 1:1-2:1. It reappears as influential in CD 6:16f, in
combination with Is 10:2, as noted above.

It is debatable whether יום תענית in 6:19 refers to general fast-days or
specifically to the Day of Atonement. In any case, we have already noted
numerous connections between Ezr 9 and CD, and the same noun, תענית,
present in both Ezr 9:5 of Ezra himself and here, constitutes another.

5.4.4 Torah in CD 7:9b-8:21

There are a number of important passages from the Torah utilized by our
author in CD 7:9b-8:21. Some are new, whilst others have already received
comment. Indeed, it is not necessary to repeat those general dependencies on

---

[104]   In contrast, scholars often argue that those at Khirbet Qumran considered
themselves to be metaphorically in exile (i.e., separated socially and religiously from
those around them) until the eschaton, while those who lived in the מחנות were
sectaries who lived a less isolated life. In this regard, 1QpHab 11:4f is noteworthy:

פשרו על הכהן הרשע אשר רדף על מורה הצדק לבלעו בכעס חמתו אבית [=אל בית]
גלותו

On this extract, Knibb, p. 243, comments: "*his place of exile*: probably the
settlement at Qumran".

[105]   Thus, note that the word שחת (CD 6:15) is found in a number of Pss. See, e.g., Ps
7:16; Ps 9:16; and 55:24; the second of these also refers to שאול and to the אביון
and the עניים (cf. CD 6:21). See Ps 84:12 and Ps 89:29, respectively, for mention of
those who walk בתמים (cf. CD 7:5) and of God's covenant (with David) as being
נאמנת (CD 7:5).

scriptural language already listed with regard to 6:11b-7:9a, including certain phrases found in the injunctions of 6:15-7:4, which are repeated in 8:5-9.[106]

Although at first sight rather speculative, it seems reasonable to see a connection between המואסים in CD 7:9 and the presence of the same root in Lv 26:15, especially given the widespread employment of Lv 26 throughout CD 1-8.

CD 7:19 contains a citation from Nu 24:17, followed by another from the same scriptural verse in CD 7:20f. Both are part of a digression within another quotation from Is 7:17, married to a citation from Am 5:26. The exegetical method employed by our author in his utilization of these passages has been the concern of several studies. However, from our perspective, it is the interconnection that exists between them and other quotations or allusions in the Admonition that is of importance.[107]

When the writer of CD complains of the "princes of Judah", in 8:7, that each does הישר בעיניו, we are reminded of Dt 12:8, a chapter we have already encountered:

לא תעשון ככל אשר אנחנו עשים פה היום איש כל הישר בעיניו:

Dt 12 stresses the central sanctuary and the abomination of blood-eating; the latter, we saw, was a theme in an earlier portion of CD.[108]

CD 8:9 utilizes a quotation from Dt 32:33, which is then interpreted in a pesher-like manner. Both the biblical and sectarian contexts contain in their vicinity a reference to a lack of understanding on the part of those criticized. Thus, with CD 8:12, לא הבינו, compare Dt 32:28,29, which reads:

כי גוי אבד עצות המה ואין בהם תבונה: ²⁹לו חכמו ישכילו זאת יבינו לאחריתם:

The first of these two verses was virtually cited by the author of CD in 5:16,17, and it seems more than likely, therefore, that we are right to see another link in the choice of words in CD 8:12.

---

106   Moreover, other possible links exhibit doubtful or extremely indirect connections:
       Emending CD 8:4 to וידבק מום, note the presence of the same verb in Dt 13:18;
       For זמה, found in CD 8:7, cf. Lv 18:17 and 20:14, where it refers to prohibitions
       on the degrees of marriage;
       Thirdly, ברית אבותיך in Dt 4:33 is parallel to CD 8:18.

107   There are significant differences between Ms A and Ms B here. For a discussion of
       how the two witnesses relate, as well as other bibliographical data, see below, pp.
       153-158. For now, it is noteworthy that, whilst the reference to the כוכב אלהיכם in
       Am 5:26 is not included in the actual citation of that passage, it is clearly
       understood, as shown by the subsequent quotation from Nu 24:17 concerning the
       כוכב. Cf. above, p. 125, for Ex 32:25f in relation to CD 4:19.

108   See above, pp. 74 and 142.

We find further dependence upon Dt in CD 8:14,15. A quotation from Dt 9:5 is used to demonstrate that the election of Israel and the sect is based upon God's goodness, not on any inherent worthiness. This is expanded by an unacknowledged virtual quotation of Dt 7:8, stating that the reason for the deliverance from Egypt was God's faithfulness to the patriarchal promises. This is used by CD as a reassurance for the sectaries in that, as God loved the ראשנים, so too does he love הבאים אחריהם.[109]

5.4.5 Nevi'im in CD 7:9b-8:21

The number of prophetic texts relevant for this part of CD are fairly numerous, primarily because more are directly quoted than has been the case up to now in 6:11b-8:21.[110]

The first citation is from Is 7:17, whose fulfilment is referred to in CD 7:11, where the realization of the prophet's words is interpreted negatively.[111]

The ארץ צפון in CD 7:14 has potential links with several occurrences of this phrase in the bible. In particular, we may note Zec 6:8, which reads:

ויזעק אתי וידבר אלי לאמר ראה היוצאים אל ארץ צפון הניחו את רוחי בארץ צפון:

The resemblance between this text and CD is so strong that ארץ צפון in CD 7:14 must connote the exile and Babylon. Especially interesting is the use of היוצאים, also present in CD 4:3 and 6:5.

We find two texts from Am behind CD 7:14-16. The quotation and interpretation of Am 5:26 is rather extensive and is supported part-way

---

[109] Note that the reason given for entering the land has been changed in CD from its former inhabitants' wickedness, as in the biblical text, to God's election of the Patriarchs' descendants (cf. Dt 9:5 and 7:8).

[110] Note the following of dubious or unclear importance:
CD 7:17's ספרי הנביאים אשר בזה ישראל את דבריהם is reminiscent of 2 Ki 17:13, mentioned briefly above, p. 96, note 82, in relation to CD 5:21, and stating:
ויעד ה׳ בישראל וביהודה ביד כל נביאו כל חזה לאמר שבו מדרכיכם הרעים ושמרו מצותי חקותי ככל התורה אשר צויתי את אבתיכם ואשר שלחתי אליכם ביד עבדי הנביאים:
In CD, it is scriptural prophetic "books" that are referred to;
In relation to CD 7:20, Ez 44:3 talks about a Davidic נשיא in association with the new temple in the new Jerusalem after the model of Ez 40-48; a connection with our document may be evident in view of this biblical text's proximity to Ez 44:15, cited in CD 3:21ff, but certainty is not possible.

[111] It is negative also in the MT and ancient versions. For the meaning of שר in CD 7:13, see above, p. 134; for סרר/סור vocabulary in the Admonition, see above, p. 58.

through by the second citation, namely, Am 9:11. Whilst the latter conforms to our present MT, the former differs considerably, as the following parallel arrangement illustrates:[112]

ונשאתם את סכות מלככם	והגליתי את סכות מלככם
ואת כיון צלמיכם	ואת כיון צלמים
כוכב אלהיכם אשר עשיתם לכם:	
והגליתי אתכם מהלאה לדמשק	מאהלי דמשק
אמר ה' אלהי צבאות שמו:	

Clearly, our author has felt free to deal with the text in his own way. Indeed, because his subsequent commentary assumes the presence of כוכב within it, it seems wise to conclude that he has merely abbreviated it. Yet, notwithstanding the great freedom with which he appears to us to be operating, it is reasonable to assume that its use relates to the exilic theme in Am 5:26 itself, as well as in Am 9:11 and the preceding reference to the ארץ צפון.

Hos 5:10 is the next text of importance, referred to in CD 8:3.[113] We have touched on this before in relation to CD 5:20. Hos 5:10-13 reads:

היו שרי יהודה כמסיגי גבול עליהם אשפוך כמים עברתי: [11]עשוק אפרים רצוץ משפט כי הואיל הלך אחרי צו: [12]ואני כעש לאפרים וכרקב לבית יהודה: [13]וירא אפרים את חליו ויהודה את מזרו וילך אפרים אל אשור וישלח אל מלך ירב והוא לא יוכל לרפא לכם ולא יגהה מכם מזור:

This biblical source of vocabulary was important for the writer of the Admonition, as demonstrated by the fact that it lies behind the document at several points.[114]

A further clear-cut allusion can also be found in CD 8:12, mentioning the בוני החיץ and the טחי התפל. These epithets derive from Ez 13:10,11, which runs as follows:

יען וביען הטעו את עמי לאמר שלום ואין שלום והוא בנה חיץ והנם טחים אתו תפל: [11]אמר אל טחי תפל ויפל היה גשם שוטף ואתנה אבני אלגביש תפלנה ורוח סערות תבקע:

We shall return to this prophetic passage below. For now, we may note that its influence here corroborates that which we posited in relation to CD 4:19, בוני החיץ.[115]

What is virtually a citation is present in CD 8:13. Behind this is Mic 2:11, where the Prophet says cynically:

לו איש הלך רוח ושקר כזב אטף לך ליין ולשכר והיה מטיף העם הזה:

---

[112]   The MT is represented on the left, and the text of CD on the right.
[113]   Ms B, in 19:15bf, makes the allusion into an explicit citation using כאשר דבר.
[114]   See above, pp. 63, 96, 128f, on CD 1:16; 5:20; 4:19, respectively.
[115]   See above, p. 127, and below, p. 167f, on CD 19:35.

Presumably, we have here ancient epithets being applied to more contemporary circumstances and personages.

In 8:16, we find reference again to the שבי ישראל, and, as previously, we are reminded of Is 59:20.[116]

It is not possible to understand the significance of the mention of Jeremiah/Baruch and Elisha/Gehazi in CD 8:20,21a; the lack of context and length render the text largely unintelligible. This is unfortunate, since what is noticeable is the two-fold coupling, presumably deliberate and counted as significant, of a prophetic master with his helper. In any case, see Jer 45:1 and 2 Ki 5:25 for the relevant references concerned.

The final eight words of Ms A revert to what is familiar from elsewhere: כל האנשים אשר באו בברית החדשה בארץ דמשק. For ברית החדשה, see again Jer 31:31, which we highlighted in relation to CD 6:19.

5.4.6 Ketuvim in CD 7:9b-8:21

Three familiar biblical contexts reappear as relevant for grasping employment of the Ketuvim in CD 7:9b-8:21.[117] Firstly, regarding CD's words in 7:9, להשיב גמול רשעים, we may gather that Ps 94:2 was of influence, given the employment of Ps 94:6 already noted in CD 6:16f.

Secondly, we came across Ps 78:62, ויסגר לחרב עמו, when we considered CD 1:4 and 3:10. It now reappears behind the language used in CD 7:13.

In interpreting the כיניי הצלמים, the writer of CD refers to the ספרי הנביאים אשר בזה ישראל את דבריהם. This reference is reminiscent of 2 Chr 36:16, which complains:

ויהיו מלעבים במלאכי האלהים ובוזים דבריו ומתעתעים בנבאיו עד עלות חמת ה' בעמו
עד לאין מרפא:

This is a general description, parallel to that in 2 Ki 17:13 mentioned above, from the hand of the Chronicler which well suits our author's view of his contemporaries.[118]   If this text were in view, it would not ·be easy to determine whether its use is metaphorical (i.e., the sectaries are like the exiles in Babylon), or literal (the author of CD views the exile's effects as lasting to his own day), or both; a similar ambiguity was found at points in CD 1:1-2:1.

---

[116]   See above, p. 62, on CD 1:8,9.

[117]   Of unclear significance, if any, is 2 Chr 21:18 in relation to כי יחלו למרפא in CD 8:4. The former describes Jehoram's end, who (along with his family) is punished thus: ואחרי כל זאת נגפו ה' במעיו לחלי לאין מרפא.

[118]   For 2 Ki 17:13, see above, note 110.

In fact, such ambiguity in the employment of exilic imagery is present in varying degrees throughout much of the Admonition.[119]

5.4.7 Summary

It is not to be denied that there are serious problems within CD 6:11b-8:21. In sum, these consist of the awkward flow of 6:11f, the matter of the identity of the מואסים and the שרי יהודה, as well as other historical questions generally relevant to the whole of the Admonition. Notwithstanding such difficulties, however, it has been possible to attempt a reading of this section as a whole, and to detect a structure. As part of this structure and in corroboration thereof, we have not been surprised to find a core of biblical quotation and allusion in 6:11b-8:21, which shares elements common to other parts of our document, as well as a number of texts not previously met.[120]

Indeed, the peculiar subject-matter and style of 6:11b-8:21 inevitably meant that we would encounter new scriptural contexts; this relates to the broadly halakhic nature of the material, distinguishing it from the historical sections dealt with in the previous chapter. At the same time, we have also referred to passages from the Torah, Nevi'im and Ketuvim that came to our attention previously with regard to CD 1:1-2:1, 2:14-4:12a, and 5:15b-6:11a, as well as in CD 4:12b-5:15a. We found ourselves invoking once more the Holiness Code, Nu 15f, and Dt 9, 12, 32, as well as Is 59, Ez 13, 44, and Hos 5, and then Ps 78, Ps 94, Ezr 9 and 2 Chr 36.

---

[119]   As far as 1,2 Chr is concerned, it is difficult to be sure about dependence on this version of Israelite history in CD or in other sectarian DSS, over against usage of 1,2 Sa and 1,2 Ki. This is especially so in the present context, in view of the similarity of CD's references to the ספרי הנביאים to 2 Ki 17:13, a context also considered in passing with regard to CD 5:21 (see above, p. 96, note 82). However, there may be sufficient cumulative pointers within CD to an interest in the last chapters of 1,2 Chr to push us in the direction of seeing another link here.

[120]   Some have argued that the repetition of vocabulary in CD 6:11b-8:21 from earlier portions of the Admonition, including that borrowed from the bible, shows that supposedly later portions of the document are secondarily dependent on earlier ones; see, e.g., Davies, p. 164, on CD 8:2b-19. However, even if this is true, which cannot be proven, the end-result of the alleged redactional process is a phenomenon worthy of study in its own right.

5.5 *Scripture in CD 19:1-33a*

CD 19:1-33a in Ms B is witness to a different form of the text paralleled in
CD 7:5b-8:19 and reads as follows:[121]

נאמנות להם לחיותם לאלפי דורות: ככ שומר הברית והחסד   1
לאהב ולשמרי מצותי לאלף דור: ואם מחנות ישבו כסרך
הארץ אשר היה מקדם ולקחו נשים כמנהג התורה וה[ו]לידו בנים
ויתהלכו על פי התורה: וכמשפט היסודים כסרך התורה

כאשר אמר^בין‎ואיש לאשתו ובין אב לבנו וכל המאסים במצות   5
ובחקים להשיב גמול רשעים עליהם בפקד אל את הארץ
בבוא הדבר אשר כתוב ביד זכריה הנביא חרב עורי על
רועי ועל גבר עמיתי נאם אל הך את הרעה ותפוצינה הצאן
והשיבותי ידי על הצוערים: והשומרים אותו הם עניי הצאן

אלה ימלטו בקץ הפקדה והנשארים ימסרו לחרב בבוא משיח   10
אהרן וישראל: כאשר היה בקץ פקדת הראשון אשר אמרי~דזקאל~
ביד יחזקאל ~והתו~ להתות התיו על מצחות נאנחים ונאנקים
והנשארים הסגרו לחרב נוקמת נקם ברית: וכן משפט לכל באי
בריתו אשר לא יחזיקו באלה החקים לפקדם לכלה ביד בליעל

הוא היום אשר יפקד אל כאשר דבר היו שרי יהודה כמשיגי   15
גבול עליהם אשפך כמים עברה: כי באו ~באו~ בברית תשובה
ולא סרו מדרך בוגדים ויתגללו בדרכי זנות ובהון הרשעה
ונקום ונטור איש לאחיהו ושנא איש את רעהו ויתעלמו איש
בשאר בשרו ויגשו לזמה ויתגברו להון ולבצע ויעשו ~אא~ ~Xא~

איש הישר בעיניו ויבחרו איש בשרירות לבו ולא נזרו מעם   20
ומחטאתם: ויפרעו ביד רמה ללכת בדרכי רשעים: אשר
אמר אל עליהם חמת תנינים יינם וראש פתנים אכזר: התנינים
מלכי העמים ויינם הוא דרכיהם וראש פתנים הוא ראש
מלכי יון הבא עליהם לנקם נקמה ובכל אלה לא הבינו בוני

החיץ וטחי תפל כי הולך רוח ושקל ~ספח~ סופות ומטיף אדם   25
לכזב אשר חרה אף אל בכל עדתו: ואשר אמר משה
לישראל לא בצדקתך וביושר לבבך אתה בא לרשת את הגוים
האלה כי מאהבתו את אבותיך ומשמרו את השבועה: כן
משפט לשבי ישראל סרו מדרך העם באהבת אל: את הראשנים

אשר העידו על העם אחרי אל ואהב את הבאים אחריהם כי להם   30
ברית אבות ושונא ומתעב אל את בוני החיץ וחרה ~אב~ אפו בם ובכל
ההלכים אחריהם וכמשפט הזה לכל המאס במצות אל XXXXX
ויעזבם ויפנו בשרירות לבם

---

121   An 'X' in the text denotes the remains of a letter now illegible.

The existence of this parallel text is one of the greatest sources of puzzlement for students of CD 1-8 and 19-20.   Unfortunately, the main obstacle to finding a solution to the problem of the relationship between the two forms of the overlapping material in the Admonition is that MS B is not extensive enough to enable a thorough analysis.   However, it does appear that MS B has been written by a hand somewhat more careless, or less skilled, than that which has penned MS A.[122]

Encouraged by Milik and Baumgarten, scholars have usually assumed that MS A and MS B are essentially the same work.[123]   With the release of the 4QD material, this, indeed, seems to be the case but we are not in a position to advance our knowledge of the precise nature of the connection between MSS A and B.   At the same time, it is clear that there are different types and varying degrees of divergence between MSS A and B, some of greater importance than others.   The following arrangement of the witnesses, therefore, may be useful.

5.5.1 A Comparison of Manuscripts A and B

The parallel material in CD 7:5b-8:21 and 19:1-34a is set out side by side, in order to view better the detail of the interrelationship, which is at times complex, between the two texts:[124]

7:6	...נאמנות להם לחיותם אלף דור	נאמנות להם לחיותם לאלפי דורות	19:1
		כך שומר הברית והחסד לאהב	19:2
		ולשמרי מצותי לאלף דור	
	ואם מחנות ישבו כסרך הארץ	ואם מחנות ישבו כסרך הארץ	19:3
		אשר היה מקדם	
7:7	ולקחו נשים	ולקחו נשים	
		כמנהג התורה	
	והולידו בנים והתהלכו על פי	והולידו בנים ויתהלכו על פי התורה	19:4
7:8	התורה וכמשפט היסורים כסרך	וכמשפט היסודים כסרך התורה	

---

[122]   Manifestations of such carelessness have been represented as best as possible in the text of 19:1-33a above, and are found chiefly in the scoring out of words or parts of words.

[123]   See above, pp. 1-4.

[124]   What follows is arranged so that, where one MS contains unique material, there is no parallel in the other.   Where, despite minor changes in spelling or word-order, the same or similar text underlies both, these are placed in parallel; unfortunately, complete consistency is impossible.   Since the Hebrew of both CD 7:6-8:21 and 19:1-33a has appeared already, the precise point at which each new line within the text of both MSS begins has not been marked again.

התורה כאשר אמר בין איש		כאשר אמר בין איש לאשתו ובין	19:5
7:9	לאשתו ובין אב לבנו וכל המואסים	אב לבנו וכל המאסים	
	בפקד אל את הארץ	במצות ובחקים	19:6
7:10	להשיב גמול רשעים עליהם	להשיב גמול רשעים עליהם	
	בבוא הדבר אשר כתוב	בפקד אל את הארץ	
	בדברי ישעיה בן אמוץ הנביא	בבוא הדבר אשר כתוב	19:7
7:11	אשר אמר יבוא עליך ועל עמך		
	ועל בית אביך ימים אשר		
7:12	[לא] באו מיום סור אפרים מעל		
	יהודה בהפרד שני בתי ישראל		
7:13	שר אפרים מעל יהודה וכל		
	הנסוגים הוסגרו לחרב והמחזיקים		
7:14	נמלטו לארץ צפון כאשר		
	אמר והגליתי את סכות מלככם		
7:15	ואת כיון צלמיכם מאהלי דמשק		
	ספרי התורה הם סוכת		
7:16	המלך כאשר אמר והקימותי את		
	סוכת דוד הנפלת המלך הוא		
7:17	הקהל וכיניי הצלמים		
	וכיון הצלמים הם ספרי הנביאים		
7:18	אשר בזה ישראל את דבריהם		
	והכוכב הוא דורש התורה		
7:19	הבא דמשק כאשר כתוב דרך כוכב		
7:20	מיעקב וקם שבט מישראל השבט		
	הוא נשיא כל העדה ובעמדו וקרקר		
7:21	את כל בני שת אלה מלטו בקץ		
8:1	הפקודה הראשון והנסוגים הסגירו		
	לחרב		

ביד זכריה הנביא חרב עורי על	
רועי ועל גבר עמיתי נאם אל	19:8
הך את הרעה ותפוצינה הצאן	
והשיבותי ידי על הצוערים	19:9
והשומרים אותו הם עניי הצאן	
אלה ימלטו בקץ הפקדה והנשארים	19:10
ימסרו לחרב בבוא משיח	
אהרן וישראל כאשר היה בקץ	19:11
פקדת הראשון אשר אמר	
ביד יחזקאל להתות התיו על מצחות	19:12
נאנחים ונאנקים והנשארים הסגרו	19:13
לחרב נוקמת נקם ברית	

וכן משפט כל באי בריתו אשר		וכן משפט לכל באי בריתו אשר	19:14
8:2	לא יחזיקו באלה	לא יחזיקו באלה	
		החקים	
	לפוקדם לכלה ביד בליעל	לפקד לכלה ביד בליעל	
8:3	הוא היום אשר יפקד אל	הוא היום אשר יפקד אל	19:15
		כאשר דבר	

8:x			19:x
	היו שרי יהודה אשר תשפוך	היו שרי יהודה כמשיגי גבול	19:16
	עליהם העברה	עליהם אשפך כמים עברה	
8:4	כי יחלו למרפא וידקמים כל		
	מורדים מאשר		
		כי באו בברית תשובה	
8:5	לא סרו מדרך בוגדים ויתגללו	ולא סרו מדרך בוגדים ויתגללו	19:17
	בדרכי זונות ובהון רשעה ונקום	בדברי זנות ובהון הרשעה ונקום	19:18
8:6	ונטור איש לאחיהו ושנוא איש את	ונטור איש לאחיהו ושנא איש את	19:19
	רעהו ויתעלמו איש בשאר בשרו	רעהו ויתעלמו איש בשאר בשרו	
8:7	ויגשו לזמה ויתגברו להון ולבצע	ויגשו לזמה ויתגברו להון ולבצע	19:20
8:8	ויעשו איש הישר בעיניו ויבחרו	ויעשו איש הישר בעיניו ויבחרו	
	איש בשרירות לבו ולא נזרו מעם	איש בשרירות לבו ולא נזרו מעם	
		ומחטאתם	19:21
8:9	ויפרעו ביד רמה ללכת בדרך	ויפרעו ביד רמה ללכת בדרכי	
	רשעים אשר אמר אל עליהם	רשעים אשר אמר אל עליהם	19:22
8:10	חמת תנינים יינם וראש פתנים אכזר	חמת תנינים יינם וראש פתנים אכזר	19:23
	התנינים הם מלכי העמים ויינם	התנינים מלכי העמים וייינם	
	הוא דרכיהם וראש הפתנים הוא	הוא דרכיהם וראש פתנים הוא	
	ראש מלכי יון הבא	ראש מלכי יון הבא	19:24
8:12	לעשות בהם		
		עליהם לנקם	
	נקמה ובכל אלה לא הבינו בוני	נקמה ובכל אלה לא הבינו בוני	
	החיץ וטחי התפל כי	החיץ וטחי תפל כי	19:25
8:13	שוקל רוח ומטיף כזב הטיף להם	הולך רוח ושקל סופות ומטיף	
		אדם לכזב	19:26
	אשר חרה אף אל בכל עדתו	אשר חרה אף אל בכל עדתו	
8:14	ואשר אמר משה	ואשר אמר משה	
		לישראל	19:27
8:15	לא בצדקתך ובישר לבבך אתה	לא בצדקתך וביושר לבבך אתה	
	בא לרשת את הגוים האלה כי	בא לרשת את הגוים האלה כי	19:28
	מאהבתו את אבותך ומשמרו את	מאהבתו את אבותיך ומשמרו את	
8:16	השבועה וכן המשפט לשבי ישראל	השבועה כן משפט לשבי ישראל	19:29
	סרו מדרך העם באהבת אל את	סרו מדרך העם באהבת אל את	
8:17	הראשנים אשר	הראשנים אשר	19:30
	הועירו אחריו		
		העידו על העם אחרי אל	
	אהב את הבאים אחריהם כי להם	ואהב את הבאים אחריהם כי להם	
8:18	ברית האבות	ברית אבות	19:31
	ובשונאי את בוני החיץ חרה אפו		
		ושונא ומתעב את בוני החיץ	
		וחרה אפו בם ובכל ההלכים אחריהם	19:32
8:19	וכמשפט הזה לכל המואס במצות	וכמשפט הזה לכל המאס במצות	
	אל ויעזבם ויפנו בשרירות לבם	אל ויעזבם ויפנו בשרירות לבם	19:33
8:20	הוא הדבר אשר אמר ירמיהו לברוך		
8:21	בן נרייה ואלישע לגחזי נערו		
	כל האנשים אשר באו בברית	כן כל האנשים אשר באו בברית	

19:34   ‏החדשה בארץ דמשק   ‏החדשה בארץ דמשק

This arrangement confirms that the differences between the two MSS are of
varying degree.[125]   There are slight discrepancies in spelling, as well as
variations over the precise reading of the text (e.g., singular or plural).
Hence, CD 8:6 has ‏שנוא, whilst 19:18 reads ‏שנא; similarly, 7:6 promises
eternal life unto ‏אלף דור, while 19:1 describes such blessing as for ‏אלפי דורות.
Some of these divergences are more interesting than others but none affects
the meaning in any great measure, as is also the case, for example, in the
variation between ‏יסורים and ‏יסודים in 7:8 and 19:4, respectively.   The same
can be said of omissions and additions of single words or a few words at
several points.   Thus, 19:14 includes ‏החקים after ‏האלה, while 19:21 has
‏ולא נזרו מהם ומחטאתם.[126] after ‏ולא נזרו מהם

A more difficult variation is where the two witnesses have approximate
equivalents which, nonetheless, are significantly different to one degree or
another in each MS.   This can be seen in the alternative ordering of the
clauses in 7:9b-10a and 19:6, or in the descriptions of the enemies in 8:13a
and 19:25b,26a.   In some cases, both readings make sense, while at other
points one seems to be a corruption of the other.   CD 7:9b-10a/19:6 is a case
of the former, while the latter would apply to ‏הועירו/העידו (19:30/8:17).

All of these types of variation are familiar from books in the bible, as well
as from other texts belonging to the Second Temple period.   However, the
main focus of attention for the differences between MSS A and B of CD is the
fact that 7:10-8:1 quotes and interprets a cluster of texts different from those
in 19:7-13.   There have been numerous attempts to explain this substantial
divergence, concentrating on accidental or deliberate omissions and
compensatory redactional additions.[127]

---

[125]   There have been several studies of the divergences between Mss A and B. See J.
Carmignac, 'Comparaison entre les Manuscrits "A" et "B" du Document de Damas',
RQ 2 (1959), pp. 53-67; S.A. White, 'A Comparison of the "A" and "B"
Manuscripts of the Damascus Document', *RQ* 12 (1987), pp. 537-553, theorizing
that all the differences are commensurate with a common original and mere
mechanical, unintentional scribal errors in copying.

[126]   Scholars have tried to explain these differences with varying degrees of success. As
reasonable as any other, e.g., is Knibb, p. 60, on ‏החקים in CD 19:40. He states that
"'the statutes' is most probably an explanatory gloss on 'these'; it does not appear in
the parallel passage in VIII.2". Such suggestions, however, often depend on a prior
commitment to a redactional theory explaining the relationship between Ms A and
Ms B.

[127]   See G.J. Brooke, 'The Amos-Numbers Midrash (CD7[13b]-8[1a]) and Messianic
Expectation', *ZAW* 92 (1980), pp. 397-404; Davies, pp. 145-153, and *Behind the
Essenes: History and Ideology in the Dead Sea Scrolls*, Atlanta (1987), pp. 38-40;

Of these, Murphy-O'Connor has gained wide acceptance in his view as to the development of 7:10b-8:1a and 19:7b-13.[128] He argued that 7:9-13b and 19:7-14 once constituted the original text. However, a copyist accidentally omitted 19:7-13a by jumping from וכל הנסוגים הוסגרו לחרב (7:13) to והנאשרים הוסגרו לחרב (19:13). This would then have led to the inclusion of the Am-Nu Midrash, with 8:1 (הנסוגים הסגירו לחרב) added to help the flow of the newly redacted version. The presence of נמלטו and אלה מלטו in 7:14 and 7:21, respectively, along with the fact that the Am-Nu Midrash apparently adds nothing to the meaning of the passage, further convinced Murphy-O'Connor of an interpolation here. Moreover, he has posited the chance omission of the Is citation in 7:10b-13a from Ms B, due to confusion over the introductory formulae.

Brooke has accepted this explanation. He disagrees, however, as to the accidental nature of it. He prefers to see Ms A's replacement of the Zec-Ez portion with the Am-Nu Midrash as deliberate, in order to introduce a concept of two messiahs into the document; this, he maintains, brought CD into agreement with 1QS, 1QSb, 4QTest, and 4QFlor.[129] Boyce, also following the view of Murphy-O'Connor, has further suggested that, although the recension of Ms B is later, smoother and more intelligible, it did not become the standard text because its interpretation of the Teacher's death proved false, since the eschaton did not arrive as heralded in that recension.[130] It should, however, be pointed out that Murphy-O'Connor has subsequently changed his view on Ms B's priority, and stated that, in fact, Ms A's Am-Nu Midrash was original. He now argues that the Zec-Ez Midrash of Ms B was added when the Am-Nu Midrash was no longer applicable, after the arrival of the Teacher of Righteousness. A similar argument is put forward by Strickert, who holds that the redactor behind Ms B omitted and

---

J. Murphy-O'Connor, 'The Original Text of CD 7:9-8:2 - 19:5-14', *HTR* 64 (1971), pp. 379-386, and 'A Literary Analysis of the Damascus Document VI.2-VIII.3', *RB* 78 (1971), pp. 210-232; I. Rabinowitz, 'A Reconsideration of "Damascus" and "390 years" in the "Damascus" ("Zadokite") Fragments', *JBL* 73 (1954), pp. 24-31; F.M. Strickert, 'Damascus Document VII,10-20 and Qumran Messianic Expectation', *RQ* 12 (1986), pp. 327-350. See now also G.J. Brooke, 'The Messiah of Aaron in the Damascus Document', *RQ* 15 (1991), pp. 215-230.

128   See J. Murphy-O'Connor, 'The Original Text of CD 7:9-8:2-19:5-14', *HTR* 64 (1971), pp. 379-386. For the main part, he has been followed by Brooke, Davies and Knibb.

129   See G.J. Brooke, 'The Amos-Numbers Midrash (CD7[13b]-8[1a]) and Messianic Expectation', *ZAW* 92 (1980), pp. 397-404.

130   See Boyce, pp. 38-42.

replaced the Am-Nu Midrash with the Zec-Ez passage to show that the Teacher's death was in God's plan.[131] Notwithstanding this reworking of his original hyupothesis, Brooke, in another article, has reaffirmed his support of Murphy-O'Connor's original view, maintaining that the Am-Nu Midrash does indeed have priority over the competing passage in Ms B.[132]

Clearly, Murphy-O'Connor's retraction of his well-argued, original proposition, and his replacement of it by a new, plausible but contrary, theory heralds caution on this whole issue. In the final analysis, the question of the relationship between Mss A and B cannot be separated from the broader issue pertaining to the transmission of many ancient biblical and Second Temple texts, as discussed earlier in association with 4QD's Address to the Sons of Light. As mentioned in that regard, it is not always clear when divergences between two copies of what appear to be an identical or similar work, including Ms A and Ms B of CD, are sufficient to render each an independent composition in its own right. However, if it could be shown to be reasonable to posit the existence of a broader set of what might be called 'Damascus' traditions, perhaps both oral and written, of which both Ms A and Ms B are particular manifestations, then scholarly discussions about the priority of one MS over the other may inappropriate. Indeed, further analysis of 4QD[a-h] may well show that this would be a more fruitful line of approach to the complex nature of the interrelation of Mss A and B - and the same may apply to 1QS/4QS and 1QM/4QM.

5.5.2 Torah and Nevi'im in CD 19:1-33a

Obviously, where the text of both Ms A and Ms B is the same or virtually duplicated, there is no need to repeat the scriptural passages already analysed above. The more substantial divergences of Ms B, however, mean that there are some references to scripture independent of Ms A. These are few in

---

[131]   See J. Murphy-O'Connor, 'The Damascus Document Revisited', *RB* 92 (1985), pp. 223-246; F.M. Strickert, 'Damascus Document VII.10-20 and Qumran Messianic Expectation', *RQ* 12 (1985-87), pp. 327-350.

[132]   See G.J. Brooke, 'The Messiah of Aaron in the Damascus Document', *RQ* 15 (1991), p. 226, stating that "the clear description of the single Messiah of Aaron [in the Zec-Ez Midrash] was displaced [by the Am-Nu Midrash]", although he acknowledges that, if the Am-Nu Midrash was in any case conjoined with CD 12:23 and 14:19, this may be of less clear-cut significance than assumed in his earlier study. See also, M. Knibb, 'The Interpretation of *Damascus Document* VII, 9b-VIII,2a and XIX, 5b-14', *RQ* 15 (1991), pp. 243-251.

number, and are only from the first two divisions of scripture. They shall, therefore, be dealt with together.

The first of these (Dt 7:9 in CD 19:1) and the last three (Hos 5:10, Jer 31:31, and Mic 2:11 in CD 19:15,16,25) involve differences within what is, in fact, usage of the same contexts. Only Zec 13:7, Zec 11:11, and Ez 9:4 in CD 19:7,9, and 12 are completely new.

The sole passage from the Torah to be noted here is the explicit citation of Dt 7:9 in CD 19:1, introduced by כב.[133] Whereas in Ms A אלף דור is a clearer allusion to Dt 7:9, which itself reads לאלף דור, the fact of the citation in Ms B means that the allusive element, לאלפי דורות, is less precise in order to facilitate the full quotation.

The first significant divergence peculiar to Ms B is the citation of Zec 13:7 in CD 19:7. The biblical text reads:

חרב עורי על רעי ועל גבר עמיתי נאם ה' צבאות הך את הרעה ותפוצין הצאן והשבתי
ידי על הצערים:

Further allusion is made to the same prophetic book in CD 19:9, where the שמרים אתו are defined as the עניי הצאן. This epithet is obviously derived from Zec 11:11, which says:

ותפר ביום ההוא וידעו כן עניי הצאן השמרים אתי כי דבר ה' הוא:

It may be presumed that, for CD, the connection between these two verses centres on the shepherd/sheep vocabulary. It is noteworthy too that the allusion to Zec 11:11 is interpreted in a pesher-like manner, demonstrating that it was in view, although it is not actually quoted. We noted a similar phenomenon above, when dealing with mention of the כוכב in CD 7:19.[134]

Another quotation is present in CD 19:12. Ez 9:4 reads:

ויאמר ה' אלו עבר בתוך העיר...והתוית תו על מצחות האנשים הנאנחים והנאנקים על
כל התועבות הנעשות בתוכה:

The interesting point here is that connections between Ez 9 and parts of Ms A have already been noted.[135] Such an overlap of interest between Mss A and B is confirmation that their relationship, however precisely it is to be defined, is real and close.

Ms B transforms an allusion to Hos 5:10 (see 8:3b) into a citation in 19:15f by the addition of the words כאשר דבר. This passage has already been cited in full, and several points of contact between Hos and CD were noticed.[136]

---

[133] כב is an abbreviation for ככתוב.
[134] See above, p. 149.
[135] See, e.g., above, p. 60.
[136] See above, p. 149.

The reading in CD 19:25, הולך רוח ושקל סופות ומטיף לאדם לכזב, is different from the similar words in Ms A. Nonetheless, Mic 2:11 stands behind Ms B too:

לו איש הלך רוח ושקר כזב אטף לך ליין ולשכר והיה מטיף העם הזה:

Finally, the phrase ברית תשובה in CD 19:11, unparalleled in Ms A, may best be related to the ברית חדשה, mentioned already in association with CD 6:19 and 8:21 and based on Jer 31:31.

In sum, we can confirm that what is distinctive about CD 19:1-33a lies chiefly in its equivalent to the Am-Nu Midrash, using Zec and Ez. Other points of divergence involve either mere variation in, or more explicit use of, the same scriptural texts found to underlie CD 7:5b-8:19.

5.5.3 Summary

It is clear from its characteristics of content and style that Ms B is related in some close way to Ms A. This is despite the over-riding difficulty, namely, the divergence between the Am-Nu and Zec-Ez Midrashes.

The question of the priority of one of these over the other may never finally be settled, if, indeed, the posing of such a question is the best approach to the issue. However, it is sufficient for the present to point out that our study indicates that there is adequate connection to the rest of the Admonition and its use of the bible for either 7:10b-8:1a or 19:7b-13b to be considered integral to the document. Indeed, as will be abundantly clear by now, numerous contexts in both Nu and Ez are very important throughout CD. Nu 24:17, used in CD 7:19f, is part of the Balaam-Balaq cycle in Nu 22-24, and we may connect this to the common dependence upon Nu 13-21 elsewhere in the Admonition. As for Ez 9, informing CD 19:12, it relates to the not infrequent likely employment of this context with its exilic imagery at other points in CD 1-8. As hinted already, such factors may well be commensurate with the view that a broad 'Damascus' tradition existed, of which both Ms A and Ms B are particular manifestations. If so, it may be inappropriate to ask which constitutes a more original version. In any case, before making any further comments in this regard, we shall move on to CD 19:33b-20:34.[137]

---

[137] Since the chief divergence from Ms A in Ms B is its Ez-Zec passage, totalling a mere six lines, it has not been thought necessary to set out the text of CD 19:1-33a with scriptural citation and allusion highlighted.

5.6 Scripture in CD 19:33b - 20:34

This portion of the Admonition contains a diversity of material. A theme of warning is continued from CD 19:33a in 19:33b-20:13a but this appears to mix admonishment directed towards temporary lapsers from the community with outright condemnation of those deserving permanent expulsion. Then, in 20:13b-17a, the reader is reminded of the fate of all the אנשי המלחמה אשר שבו עם איש הכזב. According to 20:13b-15, their end will be met some forty years after the death of the יורה היחיד; the writer is presumably expressing himself from towards the end of this interval.[138] Such ultimate misfortune is in stark contrast to the absolute blessedness of the שבי פשע יעקב, who will be in receipt of God's loving-kindness "for a thousand generations" (20:17b-22a). CD 20:22b-34 describes a group, or part of a group, called the בית פלג (22b-25a), as well as God's rejection of apostates from the sect (25b-27a).[139] The Admonition of CD concludes, as far as Ms B is concerned, with a final depiction of the sectaries and the bliss that will eventually be theirs in 20:27b-34.

It has to be said that CD 19:33b-20:34 appears repetitive and, in places, confused. At this point, therefore, it is appropriate to include the text of 19:33b-20:34, which reads:[140]

כן כל האנשים אשר באו בברית
החדשה בארץ דמשק ושבו ויבגדו ויסורו מבאר מים החיים :
לא יחשבו בסוד עם ובכתבם לא יכתבו מיום האסף יור מורה   35
מורה היחיד עד עמוד משיח מאהרן ומישראל   וכן המשפט
לכל באי עדת אנשי תמים הקדש ויקוץ מעשות פקודי ישרים
הוא האיש הנתך בתוך כור :   ה בהופע מעשיו ישלח מעדה
כמו שלא נפל גורלו בתוך למודי אל כפי מעלו ה יוכיחוהו אנשי
דעות עד יום ישוב לעמד במעמד אנשי תמים קדש אשר אין   5
גורלו בתוך א בהופע מעשיו כפי מדרש התורה אשר יתהלכו
בו אנשי תמים הקדש אל ה יאות איש עמו בהון ובעבודה
כי ארווהו כל קדושי עליון וכמשפט הזה לכל המאס בראשונים
ובאחרונים אשר שמו גלולים על לבם וישימו וילכו בשרירות
לבם אין להם חלק בבית התורה :   כמשפט רעיהם אשר שבו   10
עם אנשי הלצון ישפטו כי דברו תועה על חקי הצדק ומאסו

---

138   See P.R. Davies, 'Communities at Qumran and the Case of the Missing Teacher', *RQ* 15 (1991), pp. 275-286, for a discussion of the יורה/מורה היחיד in CD 20:1,14 in relation to other portions of the document and to 1QS.

139   Before בית פלגX, there is a lacuna with space for one or two letters but no traces remain. Most scholars assume something was present here; e.g., *DSSE*, p. 105, reads "And every member of the House of Separation...".

140   An 'X' in the text denotes the remains of a letter that is now illegible.

בברית X ואמנה אשר קימו בארץ דמשק והוא ברית החדשה:

ולא יהיה להם וּ ולמשפחותיהם חלק בבית התורה   ומיום

האסף יורה היחיד עד תם כל אנשי המלחמה אשר שבו

עם איש הכזב כשנים ארבעים   ובקץ ההוא יחרה   15

אף אל בישראל כאשר אמר אין מלך ואין שר ואין שופט וא[י]ן

מוכיח בצדק X ושבי פשע יעקב שמרו ברית אל אז נדברו איש

אל רעהו להצדיק איש את אחיו לתמך צעדם בדרך אל ויקבש

אל אל דבריהם וישמע ויכתב ספר זכרון XXXX ליראי אל ולחושבי

שמו עד יגלה X ישע וצדקה ליראי אל ושבתם וראיתם בין צדיק   20

ורשע בין עבד אל לאשר לא עבדו: ועשה חסד XXXXXX לאהביו

לשמריו לאלף דור : [   ] Xבית פלג אשר יצאו מעיר הקדש:

וישענו על אל בקץ מעל ישראל ויטמאו את המקדש ושבו על'ד

אל דרך העם בדברים מעט XXXלם אי'ש לפי רוחו ישפטו בעצת

הקדש :   וכל אשר פרצו את גבול התורה מבאי הברית בהופע   25

כבוד אל לישראל יכרתו מקרב המחנה ועמהם כל מרשיעי

יהודה בימי מצרפותיו   וכל המחזיקים במשפטים האלה ל[צ]את

ולבוא על פי התורה וישמעו לקול מורה ויתודו לפני אל חטאנו

רשענו גם אנחנו גם אבותינו בלכתנו קרי בחקי הברית צד[ק]

ואמת משפטיך בנו: ולא ירימו יד על חקי קדשו ומשפט[י]   30

צדקו ועדות אמתו: והתיסרו במשפטים הראשונים אשר

נשפטו בם אנשי היחיד והאזינו לקול מורה צדק: ולא יעזבו

את חקי הצדק בשמעם אתם ישישו וישמחו ויעז לבם ויתגברו

על כל בני תבל וכפר אל בעדם וראו בישועתו כי חסו בשם קדשו

As can be seen, CD 19:33b-20:34 presents us with a number of difficulties. It is not immediately clear whether to understand ושבו ויבגדו in 19:34 as "and turned back and acted treacherously" or "and who again betray it".[141] A further complication is caused by the form of, and variation in, the titles in 20:1 and 20:14, namely, מורה היחיד and יורה היחיד, respectively; as these titles stand, "Unique Teacher" is presumably meant but numerous scholars consider this a corruption.[142] It is not clear how to take the word ויטמאו in 20:23 in light of the preceding וישענו על אל; it could mean either "and made the sanctuary unclean" or "declared the sanctuary unclean".[143] The reading in 20:23b-24a is ושבו עד אל ו[ ]ך העם, not ושבו עוד אל דרך העם.[144] More

---

141   For the former, see, e.g., Davies, p. 261, and Knibb, p. 69; for the latter, note *DSSE*, p. 105.

142   Thus, see *DSSE*, p. 105, "Teacher of the Community", as also Davies, p. 263, and Knibb, p. 70. These all emend to מורה היחד. However, the first choice of Rabin, p. 36, is "unique teacher". It is interesting to note that we find the same variation between מורה and יורה here as that evidenced in CD 1:11 and 6:11.

143   See, e.g., Knibb, p. 74, and Boyce, p. 276, respectively.

144   Vermes was the originator of the former proposed reading (hence, "but returned again to the way of the people", *DSSE*, p. 105), which has been confirmed by

generally, CD 19:33b-20:34 contains numerous scribal errors; these have been represented above as accurately as possible and consist mostly of scored out letters or words. This characteristic suggests a somewhat hurried or inexpert hand, as was also apparent for CD 19:1-33a.

As already mentioned, there are insufficient data for us to be certain as to the precise relationship between MS A and MS B, nor is it fully clear as yet what bearing the release of the 4QD material may have on this issue. At the same time, CD 19:33b-20:34 obviously relates to MS A in some way, as does 19:1-33a. Against this background, the text of the present section is set out below (pp. 164-165), in line with our overall task, with its quotations and allusions highlighted. As before, let us consider this in more detail.

5.6.1 Torah in CD 19:33b-20:34

A number of contexts from the Pentateuch encountered in association with other portions of the Admonition, as well as several new ones, are relevant for understanding the use of the Torah in CD 19:33b-20:34.[145]

Of greater interest than might appear to be the case at first is Nu 20:26, containing אסף in the *niphal* in connection with the death of Aaron. Assuming that the writer of CD is referring to the demise of the Teacher in 19:35 and 20:14, Nu 20 is a noticeable parallel.[146] It recounts the rebellion at Meribah and the subsequent miracle of the water from the rock (verses 1-13); this is followed by Edom's refusal to allow Israel to traverse his territory (verses 14-21), and then by an account of the divinely-ordained death of Aaron and the assumption of his position by Eleazar (verses 15-29). This

---

[145] Qimron in Broshi, p. 47. For the latter, see E. Lohse, *Die Texte aus Qumran*, Darmstadt (1971), p. 106, who translates as "und umkehrten zu Gott [...] das Volk". Although it is not possible to be sure, the phraseology לצאת ולבוא על פי התורה in 20:27f may connect to Nu 27:21, recounting God's announcement to Moses that he will soon die (utilizing נאסף; cf. CD 19:35 and 20:14) and that Joshua will be his successor, although both Joshua and the people will act according to the cousel of Eleazar, Aaron's heir (על פיו יצאו ועל פיו יבאו). A link here might be rendered more likely in view of the probable use of Nu 20:26 for the language chosen to describe the death of the Teacher in CD 19:35f; see the next note.

[146] Most scholars would interpret מיום האסף מורה היחיד as a description of the death of the Teacher. For an alternative understanding, see B.Z. Wacholder, 'Does Qumran record the death of the *Moreh*? The meaning of *he'aseph* in *Damascus Covenant* XIX.35, XX.14', *RQ* 13 (1988), pp. 323-330.

Nu 20:26 *Ez 13:9*

Ez 22:22
Is 54:13

Ez 14:3

Is 28:14,22
Jer 31:31 Neh 10:1

Dt 2:14

Hos 3:4

35

5

10

15

Quotation and Allusion in CD 19:33b-20:16

	Is 59:20 Mal 3:16
	Mal 3:16 **Dn 12:3**
20	
	Dt 7:9
	Gn 10:25
	Ez 23:38
25	
	Dt 2:14 **Dn 11:32**
	Lv 26:40 1 Ki 8:47
	Ps 106:6 **Dn 9:16**
30	
	Ps 33:21 37:40

Quotation and Allusion in CD 20:17-34

general pattern, as well as some items of vocabulary, suggests Nu 20 forms the background for the sect's understanding of the death of the Teacher.[147]

Dt 2:14 provides phraseology for both CD 20:14 and 20:26. The verse reads:

והימים אשר הלכנו מקדש ברנע עד אשר עברנו את נחל זרד שלשים ושמנה שנה עד תם
כל הדור אנשי המלחמה מקרב המחנה כאשר נשבע ה' להם:

Whatever the problems in identifying the characters and group(s) in this part of CD, it is clear that Dt 2:14 was used to express their activity, status and final lot.[148]

The language in 20:21, ועשה חסד...לאהביו, is reminiscent of that in Ex 20:6 (=Dt 5:10) and Dt 7:9. The latter of these has already been viewed; the former is part of one of the commands in the Decalogue.[149]

One of the chief difficulties with CD 19:33b-20:34 is the question of the identity of the בית פלג in CD 20:22. It is unclear whether this is the historical name of a personage, or else some kind of cipher; nor is it obvious, if the latter, whether to understand an appellation, "Peleg", or merely "separation". Further, the reference may be either to part or to all of the group, depending on whether something has dropped out in the preceding lacuna.[150] If an allusion to Gn 10:25 is intended, it is presumably connected to the reason for the naming of Eber's son thus: Noah's sons were dividing the earth among themselves. The biblical text reads:

ולעבר ילד שני בנים שם האחד פלג כי בימיו נפלגה הארץ ושם אחיו יקטן:

Such "separation" might be interpreted in terms of religious disputes in the time of our author, as is the case, it would appear, in Jub.[151] If so, the writer of CD viewed the separation of the earth among the sons of Noah as another rebellion analogous to those we have already met elsewhere in Gn, but particularly in Nu.[152]

---

[147] Regarding some common terms of vocabulary, note שמעו in verse 1, as well as the verb ריב in verses 3 and 14; cf. CD 1:1-2. Also, the "rock" gives the Israelites מים רבים (v 11); cf. the באר and חקק motifs in CD 6:2-11a, dependent on Nu 21:18.

[148] עד תומם in CD 2:9 probably relates to the same biblical context; see above, p. 109.

[149] See above, p. 143, for Dt 7:9 in CD 7:6, and p. 148, for Dt 7:8 behind CD 8:15.

[150] See above, note 139.

[151] Thus, Jub 8:8f reads:
    "...And he called him Peleg because in the days when he was born the sons of Noah began dividing up the earth for themselves. Therefore he called him Peleg. And they divided it in an evil (manner) among themselves, and they told it to Noah".

[152] This would be corroborated in part by a study of the בית פלג by R.T. White, 'The House of Peleg in the Dead Sea Scrolls', in P.R. Davies, R.T. White, *A Tribute to Geza Vermes*, Sheffield (1990), pp. 67-98, whose main point is that בית פלג in CD

Lv 26:40, from a chapter already encountered, contains the theme of confession that we find in CD 20:28, and says:

והתודו את עונם ואת עון אבתם במעלם אשר מעלו בי ואף אשר הלכו עמי בקרי׃

Not a few of the biblical texts behind the Admonition contain some sort of acknowledgment of guilt; this is often one element among a number of common motifs within a wider story-line.[153] That Lv 26:40 was in mind here is confirmed by the use of the rare קרי in CD 20:29.

5.6.2 Nevi'im in CD 19:33b-20:34

Of texts from the Prophets relevant to CD 19:33b-20:34, most are familiar, while some involve new biblical contexts.[154]

We can detect a connection between CD 19:35, לא יחשבו בסוד עם, and words in Ez 13:9 regarding the exclusion of false prophets from the סוד of God's people:

והיתה ידי אל הנביאים החזים שוא והקסמים כזב בסוד עמי לא יהיו ובכתב בית ישראל
לא יכתבו ואל אדמת ישראל לא יבאו וידעתם כי אני אדני ה׳׃

This part of scripture was central in MS A, and we have referred to it before. In particular, it connects to the epithets "builders of the wall" and "daubers of plaster" found in CD 4:19 and 8:12, respectively, which reflect Ez 13:10 and 13. Further, the latter reflection of Ez 13f renders more likely a linkage

---

signifies Onias III and his followers who built a temple at Leontopolis. Whatever is to be made of this theory, he argues that the epithet is to be associated with the whole 'generation of separation', as it is in early rabbinic literature, and against the background of the preceding Flood and Eden cycles. In view of this, if correct, it was right to highlight נח ומשפחותיהם at CD 3:1 on p. 75 above.

[153] In this regard, relevant passages include Nu 13-21; Dt 28-32; Is 59; Jer 25; Ez 20; Ps 106; Ezr 9; Neh 9; Dn 9.

[154] The significance of the following will not be detailed again: Is 28:14 (cf. CD 1:14); Jer 31:31 (cf. CD 6:19); Is 59:20 (cf. CD 4:2); Ez 23:38 (cf. CD 4:18). Additional passages of little or unclear import are the following:

Is 56:1 (cf. CD 20:20) has God claim that ...וצדקתי להגלות ישועתי (vv 2,4) קרובה mention המחזיקים;

Zec 11:11 may have been connected to the use of שמר in the blessing of the "keepers" of the law in Ex 20:6/Dt 7:9, alluded to in CD 20:21;

והשארתי בקרבך עם עני וחסו בשם קדשו in CD 20:34 is reminiscent of Zep 3:12, ודל וחסו בשם ה׳. This is part of a cluster of verses, 12:11-13, which could easily have been interpreted by the sect in terms of its own existence;

For Is 11:13, which contains words not dissimilar to יכרתו...מרשיעי יהודה in CD 20:26, see below, note 156.

between Ez 14:3,4,7 and CD 20:9, גלולים, as does the liklihood that Ez 14:5 stands behind CD 4:16.

There is a virtual quotation of Ez 22:22 in CD 20:3. The biblical text uses the image of silver purified in a furnace to describe Jerusalem's approaching punishment. Presumably, the sect viewed as parallel those in their midst who defected from their covenant. Again, Ez 22 is part of a cluster of chapters from Ez which appears to have been prominent in the mind of our author.[155]

Using Is 54:13, למודי ה׳, CD 20:4 describes the sect as those who truly know God's will and way. Is 54 is a 'Song of Assurance for Zion', picturing the restored state of the people of God, and verse 13 reads:

וכל בניך למודי ה׳ ורב שלום בניך:

It may be no coincidence that Is 54:16 is quoted in CD 6:8; note also Is 54:8, הסתרתי פני (cf. CD 1:3; 2:8).

We return to another familiar passage when, in CD 20:16, our author describes the result of God's anger: a lack of king, prince, judge or one to rebuke in righteousness. Hos 3:4 reads:

כי ימים רבים ישבו בני ישראל אין מלך ואין שר ואין זבח ואין מצבה ואין אפוד
ותרפים:

This context was especially relevant in understanding the biblical background to the historical sections of CD.[156]

Mal 3:16ff is certainly in mind in 20:17,18. The biblical text relates:

אז נדברו יראי ה׳ איש את רעהו ויקשב ה׳ וישמע ויכתב ספר זכרון לפניו ליראי ה׳
ולחשבי שמו: 17והיו לי אמר ה׳ צבאות ליום אשר אני עשה סגלה וחמלתי עליהם
כאשר יחמל איש על בנו העבד אתו: 18ושבתם וראיתם בין צדיק לרשע בין עבד אלהים
לאשר לא עבדו:

This depiction of the sparing and blessing of God's true worshippers at the judgement is used by the writer of CD to refer to the state and status of his sect up to and/or at the eschaton.

A final text to consider from the Prophets in connection with CD 19:33b-20:34 is 1 Ki 8:47, part of Solomon's prayer at the dedication of the temple in Jerusalem. The whole of 1 Ki 8:46-48 is worth citing:

כי יחטאו לך כי אין אדם אשר לא יחטא ואנפת בם ונתתם לפני אויב ושבום שביהם אל
ארץ האויב רחוקה או קרובה: 47והשיבו אל לבם בארץ אשר נשבו שם ושבו והתחננו
אליך בארץ שביהם לאמר חטאנו והעוינו רשענו: 48ושבו אליך בכל לבבם ובכל נפשם
בארץ איביהם אשר שבו אתם והתפללו אליך דרך ארצם אשר נתתה לאבותם העיר אשר
בחרת והבית אשר בנית לשמך:

---

155   See above, p. 145, for Ez 22:26 in CD 6:17.

156   Also, for מוכיח בצדק in CD 20:17, cf. Is 11:4, which states of the 'messianic king', והוכיח במישור.

Here, there are items of vocabulary and phraseology that are present in CD, especially vis à vis CD 20:28, but also a general pattern, or story-line, that we have already remarked on as important for the self-identity of the sect. Hence, although we have had no occasion to appeal to this context before, it has been included in the highlighted text set out above.

5.6.3 Ketuvim in CD 19:33b-20:34

Let us turn now to the influence of the third section of the scriptures on this portion of CD. As before, ambiguity arises when turning to the Writings, especially in evaluating the possible influence of generalized religious language.[157]

A text whose possible impact is difficult to evaluate is Neh 10:1. This reads:

ובכל זאת אנחנו כרתים אמנה וכתבים ועל החתום שרינו לוינו כהנינו:

If אמנה is the correct reading in CD 20:12, certain parallels are evident.[158] Apart from the generally relevant context of the preceding Neh 9, which we have referred to before, the listing of the "princes...Levites, and...priests" may be of significance; each could conceivably be connected to the categories applied to the various types of sectarian elsewhere in CD.[159] Also, ובכל זאת at the beginning of the verse would refer to the situation described in Neh 9:2-37; this was the cause of the need for the אמנה in the first place.[160]

The epithet מרשיעי יהודה in CD 20:26 sounds similar to the appellation in Dn 11:32, מרשיעי ברית. In context, this refers cryptically, after the manner of Dn, to a conflict between the Kittim and one of the kings in Dn, that is, to action taken by Antiochus IV Epiphanes against Jerusalem in 167 BCE. The מרשיעי ברית are probably the liberal, hellenized Jews in Jerusalem. CD's מרשיעי יהודה may well represent these same people or, more likely, those

---

157   Thus, both 2 Chr 13:22 and 2 Chr 24:27 use the word מדרש. However, these merely inform us of how that term may have been used 150 years or so before the composition of CD. Similarly, the parallel between CD 20:33 and Ps 40:17 (=70:5) is clear but any conscious emulation or dependence is another, interdeterminable matter; the same applies to seeing/being shown God's ישועה, as found in both CD 20:34 and Ps 91:16.

158   Note, however, that Boyce, p. 275, emends אמנה in 20:12 to נאמנה.

159   See especially CD 3:21ff, identifying the כהנים לויים and בני צדוק of Ez 44:15.

160   From a historical-critical viewpoint, ובכל זאת may apply to the contents of Neh 13 but that would not be relevant for understanding how the text may have been read in the time of CD.

who are their successors in the eyes of the sect. Indeed, the מצדיקי הרבים in Dn 12:3 may correspondingly have been a depiction applied to members of the sect itself and CD 20:18, referring to the sectaries' disposition להצדיק איש את אחיהו, might corroborate this.

Ps 106 and Dn 9 have been mentioned on previous occasions, noting especially the pattern of events they outline, as well as their terms and manner. Both also express a sense of guilt, in Ps 106:6 and Dn 9:16, in the form of a confession, as does CD in 20:29.

The last few lines of CD 19:33b-20:34 reflect general vocabulary and phraseology from the Psalms.[161]   In particular, כי חסו בשם קדשו in 20:34 appears to be a combination of Pss 33:21 and 37:40. We have already noted that Ps 37 is an example of a number of Pss which were probably taken up and applied by members of the sect to themselves.[162]

5.6.4 Summary

Despite the problems encountered in CD 19:33b-20:34 - especially the identity of the בית פלג and confusing differences in style - there is no doubt that this section, like CD 19:1-33a, relates in some way to CD 1-8 as evidenced in Ms A. Apart from any other factor, the extent of the overlap of the usage of scriptural language is sufficient demonstration of this. We dealt with familiar passages from Lv, Nu, and Dt; from Is, Ez, and Hos; and from Ps 106, Dn and Neh.

However, the temptation to read into this more than is evident should be resisted. Without further data, the precise relationship between Mss A and B cannot be determined. That the two are connected is clear from general observations, as well as from the detail of our own study. However, our findings are commensurate with two possibilities: Mss A and B could represent two editions of the same work, on the one hand, or they could be two essentially autonomous, though interdependent, pieces, on the other. In other words, the linkage between the two Mss may be parallel to that between the remains of the Cairo and Masada copies of Ecclus; alternatively, the kinship between any two of the three Synoptic Gospels may be a more appropriate analogy. As has been remarked already, this question ultimately ties in to a wider issue, namely, that it is not always clear at what point differences between two texts are sufficient to attribute separate identities to

---

[161]   See above, note 157.
[162]   4QpPs 37 shows that this was so for Ps 37.

them.[163] This issue, in turn, relates to the methodological issues dealt with in an earlier chapter.

5.7 Scripture in the Midrashic Sections

Earlier, it was suggested that CD 2:2-13, 4:12b-5:15a, 6:11b-8:21, and 19:1-20:34 could be satisfactorily placed together for the purposes of our study. These portions are certainly more disparate than the historical sections, so that it would be acceptable, and perhaps safest, to group them together as the miscellaneous remains after the removal of the latter. Nonetheless, we observed a similarity of style in CD 4:12b-5:15a and 6:11b-8:21, which together constitute the bulk of the midrashic sections and display a mixture of midrashic and halakhic characteristics. Any doubts that may remain concern 2:2-13, which is closest in nature to the historical sections, and, to a lesser extent, 19:33b-20:34. However, even these blocks in the Admonition are set within a narrower time-frame than CD 1:1-2:1, 2:14-4:12a, or 5:15b-6:11a, giving the impression of being concerned more specifically with the contemporary situation and issues of the author's own day. This concern involves both criticism of outsiders and an assertion of the sect's superiority, two factors which are the equivalent of similar aspects expressed more historically in the historical sections. The former is paralleled in the descriptions of the wicked throughout history in CD 1:1-2:1, 2:14-4:12a and 5:15b-6:11a, while the latter is presented through the sect's claim to stand in direct line to the faithful remnant throughout the ages.

The varied nature of the midrashic portions makes it tempting to posit theories of sources, interpolations and redaction, as have been put forward by some scholars, especially in relation to the problem of priority between the Am-Nu and Ez-Zec midrashes.[164] However, we found ourselves remaining

---

[163]   There are numerous other texts from biblical and Second Temple times about which a similar dilemma is noticeable; see above, p. 43, note 21. Included here is Ac, as manifest in א and B in contrast to D, concerning which we may note the words of E. Haenchen, *The Acts of the Apostles: A Commentary*, Oxford (1973), p. 51:
> "In Acts the two text-forms show such wide divergences that Blass and Zahn supposed Luke to have issued two different editions. This hypothesis comes to grief, however, from the very fact that the texts often contradict each other, e.g., in the case of the 'Apostolic Decree' [Ac 15:29]"

[164]   They have also been used to attempt to explain the interrelation of CD 4:12b-19a and 4:19b-5:15a, and to elucidate the apparent confusion between criticism of mere

sceptical of such hypotheses, not because the text is problem-free, but because proposals of this sort do not remove difficulties present within the final form of CD 1-8 and 19-20. In view of such considerations, we attempted to keep the Admonition together for the purposes of the present study.[165]

Our examination has shown each of the midrashic sections to be heavily dependent on the bible. We found numerous citations in CD 4:12b-5:15a and 6:11b-8:21; many of the passages employed in this way appear, at first sight, conveniently open to the interpretative licence of our author.[166] Some among them are pesher-like in their arrangement and interpretation, parallel to their counterparts in the historical sections. Further, considerable virtual quotation is evident in 4:12b-5:15a and 6:11b-8:21. Although in the form of allusions, it can scarcely be doubted that, in such cases, the intention is overt reference to the bible.[167]

Only CD 2:2-13 was noticeably free of both citations and virtual quotations. However, this is only of limited significance, if both overt and subtle uses of the scriptures are part of one overall phenomenon in the Admonition. Indeed, there is much to suggest that the same basic employment of the scriptures lies behind both types of bible usage in the midrashic sections. Sometimes it manifests itself in citation and other times in allusion; cases of so-called virtual citation, difficult to categorize definitively,

---

backsliders over against apostates in 19:33b-20:34; see above, p. 120, note 48, and J. Murphy-O'Connor, 'A Literary Analysis of Damascus Document XIX,33-XX,34', *RB* 79 (1972), pp. 544-564, respectively. Such efforts may explain possible earlier editions of the document or parts thereof, as well as an alleged process of growth leading to the extant text, but not the final form itself.

[165] See above, pp. 152-158, where the limited evidence forced us to remain agnostic as to the relationship between Ms A and Ms B for the time-being, although we may suspect that both MSS are individual manifestations of what may be characterized as a broad interpretative 'Damascus' tradition.

[166] Quotations with introductory formulae are found in CD 2:2-13; 4:12b-5:15a; 6:11b-8:21 and 19:1-20:34 as follows:

4:14	Is 24:17	7:8f	Nu 30:17	19:15f	Hos 5:10
4:20	Mic 2:6	7:11ff	Is 7:17	8:9f	Dt 32:33
5:2	Dt 17:17	7:14f	Am 5:26	8:14f	Dt 9:5
5:8	Lv 18:13	19:7ff	Zec 13:7	20:16f	Hos 3:4
6:13f	Mal 1:10	7:16	Am 9:11		
19:1f	Dt 7:9	19:12	Ez 9:4		

[167] See, e.g., CD 4:21-5:1, relying on Gn 1:27 and 7:9; CD 5:13-14, using Is 50:11 and 59:5; CD 6:16-17, referring to Is 10:4 in combination with Ps 94:6; and CD 20:4, drawing upon Ez 22:22.

also belong to such a wider framework, the discovery of which has been our primary interest.

Further analysis shows that the quotations, at first sight randomly chosen for their elusive qualities, are in fact taken from parts of the bible that turn out to inform other citations and allusions elsewhere. In this regard, there were many contexts which kept reappearing in dealing with the midrashic portions. The following stand out:

Gn 7,10; Ex 31-32, 34-35; Lv 17-19, 26;
Nu 13-18, 20, 24, 30; Dt 2, 7, 9, 12, 31-32;
Ju 2; Is 7, 10, 24, 27-28, 50-51, 59; Jer 29, 31;
Ez 5, 9, 13-14, 22-23, 39, 44; Hos 3-5;
Am 5, 9; Mic 2-3; Zec 6, 11, 13; Mal 1,3;
Pss 37, 78, 94, 106; Dn 9, 11-12; Ezr 9; Neh 9, 2 Chr 36.

From this summary of our findings in this chapter, it seems fitting to suggest that citations constitute the visible part of the iceberg, as it were, while the mass remains hidden from immediate view in the form of allusion. The same phenomenon was seen to be operating in the historical parts of CD 1-8, and it is noteworthy that there is a considerable degree of overlap between the midrashic and historical sections, in terms of both allusion and quotation.[168] Thus, a core of biblical material is prominent throughout all portions of the Admonition.

This would suggest that, although it was easier to isolate the historical sections, the distinction between them and the midrashic portions is not qualitative. Even within the former we noted ambiguous characteristics - for example, the presence of pesher-like segments best paralleled in the midrashic sections, as well as an interest in correct behaviour resembling the latter's halakhic preoccupation. Similarly, there are small units within the midrashic sections which are reminiscent of the 'history-like' nature of 1:1-2:1, 2:14-4:12a and 5:15b-6:11a; see, for instance, CD 7:12b-8:1a (which includes the Am-Nu Midrash) and 20:11b-13. All in all, this is sufficient demonstration that the different parts of CD 1-8 and 19-20 interconnect with each other. While each portion makes its own contribution to the whole, it is clear that the final product was compiled with a considerable amount of care. The strongest substantiation of such a hypothesis is the interconnected web of bible usage that is perceptible throughout the Admonition, which has become evident in the course of this study.

---

168   See above, p. 101, for a list of biblical contexts prominent within the historical
         sections.

One further point may be made in relation to the 'creation of history'. It was suggested above that this might be a factor in understanding the dependence upon Ju 2:7-10, in conjunction with other passages, in CD 5:3f, inasmuch as certain scriptural texts appear to have been conjoined with a view to deducing appropriate 'information' therefrom at this point in the Admonition.[169] However, given especially that the midrashic sections are more obviously engaged in bible interpretation than the historical ones, at least at the formal level, such 'creation of history' is hardly separable from the widespread Second Temple and Rabbinic phenomenon which we may call aggadah. We shall return to this point in our concluding chapter.

---

[169]   See above, p. 131.

6 Conclusions

6.1 The Damascus Document and Scripture

The purpose of our study has been to examine the use of scripture in CD 1-8 and 19-20, for it has been our contention that the document is dependent on a relatively detectable body of biblical contexts. We have not engaged in a detailed exegesis of individual units within the Admonition in order to identify the historical or theological referents in the text, only drawing the question of the employment of scripture into the discussion secondarily when potentially helpful. Rather, it has been our intention to discover a broader framework within which it might be possible to read CD 1-8 and 19-20, while simultaneously avoiding the historical difficulties usually associated with the document. Thus, for example, we noted that the presence of the words בטוב הצואר in CD 1:19 is part of a wider dependence on Hos in the document, although we did not investigate the idiom's precise exegetical nuance.[1] As a result of our survey, therefore, we have been able to gain a different perspective on the text. Whilst scholarship in this area has, until now, concentrated on the citations in CD 1-8 or 19-20, we have sought to take into account the mass of allusive reference to the bible that is also evident in the work. The obvious dangers of subjectivity, it is hoped, have been avoided by adopting a methodology whereby only those allusions which can be confirmed by the presence of quotations or virtual citations from the same biblical context elsewhere in the Admonition have been admitted into our analysis. Only a few exceptions to this were allowed, where it was felt that

---

[1] See above, p. 62. Having traced an overarching framework of biblical texts, however, a future study may return to individual passages for detailed exegesis. Moreover, the nature of the relationship between the Admonition and CD 9-16 requires re-examination in light of our study, although the additional legal material in 4QD renders this question extremely complex. In the meantime, see P.R. Davies, 'Halakhah at Qumran', in P.R. Davies, R.T. White, *A Tribute to Geza Vermes*, Sheffield (1990), pp. 37-50.

allusive reference to a particular passage was sufficiently strong for it to be included.[2]

Even allowing for considerable misjudgement on our part in individual cases, the cumulative force of the data we have uncovered remains compelling. Indeed, at the primary level, our findings are two-fold. Firstly, there is a noticeable core of biblical texts informing the whole of CD 1-8, while CD 19:1-33a and 19:33b-20:34 also relate to this body of scriptural material, as we have seen.[3] Although the biblical passages concerned were not all universally reflected in every section, a proportion of them is found in each part of the work. It is arguable that this is too constant a feature to be put down to mere coincidence, nor is it satisfactory to relegate it to the level of an unconscious habit of little or no significance. Even if the Admonition at points does slip into subliminal literary imitation of the scriptures, this would not account for the consistent phenomenon we have been tracing.[4]

Secondly, our examination has endorsed the proposition that there is no clear-cut dividing line between citation and allusion in the Admonition. It was frequently noted that a quotation was taken from a chapter, or cluster of chapters, that would reappear in the same or another section of CD - either in the form of a further citation or as the source behind an allusion. This pattern strongly suggests that any distinction between overt and subtle references to the bible, including what we have called 'virtual citation', is formal and that all are manifestations of an underlying and overriding usage of the scriptures.[5] That biblical texts may occasionally be employed which lie outside the body

---

2   For the various sections of CD 1-8 and 19-20, set out with biblical citations and allusions highlighted, see above, p. 56 (CD 1:1-2:1); p. 110 (2:2-13); pp. 75-76 (2:14-4:12a); pp. 123-124 (4:12b-5:15a); p. 92 (5:15b-6:11a); pp. 139-141 (6:11b-8:21); and pp. 164-165 (19:33b-20:34).

3   The exact significance of this finding for the nature of the relationship between Ms A and Ms B is less than clear, however, given the lack of evidence providing a sufficiently broad framework for understanding Ms B. See above, p. 170f.

4   The Admonition, like some other Second Temple works, sometimes uses the bible in a haphazard or unwitting manner. This would appear to be the case, e.g., in the reflection of Ps 107:40/Job 12:24 in CD 1:15; cf. Is 2:22 in 1QS 5:17 for a similar example. Nevertheless, the greater part of the document's employment of biblical phraseology cannot be accounted for adequately in this way.

5   As noted earlier, this feature of the work is tacitly assumed by G. Vermes, 'Biblical Proof-Texts in Qumran Literature', *JSS* 34 (1989), p. 497, given his inclusion of virtual citations among his list of quotations in CD (and other DSS); see above, p. 29. It may be presumed that he felt a proper account of the matter had to incorporate these examples, even though they lack introductory formulae. Our study has taken the matter a stage further.

of passages that recurs frequently does not detract from the reality of this basic thesis.[6]

Before going any further, it will be useful to illustrate our findings in tabular form, in order to represent the relative proportions of biblical sources drawn upon in the various parts of the Admonition (see below, pp. 179-182). Evidence relating to dependence on the Pentateuch[7] is set out below, therefore, followed by that pertaining to the Nevi'im[8] and Ketuvim.[9] Within this layout, passages that are cited in CD 1-8 or 19-20 with an introductory

---

[6] See above, p. 29f, for a brief description of instances of such scriptural imitation.

[7] It is impossible to repeat descriptive detail from chapters 4 and 5 but a few points should be reiterated. Gn 1:27 and Dt 17:17 (in CD 4:21 and 5:2, respectively) are used straightforwardly as proof-texts, and are only on the periphery of our body of scriptures. Reference to Gn 6:17; 7:22 may be related to our author's preoccupation with rebellion in the Torah, as also may Gn 10:25,32 (CD 2:20; 3:1). Ex 7:11 (CD 5:18), regarding Egypt's magicians, is used by CD only via aggadic development of the story; Ex 32:25 (CD 4:19) is included within our tabulation of information, if somewhat speculatively, due to likely influence from the passage, given Dt 9's prominence. Similarly, it seems reasonable to incorporate Nu 18:2 and Dt 31:26 (4:3; 5:3) in view of the frequent appearance of these biblical contexts. Finally, it should again be stressed that reference to Lv 18:13 and 19:17,18 (CD 5:8; 6:20; 7:2) is part of a wider dependence on Lv 17-25 evident in CD 5ff but difficult to specify in terms of chapter and verse.

[8] Nevi'im are used chiefly for their concern with the exile and its evaluation, and this appears to explain the rarity of dependence on the Former Prophets. The main exception to this was 1 Sa 2:35 in CD 3:19, and it has not been thought necessary, therefore, to include Jos, Ju, 1,2 Sa and 1,2 Ki in the table. However, it is worth repeating several points regarding the Latter Prophets: Is 41:8 (CD 3:2), in reference to Abraham as a friend of God, is utilized in a routine manner and is not of especial significance. Is 46:3 and 55:2 (CD 2:2) are of little import, except that 55:3 may be influential in CD 7:5. Any influence from the specific language of Ez 8:6 and 9:3 (CD 1:3) is vague but the broad context and ideas of these verses are clearly important for CD. References to the minor Prophets are relatively few and difficult to interpret; the chief exception is Hos, whose influence on CD is considerable, of which Hos 4:1,6 (CD 2:3) may well be part. See below, p. 184f.

[9] Of interest are texts from Pss, as well as Dn, Ezr and Neh; the latter three works will be mentioned below. As far as Ps 81 (CD 2:17; 3:11) is concerned, some contact with CD is likely; see above, p. 85. The possible significance of 2 Chr 20:7 (CD 3:2) is fairly straightforward, whether or not any influence from it can be posited with certainty, whilst 2 Chr 36 (CD 3:10; 7:17,18) is a summary of that work's major theme. In view of the explicit exilic emphasis in the latter biblical passage, and despite E. Ben Zvi, 'The Authority of 1-2 Chronicles in the Late Second Temple Period', *JSP* 3 (1988), pp. 59-88, we may tentatively posit influence from that context, where relevant, rather than dependence upon 1,2 Sa and 1,2 Ki.

formula are highlighted.[10]   An examination of the tabulated evidence will show, however, that we should avoid overemphasizing the role of quotations, since no consistent criteria can be detected which determined whether a reference to the bible should be overt or subtle. Thus, for example, while no text from Jer is cited, our survey shows clearly that it would be wrong to suggest that Jer 23, 25, 27 are any less important in the Admonition than, say, Hos 3-4, from which verses are quoted. On the other hand, some passages that appear peripheral, when set against the entire body.of influential texts, are cited by the author, as in the case of Mal 1:10 in CD 6:12.   An acknowledgement of overt bible usage only, therefore, could lead the student of CD in the wrong direction.

Furthermore, a number of interrelated points can be made in view of the data set out in these tables. Firstly, our initial intuition that there is more to the Admonition's use of scripture than first meets the eye has received ample confirmation, for it has been possible to conduct our inquiry, while at the same time largely laying to one side the set of historical questions usually asked of CD 1-8 and 19-20.[11]   We have seen that influence from an underlying body of biblical texts is discernible throughout this material, providing the writer with a consistent framework of scriptural reminiscences to incorporate into his text.   His activity in this regard manifests itself variously in the form of quotation, virtual citation, or allusion but all of these can be seen to be part of one whole.

Secondly, our study has confirmed the centrality of exegesis in the so-called sectarian DSS, as emphasized by previous scholarly analyses. It has narrowed the gap, however, between the two types of scriptural dependency described earlier.[12]   In light of our examination of the Admonition, it may well be a mere distinction of form to posit any differentiation between works whose starting point is the bible itself over against those which use scripture secondarily to aid an independent argument. Indeed, the biblical framework evident in the above tables strongly suggests that CD 1-8 and 19-20 focus upon a selection of set portions of the bible. If this is so, it would support Davies' claim that the author found his 'message' by meditating on the

---

[10]   This is signified in **bold** script. It should be noted that, because the tables set out below are intended to facilitate an overview which concentrates on chapters and clusters of chapters, only verse numbers are highlighted for citations (e.g., Lv 18:**13**). Note also that references in square brackets ([...]) concern CD 19:1-33a in Ms B.

[11]   See above, pp. 4-8.

[12]   See above, pp. 19-24.

Torah in CD 1-8, 19-20

CD	Gn	Ex	Lv	Nu	Dt
1:1-2:1		32:8,10	26:25,40,42,45	14:23	9:12,16 27:17 28:20,29 29:20,21,26 31:17,20
2:2-13		31:2 34:6 35:30		14:18 16:2	2:14
2:14-4:12a	6:17 7:22 10:32		17:10 18:5 26:33	15:39 16:2 18:2	9:23 12:8,23 29:18,28
4:12b-5:15a	1:27 7:9	32:25	18:**13**		10:2 17:**17** 31:26
5:15b-6:11a		7:11	26:45	21:**18**	1:13 13:6 27:17 32:28
6:11b-8:21			19:17,18 26:15	13:19 15:19 18:19 24:17 30:**17**	7:8,**9** 9:**5** 12:1,8 32:28 32:**33**
19:33b-20:34	10:25		26:40	20:26	2:14 7:9

Nevi'im in CD 1-8, 19-20 (I)

CD	Is	Jer	Ez
1:1-2:1	24:5 28:14,22 30:10,11,20 51:1,7 59:10,12 60:21	25:9,31 27:6	4:5 7:22 8:6 9:3 20:27 39:23
2:2-13	27:6 46:3 55:2 51:1,7 59:20		14:22 39:23
2:14-4:12a	41:8 56:4,6 59:20 51:1,7	23:17	6:9 11:15 20:5,11,13,21 33:25,28 44:15
4:12b-5:15a	24:17,18 50:11 59:5		5:11 12:13 13:10 14:5 23:38 44:7
5:15b-6:11a	27:11 54:16 59:20	23:13,25	
6:11b-8:21	7:17 10:2 55:3 59:20	29:6,7 31:31	[9:4] 13:10 22:26 44:23
19:33b-20:34	28:14,22 54:13 59:20	31:31	13:9 14:3 22:22 23:38

Nevi'im in CD 1-8, 19-20 (II)

CD	Hos	Am	Mic	Hab	Zec	Mal
1:1-2:1	4:1,**16** 5:10 10:11,12		2:12			
2:2-13	4:1,6		3:9			
2:14-4:12a		2:9	7:10	2:1		
4:12b-5:15a	5:11		2:**6**			
5:15b-6:11a	5:10 10:12					
6:11b-8:21	5:10	5:26 9:11	2:11		6:8 [11:11 13:7]	1:**10**
19:33b-20:34	3:**4**					3:16

Ketuvim in CD 1-8, 19-20

CD	Pss	Dn	Ezr	Neh	1,2 Chr
1:1-2:1	37:29 78:62 94:21 106:18,40,45 107:40	9:7	9:8,12		
2:2-13	106:40	9:9	9:14	9:17	
2:14-4:12a	78:62 81:13 106:18,25,40	12:2		9:14,29	2 Chr 20:7 36:21
4:12b-5:15a					
5:15b-6:11a			2:63	7:65	2 Chr 36:15
6:11b-8:21	78:62 94:2,6		9:5		2 Chr 36:16
19:33b-20:34	33:21 37:40 106:6	9:16 11:32 12:3		10:1	

scriptures themselves.[13]   Moreover, as will be suggested below, the
phenomenon we have traced may be related to the need to counter competing
claims to represent the true continuation and interpretation of ancient Israel's
traditions, as put forward by rival groups or authoritites in Second Temple
times.

Thirdly, we were wise to remain agnostic about theories of redaction.
Sources may have been used, and perhaps this is more than likely in view of
other biblical or Second Temple texts with extent parallels. However, the
question, as far as the Admonition is concerned, is how can we tell? On the
contrary, sufficient connection between the different portions of the
Admonition has been found, in terms of a foundational dependence on the
bible, to lead us to posit that it is deliberate. Although it may be debatable
where precisely the locus of this phenomenon resides - in the mind of the
writer, in the text as an artefact, or in the reader's experience of the document
- such a feature must surely override any historical or theological tensions
within the work that might tempt scholars to posit the use of sources as a
means around them. At one important level, therefore, it is clear that the
Admonition is a well-constructed text, even if such a conclusion conflicts
with the modern reader's initial reaction to the work.[14]

Consequently, our distinction between the historical and midrashic
sections within the Admonition is rendered an observation relating to
structural variations in style internal to the final form of the text, and there are
no grounds for linking the associated 'paragraph' divisions with redactional
sutures. This is well illustrated by CD 5:16f and 8:9; the former passage,
from the historical sections, cites Dt 32:28f, while the latter, from the
midrashic portions, contains a strong allusion to Dt 32:33.[15] In view of the
mass of other similar data, this overlap of dependence on the bible cannot be
coincidental. Hence, we may surmise that the alternation of historical and
midrashic sections is intentional and literary, and that this may relate to what
were earlier, admittedly a little anachronistically, called their 'diachronic' and
'synchronic' characteristics.[16] We have already seen from the work of
Vermes and Schwarz that the smaller units within CD are structured; it can be

---

13   See above, p. 9.
14   See above, pp. 43-48.
15   See above, pp. 93 and 147. Our point remains valid for the structure of the final
     form of the Admonition, even if it is claimed that the context around CD 8:9
     deliberately, but secondarily, harks back to earlier portions of the document; see
     above, p. 151, note 120.
16   A different terminology is used by Schwarz for CD's alternately recurring themes;
     see above, p. 25.

added that a similarly cohesive shape is evident on a wider scale.[17]   This is
further confirmed by the close examination of CD 1-8 and 19-20 in which we
have engaged, demonstrating that a basis of biblical texts underlies both
groupings of material.   Thus, the greater number of citations present in the
midrashic sections is an essentially formal feature.

Fourthly, it is possible to specify the passages within the bible that are
regularly used in CD 1-8 or 19-20.   What is noticeable about texts drawn
from the Torah is their emphasis upon two interrelated themes: firstly,
situations of rebellion in the aftermath of the exodus but before entry into the
land, as reflected in Ex 32 and, especially, passages from Nu (but also Gn 6,7
and 10); secondly, Lv 26 and Dt 27-32, which centre on the related story of
the sin-exile-restoration of the people after initial residence in the land - what
we may characterize as the rebellion *par excellence*.   Other parts of the
Holiness Code (i.e., Lv 17-25) employed by our writer are echoed in such a
way as to allow their language to be conveniently related to the specifically
legal aspect of the rebellions concerned.   It should be noted, of course, that
'rebellion' here, like exile, covers a process including purging and restoration.
Due to the extent of linguistic and thematic connections between these
pentateuchal contexts, of which our author appears to have been well aware,
there is no great problem in assuming that, for any pious Jew familiar with the
scriptures in Second Temple times, one passage or part thereof would easily
connote another.

As for prophetic texts exploited by the writer of CD, we find a similar
preoccupation with the exile in its broadest sense.   This accounts for most of
the frequently recurring contexts from Is, Jer and Ez, to which the
Admonition appeals for most of its prophetic quotations and allusions; it
probably also lies behind the somewhat rarer dependence on texts from the
twelve minor Prophets - Hos, Am, Mic, Hab, Zec, and Mal - although some
of these books inform the author's eschatological picture, as in the cases of
Mic 7:10, Hab 2:1, and Mal 3:16 (see CD 4:11f and 20:17).[18]   Nearly all of

---

17   See above, p. 22f, for Vermes' argument as to the internal arrangement of small
      units within the Admonition around citations; see p. 25f, for Schwarz on the
      structured interrelation of three types of material in CD 1-8 and 19-20.

18   Regarding the employment of Am 9:11 in CD 7:16, note a possible connection, via
      גזרה שוה, between Am 9:13, ונגש חורש בקצר ודרך ענבים and Lv 26:5, ...והגיש לכם
      דיש את בציר; the latter context is certainly influential in CD, as we have seen.
      Similarly, Am 9:11ff is probably linked to Am 5:26 (see CD 7:14ff) due to the
      presence of סכות/סכה in both contexts, as well as the mention of king David.   If
      correct, such links reflect the same conscious linguistic and thematic connections
      evident behind the employment of more prominent scriptural passages.

this prophetic material acts as a commentary on the various participants in the exilic saga, or represents a broader but similar cycle; the latter is exemplified in Is 59, while the former can be seen in use of Ez 13f. Although some caution is in order concerning the supposition that one verse in a particular context might evoke others in the same or surrounding passages, the extent of thematic overlap and linguistic interconnection between the prophetic chapters we have had occasion to mention confirms our overall thesis.

Turning to the Ketuvim, the situation is less easily defined. However, Pss texts would appear to concentrate either on a recurrent cycle of sin-punishment-restoration within Israelite history (e.g., Ps 106), as underlies the utilization of some prophetic passages, or on generalized religious language, easily applicable to the individual sectarian or the community as a whole (e.g., Ps 94). More concretely, reflections of Ezr 9 and Neh 9 echo a similar cycle of events, focused more especially on the exile. The same would apply to any dependence on 1,2 Chr or Dn, if this can be posited, because the relevant contexts in these works turn on the exile too.

Further, when we found that a phrase in the Admonition appeared to reflect language from more than one scriptural passage, it often seemed reasonable to conclude that two or three contexts were being utilized deliberately. For instance, CD 3:15f (אשר יעשה האדם וחיה בהם) reflects Ez 20:11,13,21 and Neh 9:29, as well as Lv 18:5, given other citations or allusions which draw on Neh 9, Ez 20, or the Holiness Code. Indeed, in such cases, our writer's starting point may have been to link certain biblical passages, via גזרה שוה, in view of the obvious linguistic connections between them.[19]

Returning to the notion of a canon of scripture, it was concluded above that the only writing accorded canonical status during the Second Temple period was the Torah itself.[20] Around this was an open-ended grouping of texts deemed to stem from the heroes of ancient Israel up to the time of Ezra, which might loosely be called 'prophets'. However, some delimitation of the large number of potential sources had to be made if our study was to remain manageable. Since it can be stated with relative safety that what was later

---

[19] We must leave to one side the historical-critical question of whether one scriptural context may have utilized another as a source, because it is not directly relevant for understanding bible exegesis in the late Second Temple period. From the perspective of exilic or early post-exilic Israelite history, however, material in Lv and Ez may well be related, while Neh 9 may have drawn upon such earlier traditions; see in the first instance the relevant portions of J.A. Soggin, *Introduction to the Old Testament*, London (1989).

[20] See above, pp. 15-18.

included in the second and third divisions of the three-fold canon would have
been viewed as 'prophetic' by those for whom they were available in Second
Temple times, it was decided to limit ourselves to this selection of books,
although our arrangement of data in terms of the later three-fold canonical
division within chapters 4 and 5 above was for the sake of convenience
only.[21] Regarding the community at Khirbet Qumran in particular, the vast
library in the surrounding caves renders the presence and use of all these texts
virtually beyond doubt. This means that, as far as the Admonition is
concerned, the main difficulty, apart from a number of unclear cases, is how
to judge whether apparent links between CD 1-8 or 19-20 and Dn, the latter
of which in its final form stems from a time not long before CD, constitute
dependence of the former on the latter or a mere common reliance on older
texts (like Ezr 9). As predicted, however, this quandary, even if it cannot be
settled definitively for the time being, was more of a problem in theory than in
practice. Similarly, whatever was believed about 1 En, Jub, or TestXII, they
are considerably later in origin than the majority of the contents of the three-
fold canon. As such, it is the latter that are likely in reality to have exercised
the greatest influence on the Admonition, simply because of their
chronological head-start. In any case, we found that the former were less
important for understanding CD 1-8 and 19-20 than the Torah and the three
main and twelve minor Prophets, and do not affect the substance of our
thesis. This puts into perspective a reference to what is often thought to be a
form of TLev in CD 4:13 (as also that to Jub in CD 16:3f). Whilst worthy of
further investigation, this reference appears to be of little significance for the
present study, inasmuch as it stands on the periphery of the basic core of
scriptural texts influential in the Admonition, in terms of allusion as well as
citation, rather like Hab 2:1 in CD 4:11.[22]

Finally, and in support of our work, it is important to mention an article by
Brooke, who, via a different route, has made some observations which are
similar to our own.[23] His main subject is the stabilization of the content and
order of the proto-Masoretic Psalter, especially Pss 100-150. He argues that
this was not complete until the turn of the eras, as evident from the remains
of Pss MSS from Cave 4.[24] At about this time, it would appear that Book

---

21   Generally speaking, younger works like Ezr, Neh, 1,2 Chr and, more especially, Dn,
but also 1 En, Jub or TestXII, and perhaps 11QT, may have been less readily
available in both Palestine and the diaspora and, therefore, less well-known.

22   See above, p. 84.

23   G.J. Brooke, 'Psalms 105 and 106 at Qumran', *RQ* 14 (1989), pp. 267-292.

24   These MSS have been studied by G.H. Wilson, *The Editing of the Hebrew Psalter*,
California (1985), on whose conclusions Brooke draws.

Four of the Psalter was taking shape (alongside other arrangements), with Pss 105 and 106 bringing it to a close. Contending that these two Pss were originally not conjoined, he further maintains that Ps 106 was composed at the end of the third or the beginning of the second century BCE. There are two reasons for this: Ps 106 is probably dependent on 1 Chr 16, not *vice versa*; and, surprisingly, Ps 106 is itself nowhere surely present in any Qumran Pss MS.[25]

These two propositions are not directly relevant to our own analysis but, as part of his argument, Brooke makes a number of points that are pertinent.[26] Firstly, he observes that Pss 105 and, especially, 106 are interpretative pastiches of parts of the Torah - Ex 32ff, Lv 26, Nu 14ff, and Dt 27-33. Moreover, an interest in Ex 34 and Dt 7, concerning the second giving of the Law, is noticeable in this regard.[27] Secondly, he maintains that there are a number of Second Temple texts which, following Ps 106, centre on the same passages, all of which are subsumed under a controlling use of Dt; some of these also evince an overall levitical or priestly interest.[28] One of them is CD itself, and we may note Brooke's description of the work:

> "Characteristic of *CD*...is its exhortatory use of its view of God's saving plan in history, a very similar phenomenon to what can be found in *Psalms* 78, 105 and 106. This is most explicit in *CD* I, 1-IV, 12a but can apparently be found also in the *4Q* texts which offer introductory remarks that probably precede *CD* I. But not only is the use of historical exhortation similar to that of the three *Psalms* mentioned, it is also similarly oriented around *Leviticus* 26. In *CD* I, 3-5 we read: "For *when they were unfaithful in that they forsook him*, he hid his face from Israel and his sanctuary and gave them to the sword. But when *he remembered his covenant with the men of former times*, he left a remnant to Israel and did not give them to destruction". The reference to *Lev.* 26, 40 here follows an allusion to *Num* 14, 23, part of a chapter which with *Leviticus* 26 plays a key role in *Psalm* 106. *Lev.* 26, 45, here in *CD* I, 4, is repeated in *CD*

---

25   See Brooke, *op. cit.*, p. 275f, 283f. He also maintains, pp. 273 and 277f, that Ps 106 has drawn from 4Q380, a text from Persian or Hellenistic times according to E.M. Schuller, *Non-Canonical Psalms from Qumran: A Pseudepigraphic Collection*, Atlanta (1986).

26   Two factors may elicit caution regarding Brooke's main argument: firstly, his willingness to draw conclusions from the lack of evidence that Ps 106 was present at Qumran may not be justified; secondly, it is not easy to decide which way dependency of one text on another operates, when those two texts may be of a similar age. However, it ought to be said that Brooke is aware of these dangers.

27   See above, p. 112.

28   See Brooke, *op. cit.*, p. 280f, for examples, including passages in 1 Mac, 3 Mac, 4 Mac, Wis, Sir, 4 Ezr, and Lk.

> VI, 2 after which God is described as raising up men of understanding from
> Aaron and men of wisdom from Israel to dig the well which is the Law".[29]

These observations remove any doubt as to our own basic conclusions. They confirm that the mass of allusions to Nu 14ff, Lv 26, Dt 28ff, apparent throughout the Admonition, are not the product of our own imagination, and we have seen that they inform most of the work, not just CD 1:1-4:12a. That Brooke, concentrating on Pss 105 and 106, has focused on the Torah is not problematic, since the prophetic texts that we have considered as influential in the Admonition are additional, not oppositional, to those from the Law.[30]

That the Admonition belongs to a broader exegetical tradition, which has connected a number of biblical passages, can be seen from another example, 4Q504 (4QDibHam[a]). It is worth borrowing Brooke's own words again:[31]

> "*4Q504*....may have been a weekly liturgical recollection of creation, the patriarchal episodes, the exodus from Egypt, the covenant at Horeb (Frg. 3, II, 13), the wilderness rebellions (especially recalling the language of *Numbers* 14: Frgs. 1-2, I, 8-10, II, 7-10, Frg. 6, 10-14), leading up to *Psalms* of confession and praise akin to *Daniel* 9 and *Nehemiah* 9 together with some element of the *Psalms* of praise (105, 106, 145-150, 1 *Chronicles* 16). Some biblical pericopae seem to influence more than one section of the composition and may be considered as important for the overall appreciation of the text. One such biblical text is *Lev.* 26, 40-46: it almost certainly lies behind Frgs. 1-2, V, 6-10, VI, 6-8, Frg. 3, II,14. Another is *Psalm* 78, an Asaph *Psalm*, with the important description of the choice of Judah: Frgs. 1-2, IV, 5-7, also V, 6, Frg. 7, 16, Frg. 8 (recto), 9".[32]

Once more, this bears out the general thrust of our examination of CD 1-8 and 19-20. Not only does a similar combination of biblical texts appear in another non-biblical Qumran work, but it is also worthy of note that 4Q504 appeals to a core of biblical passages which consistently reappears as

---

[29] Brooke, *op. cit.*, p. 286.

[30] Note that Brooke, *op. cit.*, p. 276, does discuss Ez 4:16; 5:16; 14:13 in connection with Ps 105 and, in 'The Messiah of Aaron in the *Damascus Document*', *RQ* 15 (1991), pp. 215-230, he notes the importance of several other passages in CD, including Ez 20 and 44. Further, our own references to Ez 44 would corroborate the reality of the priestly/levitical interest just mentioned.

[31] According to Brooke, who follows M. Baillet, *Qumrân Grotte 4: 4Q482-4Q520*, Oxford (Discoveries in the Judaean Desert VII; 1982), p. 137ff, 4Q504 probably dates from the mid-second century BCE. However, cf. *DSSE*, p. 250, "The editor of the document, M. Baillet (*DJD* VII...), attributes to it an exaggeratedly early date, the mid second century B.C.".

[32] Brooke, *op. cit.*, p. 272. For 4Q504, some of it rather fragmentary, see DJD, VII, pp. 137-168.

influential at various points within the same document.[33]   Brooke's mention of Neh 9 and Dn 9 is significant, in that it justifies the inclusion of these in our own study, although, as was the case with CD, it may be difficult to tell whether parallel usage of older scriptures is in operation or dependence of one recent text (4Q504) upon another (Dn).

6.2 The Damascus Document and History

Throughout our analysis, we have deliberately refrained from entering into the detail of the debate over the significance of the Admonition for understanding the origins of the Essenes, although the main difficulties involved were outlined by way of introduction.   Also, inasmuch as our examination of CD 1-8 and 19-20 has sought to bypass them, such difficulties have been kept in the background of our study for the sake of contrast. Clearly, however, our findings must have some bearing on the problems that scholars have come up against in trying to read the Admonition as a historical source.   The remainder of this chapter will, therefore, seek to place our results within the wider context of scholarly debate concerning CD 1-8 and 19-20. In order to set the scene, we shall initially review two attempts to deal with some of the issues involved in using the Admonition to reconstruct Qumran origins.

As has been explained, two main theories as to the emergence of the Qumran sect have gained currency among scholars, if we leave to one side some extreme and untenable hypotheses.[34] Most place the beginnings of the community, with its headquarters at Qumran, in the second half of the second century BCE, and consider the sect's outlook and aims to be reflected in the non-biblical DSS. Others, in view of certain features within the Admonition, place the inception of a broader movement further into the past and propose an association with Babylon; from this wider grouping, a splinter formed under the leadership of the מורה צדק who established a seceding faction at Qumran. A mid-way position, which combines elements from each of these

---

33   Note that an as yet unpublished text, 4Q393, possibly a Qumran liturgy or communal confession, also seems to echo language from Nu 14; Lv 26; Dt 9; Ps 106. See the photograph in R.H. Eisenman, J.M. Robinson, *A Facsimile Edition of the Dead Sea Scrolls*, II, Washington (1991), plate 1457.

34   For the former, see above, p. 5f. For the latter, see the bibliographical data on the views of R.H. Eisenman, J.L. Teicher, and B. Thiering, above on p. 6, note 18.

theories and adds others of its own, has also been put forward.[35]   While numerous scholars have contributed to this debate on Qumran origins over the past two decades - including Vermes, Stegemann, Charlesworth, García Martínez, van der Woude, Murphy-O'Connor, Davies, and Knibb - it is not within our remit to enter into a detailed study of their views.[36] However, it will be worth examining the theories of Knibb and Davies, before proceeding to relate our analysis of CD 1-8 and 19-20 to the historical question. Knibb has defended the consensus view on Qumran origins via a study of the exile motif in Second Temple literature, including CD, while Davies, on the other hand, has argued for claims to an exilic foundation within the document.[37]

---

[35]   Thus, F. García Martínez, A.S. van der Woude, 'A Groningen Hypothesis of Qumran Origins and Early History', *RQ* 14 (1990), pp. 521-542, have five main proposals:

i   the Qumranites and the Essenes were not the same;

ii   the Essenes originated in Palestine in apocalyptic circles at the end of the third century/beginning of the second century BCE before the accession of Antiochus IV Epiphanes;

iii   a split occurred within this group under the Teacher, leading to the settlement at Qumran;

iv   the כהן הרשע in the sectarian DSS refers to a succession of Hasmonean rulers in chronological order;

v   it is possible to reconstruct the formative period, before the Qumranites absconded to the desert, noting various ideological, halakhic, and political factors.

Regarding item v, the Groningen hypothesis parts company with the consensus view by suggesting that the Qumran sect was not coterminous with the Essenes but was a splinter-group from that wider movement. It disagrees with Murphy-O'Connor and Davies, however, by retaining a thoroughly Second Temple, Palestinian origin for both the Essenes and the Qumran sect.

[36]   See J.H. Charlesworth, 'The Origin and Subsequent History of the Authors of the Dead Sea Scrolls: Four Transitional Phases among the Qumran Essenes', *RQ* 10 (1980), pp. 213-233; J. Murphy-O'Connor, 'The Essenes and their History', *RB* 81 (1974), pp. 215-244; H. Stegemann, 'The Qumran Essenes - Local Members of the Main Jewish Union in Late Second Temple Times', in *Madrid*, I, pp. 83-166; G. Vermes, 'The Essenes and History', *JJS* 32 (1981), pp. 18-31. For García Martinez and van der Woude, see the preceding note; for Davies and Knibb, see the next note.

[37]   See M. Knibb, 'The Exile in the Literature of the Intertestamental Period', *Heythrop Journal* 17 (1976), pp. 253-272; 'Exile in the Damascus Document', *JSOT* 25 (1983), pp. 99-117; 'Jubilees and the Origins of the Qumran Community', Inaugural Lecture at King's College London (1989), pp. 1-20; P.R. Davies, 'Hasidim in the Maccabean Period', *JJS* 28 (1977), pp. 127-140; *Behind the Essenes: History and Ideology in the Dead Sea Scrolls*, Atlanta (1987); 'The Birthplace of the Essenes: Where is 'Damascus'', *RQ* 14 (1990), pp. 503-520.

Knibb maintains that a number of Second Temple texts consider the exile, inaugurated under Nebuchadnezzar, as continuing well beyond the time of Cyrus' decree (538 BCE). This view may be expressed through an interpretation of the "70 years" found in Jer 25:11 and 29:10 (as in Dn 9:24-27, 1 En 85-90, 1 En 93:1-10, 91:11-17, perhaps also TLev 16:1, and AssMos 3:14), or, as in CD, by the use of Ez 4's "390 years".[38] While such works place their narrative in the past, differing in precisely how far towards the present they bring the reader, they address a contemporary Second Temple situation which is viewed as a prolongation of the exile. The return under Cyrus and, later, under Ezra and Nehemiah, may be mentioned either half-heartedly or else not at all. Thus, while CD's historical sections appear to connect the founding of the community with the exile, this motif is to be viewed as a theological pattern, from which few, if any, historical or geographical facts can be deduced.[39] Indeed, the writer of CD does not mention the sixth century BCE return specifically, simply because he considered the exile to be continuing until the foundation of his own community. This should not lead modern scholars to conclude that the jump from Nebuchadnezzar's deportation to the sect's foundation is historically accurate. Rather, it signifies only that nothing worthy of note took place in between these two episodes, with no implications as to the duration of the intervening period. According to Knibb, therefore, since there is much that points to a religious reform in the second century BCE, we should continue to posit that same milieu as the appropriate context for the founding of the Essene community at Qumran.

Acknowledging that the historian has a difficult task, Knibb states that it must be remembered that the sectarian DSS are not to be treated as historical documents. He points out that the use of nicknames limits our ability to penetrate the historical development of the sect; they predominate in CD 1-8 and 19-20, in which we ourselves have noted that the epithets concerned are

---

[38]   M. Knibb, 'The Exile in the Literature of the Intertestamental Period', *Heythrop Journal* 17 (1976), pp. 253-272, points to a similar motif in the 'Sin-Exile-Return' passages of TestXII, as well as in Bar, 2 Esd, 2 Bar, although the latter are not based so closely on biblical texts.

[39]   1 En 93:1-10 and 91:11-17 are of a similar nature. In view of this, M. Knibb, 'Exile in the Damascus Document', *JSOT* 25 (1983), p. 103f, proposes that the supposed Babylonian influence on CD can be viewed otherwise, as can also Murphy-O'Connor's interpretations of דמשק, שבי ישראל, and ארץ יהודה.

often based on scripture, as well as 1QpHab, 4QpNah, and 4QpPs.[40]   He says:

> "The statements of a historical kind [in CD] are found within the exhortation, and because of the very context in which they occur they lack any precision. The historical statements in the biblical commentaries...and...some...in the Damascus Document...are based on the interpretations of biblical passages, and the language used is often strongly influenced by the language of the biblical passages commented on rather than by the actual characters of the persons and events described."[41]

Therefore, "the link between the origins of the Essene movement and the events of the exile - which is certainly present in the Damascus Document - [has]...a significance other than that suggested by Murphy-O'Connor...and Davies".[42]   The link is theological, not historical, and similar to a pattern in other texts, where Israel is in exile for both the exilic and post-exilic periods; this situation is only brought to an end with the rising of the "plant of righteousness" in 1 En and with the formation of the sect in the Admonition.[43]   Since Sir, Dn, 1 En, and Jub all witness to a reform movement in Palestine towards the end of the third and beginning of the second century BCE, this remains the best context in which to view CD 1-8 and 19-20.   Indeed, Jub 1:10-18 and 23:14-31 provide a useful parallel, for, although the restoration described could denote that which took place in the sixth century BCE, the fact that the author is obviously unhappy with the state of religion and its practice in his own day means that, as far as he is concerned, the exile continues and salvation will only occur in the eschatological future.[44]

---

40   As is well known, 4QpNah also refers to a certain [דמי]טרוס and one אנתיכוס in 1:2,3.   These are almost certainly Demetrius IV (95-88 BCE) and Antiochus IV Epiphanes.

41   M. Knibb, 'Jubilees and the Origins of the Qumran Community', p. 4.

42   M. Knibb, 'Jubilees and the Origins of the Qumran Community', p. 6.

43   Cf. J. Murphy-O'Connor, 'The Damascus Document Revisited', RB 92 (1985), p. 228, responding to M. Knibb, 'Exile in the Damascus Document', JSOT 25 (1983), pp. 99-117, that this pattern only applies to the reworking of CD 1:1-2:1, not to the other two historical portions.

44   M. Knibb, 'Jubilees and the Origins of the Qumran Community', pp. 10-16, points to numerous parallels between Jub and the sectarian DSS over the notion of covenant, the calendar, the importance of שבת, the need for separation, as well as the dualism present in both contexts.   Jub, therefore, along with other texts such as 1 En, can be viewed as belonging to the pre-history of the Qumran sect.   Further, if Jub dates to 175-167 BCE (175 BCE, because Jub reflects sufficient increase in hellenization to require the assession of Antiochus IV Epiphanes; 167 BCE, since there is no hint that the excesses of 167-164 have yet taken place), and is an appeal

In Davies' view, as will be clear already, a pre-Qumran group was responsible for an original edition of the Admonition; its members viewed themselves as originating in exile. This is related in CD 2:14-4:12a and 5:15b-6:11a; at one time, the same was the case for 1:1-2:1 but additions from the later Qumran community have created a competing point of reference - the split that led to the formation of the seceding Qumran party in the second century BCE.[45] In a comparison of CD 1:1-2:1, 2:14-4:12a, and 5:15b-6:11a with Jub 1, 1 En 93:1-10, and 91:11-17, Davies has argued that all of these passages share certain characteristics but were not penned by Qumranite authors. In his judgement of Jub and 1 En, he differs little from that of Knibb, in that these works seem to stem from an earlier, broader movement, from which those who went to Qumran separated. However, in contrast to Knibb's views, Davies labels the wider group 'Essene' and believes his overall thesis on CD is confirmed by a comparison of the *Heilsgeschichten* of the above-mentioned texts. Summarizing the similarities and differences, he draws a number of observations from his consideration of the story-lines in these books.[46] In particular, Davies points out that both the Admonition and Jub have a picture of repentance, forgiveness and renewal of the covenant taking place in exile, only then followed by a return to the land, linked to obedience to a true interpretation of the Law. He argues that, even if the modern historian has to conclude otherwise, the Essene movement believed it originated in exile and returned to Palestine at a some point in time before the secession of the Qumran community from a wider Essene movement in the second century BCE.[47] Moreover, although the Admonition's assertion that all of its traditions *in toto* stem from the exilic remnant may be idealized, its claim should be treated seriously, if, as is likely,

---

to renew the covenant and observe the Law in Palestine, then, as precursor to the Essene movement, the latter too, including the Essenes at Qumran, must belong to the second century BCE.

45   See especialy Davies, pp. 173-201.

46   In particular, note P.R. Davies, *Behind the Essenes: History and Ideology in the Dead Sea Scrolls*, Atlanta (1987), p. 125:
"For there can hardly be any doubt that the correspondences of these texts...oblige us to regard them as products of a single movement... It is unnecessarily pedantic to withhold from this group the name "Essene". But the use of this designation does not have to imply a tightly-organized movement...such organisation is attested by Josephus...and the Qumran evidence is not indicative of the Essenes as a whole, but...a particular...sect".

47   Cf. J. Murphy-O'Connor, 'The Essenes and their History', *RB* 81 (1974), p. 224f, who posits that the time concerned was that of the campaigns of Judas Maccabee.

interchange between Jews in Babylon and Palestine in the late Persian and Hellenistic periods was more extensive and complex than is often assumed.[48]

It is difficult not to be in sympathy with Davies' work, not least due to the fact that he posits an exilic connection for the group commended in the Admonition, which is the most natural reading of CD 3:10ff and 5:20ff. Indeed, given that we have highlighted the centrality of the exilic motif in the document's employment of scripture, this connotation is even clearer. However, our chief point of departure from his theory is that the supposed secondary additions to CD 1:1-2:1 link up with the underlying body of scriptural contexts informing the rest of the Admonition. It is difficult to reconcile any theory of redaction, which necessarily assumes an awkwardness in the text, to this fact.

Our appreciation must also lie with Knibb, for he is aware that the document's use of scripture may have shaped its presentation of events.[49] However, he maintains that the connection between the Babylonian exile and the formation of the sect, despite *prima facie* historical appearances, is theological and of no historical value. While at first sight this makes sense in view of the well-known inadequacies of Jewish chronology during this period, we may suspect that it is not a distinction that would have made sense to the ancient readers of CD 1-8 and 19-20.[50] Moreover, while similarities between CD and Jub are certainly noticeable, Knibb oversimplifies them. In particular, our document in its final form has two clearly-articulated points of reference - one exilic and the other considerably later. If the text were advancing some theological pattern, we should expect only one of these points in time to be specified; and, only if it were the latter, would it allow a mere typological use of the exilic motif.[51] Similarly, it is not clear that the Admonition implies simply that the formation of the sect constituted the end of the exile. Although the document may imply that the members of the community experience a foretaste of the divine restoration, the rest of the world is still in a perilous exilic state, according to CD 4:12b-5:15a, while CD 4:11f suggests that this will not be remedied until the eschaton.

---

[48]   See P.R. Davies, 'The Birthplace of the Essenes: Where is 'Damascus'', *RQ* 14 (1990), pp. 503-520, and, more generally, *In Search of 'Ancient Israel'*, Sheffield (1992).

[49]   His view as outlined here has been reaffirmed in a study discussing whether or not מורה צדק was a messianic title and concluding that it was not; see 'The Teacher of Righteousness: A Messianic Title?' in P.R. Davies, R.T. White, *A Tribute to Geza Vermes*, Sheffield (1990), pp. 51-65.

[50]   On Second Temple Jewish historiography, see above, p. 28, note 58.

[51]   See above, p. 102.

Nevertheless, it can be seen that both scholars have contributed significantly to the debate concerning the Admonition and Qumran origins. More specifically, it may be possible to conjoin Davies' acceptance of the plain sense of the Admonition's exilic claim with Knibb's realization that the document's presentation of history may be shaped by a theologizing use of biblical language. Indeed, we shall now attempt to draw into the discussion our own observations about the employment of scripture in CD 1-8 and 19-20, coupled with the notion, mentioned several times during our survey, of the 'creation of history'.

6.3 Mark 15:22-37 and Scripture

In order to clarify the possible linkage between bible usage in CD 1-8 and 19-20 and the idea of the 'creation of history', it may be helpful to take a brief look at an entirely different passage, namely, Mk 15:22-37, which forms part of the Marcan Passion Narrative. There are, of course, may differences between Mk 15:22-37 and the Admonition, not least the fact that the latter covers a much broader span of time in its historical sections than does Mk 14-16; moreover, we have been able to take advantage of the opportunity to examine the whole of CD 1-8 and 19-20, not just a part of it. Nevertheless, many of the points that have been found to apply to the Admonition and its utilization of scripture can be seen to be operating in this Marcan passage.

Mk 14-16, like the parallel accounts in Mt and Lk, appears to be particularly old and interconnected; it makes sense as a narrative on its own. Thus, while Mk 1-13 consists of various pericopae and traditions brought together by the evangelist, it is noticeable that chapters 14-16 flow in a more integrated and coherent way. Presumably, such a narrative concerning Jesus' arrest, death and resurrection existed earlier rather than later in the Gospel tradition, not least due to the importance attached to explaining his suffering and death and to proclaiming his subsequent vindication. The relative age and coherence of Mk 14-16 are shown partly by the fact that the evangelist appears less free in dealing with his material in Mk 14-16 than with other stories and sayings.[52] Indeed, one of the main concerns of the earliest

---

52 See M. Dibelius, *From Tradition to Gospel*, Cambridge-London (1971), p. 178ff. Of course, there are many differences of detail between the three Synoptic Passion Narratives, especially between Lk over against Mt and Mk. Nevertheless, the agreement of a basic framework and much detail is noticeable, and this even

Christians from the outset was to show Jesus' death to be in God's plan - contrary to most people's expectation of what God's anointed would accomplish.[53] They were eager to show to themselves and to others that the events surrounding Jesus' death were divinely ordained. Only from such a viewpoint would recounting the story make sense.

Allied with this evangelical concern, Mk's Passion Narrative also evinces a pronounced employment of scripture by both quotation and allusion. Indeed, there is a relatively small number of citations (in relation to the length of the text), accompanied by a somewhat greater amount of allusion; the body of allusion relates to the quotations in more than a coincidental or haphazard way. This can be observed well in the crucifixion narrative in Mk 15:25-39, which reads as follows:[54]

[22]Και φερουσιν αυτον επι τον Γολγοθαν τοπον, ο εστιν

Ps 69:21   μεθερμηνευομενος Κρανιου Τοπος. [23]**και εδιδουν αυτω εσμυρνισμενον οινον**, ος δε ουκ ελαβεν. [24]Και σταυρουσιν

Ps 22:18   αυτον και **διαμεριζονται τα ιματια αυτου βαλλοντες κληρον επ αυτα** τις τι αρη. [25]ην δε ωρα τριτη και εσταυρωσαν αυτον. [26]και ην η επιγραφη της αιτιας αυτου επιγεγραμμενη, Ο βασιλευς των Ιουδαιων. [27]Και συν αυτω σταυρουσιν δυο ληστας, ενα εκ δεξιων και ενα εξ ευωνυμων αυτου. [[28]και

[Is 53:12]   επληρωθη η γραφη η λεγουσα, *Και μετα ανομων ελογισθη*]

Ps 22:7   [29]Και οι παραπορευομενοι εβλασφημουν αυτον **κινουντες τας κεφαλας αυτων** και λεγοντες, Ουα ο καταλυων τον ναον και

Ps 22:8   οικοδομων εν τρισιν ημεραις, [30]**σωσον σεαυτον** καταβας απο του σταυρου. [31]ομοιως και οι αρχιερεις εμπαιζοντες προς

---

extends to Jn. On the other hand, it is clear that Mk's Passion Narrative is made up of blocks of text, some of which could exist autonomously. In particular, this applies to Mk 14:22-25 with its parallel in 1 Cor 11:23-26. The same is the case for the tradition about the anointing of Jesus at Bethany, found in Mk's Passion Narrative but not in Lk's, which places it at 7:37-39; conversely, Jesus' teaching on humility is placed in Lk 22:24-27, but in Mk 9:33-37.

53   It is not to be suggested, of course, that the Jews *en masse* 'believed' this or that about a messiah(s) during the Second Temple period. Indeed, see Schürer, II, pp. 488-554, on the wide variety of messianic hopes, which suggests that the notion of 'the Messiah' as a title for a figure with a fixed role belongs to later Jewish and Christian tradition after 70 CE. Nevertheless, it seems probable that Jesus' end would not have been expected by most, if not all, of those who were waiting for the advent of an anointed(s) of some description.

54   Quotations or allusions to the Prophets and Writings are represented in *italics* or **bold** script, respectively. The numbering of the Pss and their verses here is in accord with NRSV.

Ps 22:8   αλληλους μετα των γραμματεων ελεγον, **Αλλους εσωσεν, εαυτον**
ου δυναται σωσαι. ³²ο Χριστος ο βασιλευς Ισραηλ καταβατω
νυν απο του σταυρου, ινα ιδωμεν και πιστευσωμεν. και οι
συνεσταυρωμενοι συν αυτω ωνειδιζον αυτον. ³³Και γενομενης
ωρας εκτης σκοτος εγενετο εφ ολην την γην εως ωρας ενατης.

Ps 22:1   ³⁴και τη ενατη ωρα εβοησεν ο Ιησους φωνη μεγαλη, **Ελωι**
ελωι λεμα σαβαχθανι; ο εστιν μεθερμηνευομενον
Ο θεος μου ο θεος μου, εις τι εγκατελιπες με; και
³⁵τινες των παρεστηκοτων ακουσαντες ελεγον, Ιδε Ηλιαν φωνει.

Ps 69:21   ³⁶δραμων δε τις και γεμισας σπογγον **οξους περιθεις καλαμω**
εποτιζεν αυτον, λεγων, Αφετε ιδωμεν ει ερχεται Ηλιας καθελειν
αυτον. ³⁷ο δε Ιησους αφεις φωνην μεγαλην εξεπνευσεν.

A number of points can be made by examining this arrangement. Firstly, it is possible to conduct an inquiry into scriptural quotation and allusion in Mk 15:22-37, despite obscurities regarding the fluidity of the biblical text and the limits of the canon, which apply to the world informing the NT as much as to that behind the sectarian DSS.[55] Thus, the presence of Ps 22:1 in verse 34 is clear and, in effect, constitutes a citation; Ps 22:18 in verse 24 is similar.[56] In addition, an unmistakable allusion to Ps 69:21 is to be found in verse 36, which might also lie behind the analogous reference in verse 23. Details such as these point to an underlying structure of exegetical traditions, involving what were thought to be related passages (i.e., Pss 22 and 69), surfacing in both overt and subtle references to the bible. Secondly, on the other hand, there are certain ambiguities present too. Thus, the question of an allusion to Ps 22:8 in the use of σωζειν in verse 30f is more difficult to decide, although the wagging of the head in verse 29, based clearly on Ps 22:7, might confirm it.[57] Less likely, perhaps, is a reference to Lam 1:12; 2:15 in verse 29 but it is not possible to be sure.

Nevertheless, there is a body of citation and allusion which is unmistakably present in Mk 15:22-37, as was found to be the case in CD 1-8 and 19-20, even if its precise limits, as with the Admonition also, are not detectable. It is reasonable to suppose that each relates to the other and that both are, in fact, part of the same process. Furthermore, it appears that a proper understanding of the quotations cannot be gained without fully appreciating

---

[55]   On a wider front, see D.J. Moo, *The Old Testament in the Gospel Passion Narratives*, Sheffield (1983); M.D. Hooker, *The Gospel according to St. Mark*, London (1991), pp. 371-377.

[56]   Jn 19:24f changes this into an explicit quotation.

[57]   As far as the former is concerned, the allusion in Mt 27:43f is considerably clearer.

the extent of the presence of allusive references to the bible. Hence, an acknowledgement of the allusive background leads to the realization that Jesus' cry on the cross in Mk 15:34, citing Ps 22:1, is not intended to express complete despair.[58] Rather, it is demonstration of the fact that the awful event described is part of a wider divine plan, manifest in the parting of the clothes, the shaking of heads, and other aspects of the narrative.

It would be of interest to examine the relation between Mk 15:22-37 and the remainder of the Marcan Passion Narrative (as well as the rest of that Gospel) in terms of the usage of scripture but, obviously, this is beyond the scope of the present study. One point worth mentioning, however, concerns the citation of Is 53:12 in verse 28, which is present only in a number of late MSS.[59] Whilst, within the confines of the above layout, it seems out of place and secondary, this reference, with its allusion to Is 53:12, not Ps 22 or Ps 69, is what intermeshes with other bible usage in Mk 14-16 and elsewhere; dependence on Ps 22 in the rest of the work appears to be non-existent.[60] Thus, from a literary point of view, it may be best to retain verse 28 within Mk 15:22-37, when the passage is viewed against the background of the rest of Mk's dependence on scripture. Whether or not verse 28 should be deemed 'original' to the pericope is another matter.

We may connect our remarks about Mk 15:22-37 to the summary of our findings on CD 1-8 and 19-20, expressed at the start of this chapter. This study has aimed to show that the Admonition can be viewed as a unified document when its employment of scripture is taken as the main criterion for establishing its credentials as a well-constructed text. Paradoxically, this is in contrast to the problems scholars have experienced in understanding the work, especially in harmonizing its accounts of the origins of the community and relating them to other sectarian DSS. Similarly, it is clear that, at the level of its usage of the bible, an integrated literary structure underlies Mk 15:22-37, from which it can be inferred that not a little effort went into shaping the story. On the other hand, Mk 14-16 is made up of a number of pericopae that could exist separately, as the luxury afforded by parallel texts demonstrates. More seriously, the weighty historical problems that have perplexed the minds of many scholars - both internal tensions within the

---

[58]   It may be that the danger of misunderstanding was what led to the replacement of Ps 22:1 with other statements by Jesus in Lk 23:46 and Jn 19:30.

[59]   This verse is found, *inter alia*, in L and Q.

[60]   For relevant data, see the tables in Moo, *op. cit.*, pp. 52-56, concerned in large measure with Mk's use of LXX. Regarding the use of Is in Mk, note, e.g., the probable link between Is 53:7 and the silence of Jesus in Mk 14:61 and 15:5.

Marcan account and difficulties in relation to Mt and Lk and to rabbinic sources - conflict with this evidence showing a creative final hand.[61] Such tensions within Mk 15:22-37 can be deemed analogous to those in the Admonition. Likewise, the main problem in the Marcan Passion Narrative on a wider front concerns its relation with Mt and Lk and with rabbinic material in the data they may or may not provide for an accurate reconstruction of the events surrounding Jesus' arrest, trial and death; this parallels the difficulties encountered in relating CD 1-8 and 19-20 to other Qumran texts.[62] However, as was suggested in an earlier chapter with regard to the Admonition, it may be possible to view these conflicting observations in cultural terms. In other words, although the modern person has a tendency to notice first the historcial tensions in Mk and in the Admonition, the writers responsible for these works may have had a different perspective. For them, the most distinctive characteristic about their respective texts was the prominence of certain biblical passages.

It is precisely this feature which links in to the aforementioned notion of the 'creation of history'. This expression is derived from Dibelius, who maintained that in a number of places in Mk "...the biblical passages have begotten history".[63] In other words, reflection by the author or his community upon scripture, coupled with a zeal for the basic message to be communicated, may have led to the addition of details or even of an overall pattern to the events described in the Gospel. We have already allowed the tacit inference of such a phenomenon in our brief description of scripture in Mk 15:22-37, especially given its clear employment of Ps 22. Thus, even a

---

61   In this regard, it can be noted that the author has left Mk 14:1f, stating that Jesus' arrest and death should occur before the Feast, while proceeding to describe those events as taking place during it. Similarly, Mk 14:28 would lead the reader to expect an appearance of Jesus to Peter in Galilee, an expectation which is not met (although Mk 16:7 may be tackling this problem).

62   For a discussion of some of these and other issues, see D. Juel, *Messiah and Temple: The Trial of Jesus in the Gospel of Mark*, Missoula (1977); E.P. Sanders, *Jesus and Judaism*, London (1985), pp. 270-318; and F. Millar, 'Reflections on the Trial of Jesus', in P.R. Davies, R.T. White, *A Tribute To Geza Vermes*, Sheffield (1990), pp. 355-381.

63   Dibelius, *op. cit.*, p. 188f. Cf. Moo, *op. cit.*, pp. 351-97, who rejects this. However, Moo's evaluation of his own useful analysis does not stand on this point, not least because he uses the unhelpful term "fabrication" (e.g., p. 381). More appropriate is an analogy with the historico-theological development in the early Church's beliefs about Jesus: the significant starting-point for his role gradually moved backwards from death/resurrection (Rm 1:2ff) to baptism in the Jordan (Mk) to his conception and birth (Mt, Lk) to his pre-existence with God (Jn).

conservative scholar such as Taylor argues that the presence of the αρχιερεις in Mk 15:31 is not historical.[64] Indeed, there are real problems in positing the presence of these people at the crucifixion of Jesus, and it seems highly reasonable that their attendance is inspired by Ps 22 itself, in which the enemies of the Psalmist mockingly confront him in his misfortune. Such developments within the Passion Narrative may be seen as an ongoing process, continued by other evangelists.[65] Yet, while such a phenomenon may be classed as the creation of history, this description is somewhat anachronistic, for we cannot doubt that, as far as the writer of Mk was concerned, what is recounted actually happened and was believed to have been foreshadowed in the bible. Because the scriptures so spoke, certain details 'must' have taken place.

The same possibility presents itself with regard to the Admonition, even if, as far as the historian is concerned, it would result in the removal of all or part of the stories involved from the realm of history. This, however, would not have been the case for the relevant Second Temple readers of the document. Hence, it would appear that one of the prime concerns of the writer of the Admonition within his own *Sitz im Leben* - to impress the audience with his authoritative and convincing use of scripture - may have led to the creative addition of historical details which, ironically, may have caused serious difficulties for modern scholars trying to understand the text.

6.4 The Damascus Document, Scripture, and History

In view of the above discussion, in which the question of bible usage and its relation to the notion of the creation of history in Mk 15:22-37 may have important implications for the Admonition, we may be able to begin to conjoin the insights of Knibb and Davies outlined earlier.

First of all, therefore, we shall reconsider Knibb's cautionary warning that the language of the Admonition's narrative portions is strongly influenced by

---

[64] See V. Taylor, *The Gospel according to St. Mark*, London (1952), p. 592.

[65] According to Dibelius, *op. cit.*, p. 188f, another example may be found in Lk 24:39 and Jn 20:25, 27, where we find references to the piercing of Jesus' hands and feet. It is reasonable to suppose that "[Mk] conceived the event otherwise and assumed that the body was made fast by binding". Thus, Lk and Jn, aware of Ps 22:17, realized that Jesus' hands and feet 'must' have been nailed (assuming a reading כרו/כארו for MT כארי, following LXX, ωρυξαν), although the detail has not been added to the crucifixion pericope itself.

scripture, which renders their contents of little historical value. Certainly, our own survey has shown that certain biblical passages are consistently influential throughout not only the historical sections of the document but also those portions we have designated midrashic. For example, we noted that the manner in which events are described in CD 1:3,4 and 17 is shaped by the language of Lv 26:40, 45 and 25, respectively. Lv 26 also contains a story-line similar, at least in general terms, to that in CD 1:1-2:1 and the other historical sections. Moreover, that same scriptural context is influential in CD 3:10 (cf. Lv 26:33), 6:2 (see Lv 26:45), and 7:9 (Lv 26:15).

As part of the intricate appeal to a selection of scriptures exemplified in the employment of Lv 26 in CD 1:1-2:1 and elsewhere, it appears that certain details within the Admonition's story-line can be attributed to aggadic elaboration, both in the descriptions of ancient Israel and of the development of the sect. This is parallel, in general terms at least, to what was found in Mk 15:22-37, and it will be helpful to remind ourselves of several examples within the Admonition encountered in earlier chapters. First of all, the mention of Eleazar, alongside Joshua and the elders, in CD 5:3 can be put down to an interpretative combination of Ju 2:7-10 and Jos 24:29 on the part of our author. Secondly, and leaving to one side the question of the relation between the marriage laws in CD and 11QT, a simple deduction has been made regarding an aspect of king David's behaviour in CD 5:2-4. In short, because Dt 17:17 states that the king should not have many wives, the fact that David did so must be explained by his ignorance of this law, which in turn can be accounted for by the supposition that the Torah was not available to him at this time. As a third example, we noted that the attribution of blood-eating to the Israelites who were refused entry to the land in CD 3:6f is probably based on an interpretation of Lv 17:10 and Dt 12:23, in conjunction with Ez 33:25,28. Finally, an instance of scripture controlling the presentation of prospective history may be found in CD 20:14f, based on Dt 2:14.[66]

Upon reflection, these examples of aggadah do not seem out of the ordinary. As we saw in an earlier chapter, they are only to be expected in a text which utilizes a set of scriptural works which are at once authoritative and call out for interpretative supplementation.[67] As far as the author of the

---

[66] See above, pp. 87f, 126, 131, 166 for these examples.

[67] See above, p. 46f. Halakhic embellishment is also inevitable, as found in some parts of the Admonition but more fully present in CD 9-16 and other legal works among the sectarian DSS. Thus, CD 5:7-10 deals with Lv 18:3, prohibiting marriage between a man and his aunt. Because the biblical text does not spell out, however,

Admonition was concerned, we may presume that certain events or details about events in the biblical past 'must' have taken place, even if not explicitly stated in the scriptures, given various associations and deductions that can be made within and between biblical passages. The end-result is an interpreted version of the scriptural account, connecting words and phrases, smoothing out unevennesses, and adding clarificatory details when deemed necessary, although other elements in this or that episode might ostensibly be omitted because taken for granted.[68]

Nonetheless, it is important to remember that the Admonition has a polemical edge to it, as is clearly evident, for example, in CD 4:12b-5:15a. It remains true that the narrative sections simply recount the familiar story of ancient Israel in a way that seeks to impart understanding of how God dealt with the righteous and the wicked in the past and how he always ensured the existence of a faithful remnant. Allied with this, however, part-way through the story there is a shift from ancient Israel to the formation and development of the group behind the Admonition. Thus, the story of the God's involvement with biblical Israel culminates in the establishment of the community commended in CD 1-8 and 19-20, as has been highlighted by Laato and Fraade.[69] It is now the locus of divinely-inspired insight into the historical process that eventually led to its own formation and, concomitantly, of the true interpretation of the Law.

Yet, it is precisely at those points dealing with the shift to the sectarian Israel that scholars have found the greatest difficulty in reading the Admonition. However, if we rename the aggadic phenomenon just described as 'the creation of history', a related feature comes to the fore. In other

---

whether the same prohibition extends to a woman and her uncle, the law could be interpreted in two directions. The opponents of those behind the Admonition presumably believed that, if God had intended a ban on the latter, the scriptures would have so stated; CD 5:7ff, on the other hand, argues that a ban on niece-marriage is implied by the explicit prohibition of union between a nephew and an aunt. For examples within CD 9-16, see Schürer, III.1, p. 392, note 7.

68   This applies, e.g., to CD 3:6ff, where the golden calf incident is not mentioned but, in view of other hints that the author had meditated on Ex 32, assumed; see above, p. 77.

69   Thus, A. Laato, 'The Chronology of the *Damascus Document* of Qumran', *RQ* 15 (1992), p. 607, states: "...the writer of CD has intentionally tried to place the birth of the community within the chronology of the history of Israel". Also, S.D. Fraade, 'Interpretative Authority in the Studying Community at Qumran', *JJS* 44 (1993), p. 69, comments: "...the movement experienced its collective life of study and practice...as the revelatory link to the biblical past that justified its rules and teachings, just as its life of purity and prayer linked it to heaven".

words, it is worth recalling that there are specific words and phrases within the historical sections recounting the origins of the sect that are taken from prominent biblical passages with a parallel narrative: נבוכדנאצר מלך בבל פקדם in CD 1:6 (cf. Jer 27:6,22); דור אחרון in CD 1:12 (Dt 29:21); נסתרות at CD 3:14 (Dt 29:28), and others. The Admonition's presentation of events may well have been influenced by such scriptural precedents, not only in a general way but also in the manner in which the text has recounted the exilic origins of the community. That such a narrative pattern, based on the cycles of Israelite history recounted in Is 59 and Ps 106, as well as on passages like Dt 29ff concerned with the exile, has shaped the account of the origins of the sect may be confirmed by the ambivalent status of those mentioned in CD 3:10ff, for it is not clear whether they were an obedient, righteous remnant, or else a sinful group which repented of its former ways. Precisely the same sort of ambiguity can be found in a number of biblical passages, especially Is 59, from which we cannot doubt that our author has drawn.[70] Or again, in dealing with the account of the sect's exilic origins in the third historical section, we noted the poignant use of the terms נבונים and חכמים in CD 6:2f, derived from Dt 1:13.[71] Observations such as these seem to confirm that we should accept Knibb's advice and take the historical portions of the Admonition, in the words of another scholar, "*cum grano salis*".[72]

However, this line of argument might seem somewhat anachronistic, for we cannot doubt that the person or group responsible for the Admonition thought that its descriptions of Israelite and sectarian history were accurate. It is appropriate at this point, therefore, to return to Davies' insistence that we take the document's claim to exilic origins seriously, because, at the very least, the writer believed this element to be true. Indeed, given his place within the mythology of the sect with its presuppositions about the bible, we may take it for granted that the author would not have distinguished between those details in biblical or sectarian history which, from a historical-critical viewpoint, really took place and others which may have been the product of an imaginative meditation on the scriptures.

We witnessed a similar state of affairs in considering Mk 15:22-37. Thus, while we may be obliged to accept that the αρχιερεις of Mk 15:31f were not present at Jesus' crucifixion but were inspired by the role of the enemies of the psalmist in Ps 22:7f, the writer of this Marcan pericope doubtless believed

---

[70]   See above, p. 102, note 89.
[71]   See above, p. 94.
[72]   E. Wiesenberg, 'Chronological Data in the Zadokite Fragments', *VT* 5 (1955), p. 308.

they were there. However, matters are rarely as clear-cut as this relatively certain instance of the creation of history might seem to imply at first sight. What, for example, is to be made of the parting of Jesus' garments (cf. Ps 22:18) or the offering to him of "sour wine" to drink (cf. Ps 22:15)?[73]

Returning to CD 1-8 and 19-20, it was suggested above that the exilic origins ascribed to the community in the historical sections of the document might constitute an instance of the creation of history, formed on the basis of a number of biblical texts whose story-line the Admonition seems to follow. Nevertheless, this attribution of a foundation in the exilic period might contain a historical kernel, even if it has been overlaid with a veneer of language derived from scripture and even if it has accrued some unhistorical embellishments. After all, few would deny that Jesus was crucified, whatever elaborative details the tradition behind Mk 15:22-37 may have picked up in transmission. Similarly, as we noted earlier, Davies has suggested that an exilic origin for the community behind the Admonition is not as impossible to envisage as many have assumed, especially if the situation that predominated at the time of the fifth century return was more complex than the surviving accounts imply.[74] Indeed, there is an increasing tendency among scholars to acknowledge that the narrative in Ezr, for example, is idealist in its presentation and propagandist in its aims.[75] If it is reasonable to assume an interchange between Babylon and Palestine at the time of the return under Ezra and in subsequent centuries more extensive than the 'official' records of the Jerusalem authorities would suggest (whether Ezr or, later, Josephus), it may not be surprising to find a sect such as that at Qumran, with alternative legal and historical traditions in opposition to those of such authorities, in possession of a work asserting its own exilic origins.

Such a claim places the writer of the Admonition and his community in an extremely authoritative position. Central to the affirmation is a controlling interpretation of the scriptures so that, in view of the apparent priestly and

---

[73]   Indeed, it should be noted that the Babylonian Talmud (Sanhedrin 43a) refers to the custom of offering a painkilling concoction to criminals about to be executed.

[74]   See again P.R. Davies, 'The Birthplace of the Essenes: Where is 'Damascus'', *RQ* 14 (1990), pp. 503-520, and, more generally, J. Blenkinsopp, *Ezra-Nehemiah*, London (1988); J.H. Hayes, J.M. Miller, *Israelite and Judaean History*, London (1990), pp. 489-538.

[75]   Thus, note Davies, *op cit*, p. 515, that "The so-called "exile" was in fact the deportation of a small number of Judean aristocrats. An even smaller number were sent back by the Persians to form a pliable ruling elite in the new province of Yehud".

levitical interest in some of the biblical texts employed in the document, a comment by Vermes referred to earlier is again relevant:

> "...exegetical elasticity matches the textual elasticity of the Qumran Bible. It still requires an explanation. I believe this should be sought in the paramount doctrinal authority of the Priests, the Sons of Zadok, the guardians of the Covenant".[76]

If the leadership of the group behind the Admonition included a Zadokite elite, entitled above all others to interpret the scriptures in view of their inherited status, this factor might explain CD's interest in Nu 16 and Ez 44 and the surrounding material, where corruption of correct priestly ordering and practice in both contexts appears to be a large part of what calls forth divine wrath and the preservation of a remnant.[77]

In sum, it appears that details in the Admonition, as well as the overall story-line, may have been inspired by the scriptures themselves, at least in part. At the same time, however, this is not to say that the events described, whether biblical or post-biblical, have no historical basis whatsoever. Rather, the historical and theological, in association with scripture, are inseparable and, from a historiographical viewpoint, the former is, perhaps, largely impenetrable. If so, the question of the origins of the Qumran community might be placed into the same category as a number of other problematic biblical and Second Temple events with which it bears similarly complicated characteristics: the exodus story, the return from Babylon, the Passion Narratives in general, Josephus' account of the causes of the First Revolt, and the emergence of Rabbinic Judaism in the first and second centuries CE.[78]

6.5 Use of Scripture in the Damascus Document 1-8, 19-20

Our analysis has proved more fruitful than might have been expected at the outset, and it has provided an alternative perspective on the text of the Admonition. Contrary to the difficulties usually encountered upon an initial

---

[76]   G. Vermes, 'Biblical Proof-Texts in Qumran Literature', *JSS* 34 (1989), p. 508; see above, p. 24.

[77]   See too M.A. Knibb, 'The Interpretation of *Damascus Document* VII, 9b-VIII,2a and XIX, 5b-14', *RQ* 15 (1991), p. 250, pointing to Ex 16, 34 and Nu 16, *inter alia*, as informing the background of the choice of language at CD 7:20. However, see above, p. 83, note 55, on the absence of the בני צדוק in 4QS.

[78]   This does not mean, of course, that the precise reasons for the difficulties in each case are the same.

reading of the work, it appears that it is in the document's skilled employment of the bible that its integrity and unity can be found. Although CD 1-8 and 19-20, like some other Second Temple texts, may at times employ biblical language simply because of the generally pervasive, but unconscious and hence largely insignificant, saturation of the author's mind with the vocabulary of the scriptures, most of the quotations, virtual citations, and allusions we have considered do not fall into this category. Indeed, notwithstanding some cases of bible usage which, for the time-being, lie beyond any detectable structure, we found ourselves returning to a distinct corpus of scriptural passages. This demonstration of the existence of a biblical framework underlying the Admonition has confirmed the interest placed by earlier scholarship on exegesis in the so-called sectarian DSS and carried it forward. However, it has also meant that we have had to reorient ourselves towards finding a suitable way of reading the document which takes its employment of the bible seriously.

A good random example, among the many we have sifted through in the preceding two chapters, of the document's utilization of the scriptures is its employment of language from Ex 32:25, Dt 9:5,23, Is 28:8,13f, and Hos 5:10,11 in several sections of the Admonition. Thus, CD 3:7 and 8:14 cite Dt 9:5 and 9:23, respectively, while this biblical context contains a summary of the rebellion recounted in Ex 32. Although Ex 32 itself is not explicitly mentioned in the Admonition, we may suspect that it was in the mind of our author, both because of his clear dependence on Dt 9 and, more interestingly, because לשמצה in Ex 32:25 may well have been understood as לשם צאה by our writer, inasmuch as such an interpretation would link in with his allusions to Is 28 and Hos 5. Regarding the former, it is the source for the epithets איש הלצון in CD 1:14 and אנשי הלצון in 20:11 (cf. Is 28:14, אנשי לצון) and contains the word צאה in verse 8 (cf. לשם צאה) and צו in verses 10 and 13 (cf. CD 4:19). The latter sound, apparently mimicking prophetic speech, also occurs in Hos 5:11 ("because he was determined to go after צו"), which clearly informs CD 4:19 (הלכו אחרי צו), while the same context in the form of Hos 5:10 stands behind the negative designation employed in CD 5:20 and 19:16 (cf. CD 8:3), namely, מסיגי הגבול.

The scriptural contexts that predominate in the Admonition have to do with various momentous Patriarchal or Israelite rebellions (e.g., Gn 6-7, Ex 32, Nu 14ff, 1 Sa 2) and, more particularly, with the rebellion *par excellence*, the exile (Lv 26, Dt 28ff, the Latter Prophets). As far as the historical sections of the work are concerned, language from such passages tends to be utilized in one of three ways:

(i)   Most straightforwardly, phraseology from a particular biblical incident or scenario is incorporated into an account of the same in CD. An instance of this can be found in CD 2:20f, drawing on Gn 6:17 and 7:22 in a description of the Flood.

(ii) At other points, it seems that language originating from an event narrated in a given biblical context is transferred within the Admonition to another incident deemed analogous by the writer. An example can be seen in CD 2:17, employing words from Dt 29:18 and Jer 23:17, scriptural passages concerned with the exile, to picture the obstinacy of the Watchers of primordial times.

(iii) Thirdly, phraseology from the bible is sometimes taken up and used to describe the origins of the sect, its development, or the eschaton. This adaptation of scriptural language can be illustrated in CD 1:8,9, which borrows words from Is 59:10,12 regarding the שורש מטעת, in CD 1:11, drawing on Hos 10:12 and Is 30:20 for the epithet מורה צדק, and in CD 20:14, which echoes Dt 2:14 in a description of the lot of the אנשי המלחמה.

Further, and as the tables above demonstrate (see pp. 179-182), we saw that many of the scriptural contexts informing the language of the historical sections were also influential in the document's intervening midrashic portions.

With regard to the significance of the use of scripture in CD 1-8 and 19-20, we may go one stage further in view of the polemical air of much of the document. This adversarial tone, as already implied in our consideration of the sect's supposed exilic origins, may profitably be related to conflicting claims in the second half of the Second Temple period truly to represent and continue ancient Israel's traditions. Indeed, rival interpretations of revelation held in common among the various Jewish groups at this time have been highlighted by Vermes, whose own words we may borrow once more:

> "From the one body of sacred writings...and employing the same methods of interpretation, each evolved a distinct religious outlook and way of life in conflict, very often, with those of the others".[79]

The way in which the Admonition goes about justifying its own claim to authority, as well as its own historical and legal traditions, therefore, is essentially through a subtle and complex use of the bible, coupled with and

---

[79]   See *PBJS*, p. 38, to which attention was drawn above, p. 9, note 23. Cf. also 4QMMT as presented and interpreted in the recently published E. Qimron, J. Strugnell, *Qumran Cave 4: Miqsat Ma'ase ha-Torah*, Oxford (Discoveries in the Judaean Desert, X; 1994).

authenticated by an appeal to the Zadokite status of its leadership or part thereof.

The manner in which the writer of CD 1-8 and 19-20 employs the bible is by regularly incorporating into his work reminiscences of language from scriptural contexts which recount a series of Israelite and, occasionally, pre-Israelite crises, in which the 'sheep' are separated from the 'goats'. Although our author was presumably aware that these rebellions and their accompanying restorations took place in a more-or-less linear fashion, he seems to have viewed them as analogous and interchangeable. Hence, the exile is a state that has been in force from ancient times until the present, along with concomitant righteous and apostate factions. This explains the Admonition's usage of certain prominent pentateuchal passages: Gn 7f, Ex 32, Nu 13-21, Lv 26, Dt 28ff, as well as contexts outside the Torah dealing with the exile or a parallel cycle of rebellion and restoration. As for the second century crux which is narrated in CD 1:5b-11a, we may suspect that it was viewed as yet another instance of Israelite rebelliousness, like those narrated in Nu after the exodus and, of course, the rebellion *par excellence*, the exile itself. This explains a certain vagueness in some of the document's descriptions, so that it is not always clear who is being talked about nor when (see, e.g., CD 1:4ff, 1:9ff, 3:10ff). Such ambiguity, along with the fact that the historical portions are interspersed with more ahistorical material (see especially CD 2:2-13), suggests that the writer thought that one age is much the same as any other vis à vis God and his relationship with his chosen people and their enemies. Accordingly, an understanding of this essentially timeless state of affairs, which explains the religious conditions of the author's own day, can be gleaned from accounts of biblical rebellion, purging and restoration, as well as from the circumstances of the sect's formation in exile (CD 1:4f, 3:12ff, 6:2ff) and subsequent experience (1:5b-11a). Moreover, it is a state of affairs which will only cease with the arrival of the approaching eschaton (cf. CD 4:11-12a, 6:8b-11a, 20:13b-22a).

Abbreviations

The following abbreviations have been used for books of the Hebrew Bible, New Testament, Apocrypha and Pseudepigrapha:[1]

Gn	Genesis	1,2 Esd	1,2 Esdras
Ex	Exodus	Tob	Tobit
Lv	Leviticus	Jud	Judith
Nu	Numbers	Wis	Wisdom
Dt	Deuteronomy	Sir/Ecclus	Sirach/Ecclesiaticus
Jos	Joshua	Bar	Baruch
Ju	Judges	LettJer	Letter of Jeremiah
1,2 Sa	1,2 Samuel	1,2,3,4 Mac	1,2,3,4 Maccabees
1,2 Ki	1,2 Kings	Mt	Matthew
Is	Isaiah	Mk	Mark
Jer	Jeremiah	Lk	Luke
Ez	Ezekiel	Jn	John
Hos	Hosea	Ac	Acts
Joel	Joel	Rom	Romans
Am	Amos	1,2 Cor	1,2 Corinthians
Ob	Obadiah	Gal	Galatians
Jon	Jonah	Eph	Ephesians
Mic	Micah	Phil	Philippians
Nah	Nahum	Col	Colossians
Hab	Habakkuk	1,2 Thes	1,2 Thessalonians
Zep	Zepheniah	1,2 Ti	1,2 Timothy
Hag	Haggai	Tit	Titus
Zec	Zecheriah	Philem	Philemon
Mal	Malachi	Heb	Hebrews
Ps	Psalm	Jas	James
Pr	Proverbs	1,2 Pet	1,2 Peter
Job	Job	1,2,3 Jn	1,2,3 John
Song	Song of Songs	Jude	Jude
Ru	Ruth	Rev	Revelation

---

[1] For the sake of completeness, all of what are normally considered to be the contents of the Hebrew Bible, NT and Apoc are included in what follows, whether or not cited or discussed in our study.

Lam	Lamentations	Jub	Jubilees
Eccl	Ecclesiastes	1,2 En	1,2 Enoch
Est	Esther	TestXII	Testaments of the
Dn	Daniel		Twelve Patriarchs
Ezr	Ezra	TLev etc	Testament of Levi etc
Neh	Nehemiah	AssMos	Assumption of Moses
1,2 Chr	1,2 Chronicles	2 Bar	2 Baruch

Other abbreviations, including periodicals, frequently cited works, and texts
and versions, are as follows:

א	Codex Sinaiticus
AJ	Josephus, *Jewish Antiquities*, I-XX, Cambridge-London (1930-65)
Apoc	Apocrypha
Aq	Aquila
ASTI	*Annual of the Swedish Theological Institute (in Jerusalem)*
B	Codex Vaticanus
BA	*Biblical Archaeologist*
BJ	Josephus, *The Jewish War*, I-VII, Cambridge-London (1927-79)
Boyce	M. Boyce, *The Poetry of the Damascus Document*, Edinburgh (PhD, 1988)
Broshi	M. Broshi (ed.), *The Damascus Document Reconsidered*, Jerusalem (1992)
CA	Josephus, *Against Apion*, I-II, Cambridge-London (1926)
CBQ	*Catholic Biblical Quarterly*
CD	The Damascus Document from the Cairo Genizah
Charles	R.H. Charles, *Apocrypha and Pseudepigrapha of the Old Testament*, I-II, Oxford (1912-13)
D	Codex Bezae
Davies	P.R. Davies, *The Damascus Covenant*, Sheffield (1982)
DJD III	M. Baillet, J.T. Milik, R. de Vaux, *Les 'Petites Grottes' de Qumrân*, Oxford (Discoveries in the Judaean Desert, III; 1962)
DJD VII	M. Baillet, *Qumrân Grotte 4: 4Q482-4Q520*, Oxford (Discoveries in the Judaean Desert VII; 1982
DSS	Dead Sea Scrolls
EW	R.H. Eisenman, M. Wise, *The Dead Sea Scrolls Uncovered*, Shaftsbury (1992)
DSSE	G. Vermes, *The Dead Sea Scrolls in English*, London (1994)
ed.(eds.)	editor(s)
FO	*Folio Orientalia*
Forty Years	D. Dimant, U. Rappaport, *The Dead Sea Scrolls: Forty Years of Reserach*, Leiden (1992)

HUCA	*Hebrew Union College Annual*
JBL	*Journal of Biblical Literature*
JJS	*Journal of Jewish Studies*
JPSA	Tanakh, the Holy Scriptures (Jewish Publication Society, 1985)
JQR	*Jewish Quarterly Review*
JSOT	*Journal for the Study of the Old Testament*
JSP	*Journal for the Study of the Pseudepigrapha*
JSS	*Journal of Semitic Studies*
JTS	*Journal of Theological Studies*
Knibb	M. Knibb, *The Qumran Community*, Cambridge (1987)
L	Codex of the Gospels from the eighth century CE
LXX	Septuagint
Madrid	J.T. Barrera, L.V. Montaner, *The Madrid Qumran Congress: Proceedings of the International Congress on the Dead Sea Scroll Madrid 18-21 March, 1991*, I-II, Leiden (1992)
MS(S)	manuscript(s)
MT	Masoretic Text
NJB	New Jerusalem Bible (1985)
NRSV	New Revised Standard Version (1989)
NT	New Testament
NTS	*New Testament Studies*
OTP	J.H. Charlesworth (ed.), *Old Testament Pseudepigrapha*, I-II, London (1983-85)
PBJS	G. Vermes, *Post-Biblical Jewish Studies*, Leiden (1975)
Pseud	Pseudepigrapha
Rabin	C. Rabin, *The Zadokite Documents*, Oxford (1958)
RB	*Révue Biblique*
REB	Revised English Bible (1989)
RQ	*Révue de Qumrân*
RSV	Revised Standard Version (1946-53, 1976)
Schürer	E. Schürer, G. Vermes, F. Millar, M. Goodman, *The history of the Jewish people in the age of Jesus Christ*, I-III.2, Edinburgh (1973-87)
Schwarz	O.J.R. Schwarz, *Der erste Teil der Damaskusschrift und das alte Testament*, Diest (1965)
Syr	Syriac
Q	Codex of the Gospels from the ninth century CE
Theod	Theodotian
v(v)	verse(s)
Vermes	G. Vermes, *Discovery in the Judean Desert*, New York (1956)
VT	*Vetus Testamentum*

Vulg	Vulgate
WA	B.Z. Wacholder, M.G. Abegg, *A Preliminary Edition of the Unpublished Dead Sea Scrolls: the Hebrew and Aramaic Texts from Cave Four*, Fascicle One, Washington (1991)
ZAW	*Zeitschrift für die Alttestamentliche Wissenschaft*
ZRGG	*Zeitschrift für Religions- und Geistesgeschichte*
1QapGen	The Genesis Apocryphon from Qumran Cave 1
1QH	The Hymns Scroll from Qumran Cave 1
1QM	The War Scroll from Qumran Cave 1
1QS	The Community Rule from Qumran Cave 1
1QSa	The Messianic Rule from Qumran Cave 1
1QpHab	The Habakkuk Pesher from Qumran Cave 1
1QpMic	The Micah Pesher (1Q14) from Qumran Cave 1
4-6QD	The Damascus Document from Qumran Caves 4-6
4QFlor	A Midrash on the Last Days (4Q174) from Qumran Cave 4
4QM	The War Scroll (4Q491-6) from Qumran Cave 4
4QMMT	Some Observances of the Law (4Q398-9) from Qumran Cave 4
4QpHos	The Hosea Pesher (4Q166-7) from Qumran Cave 4
4QpNah	The Nahum Pesher (4Q169) from Qumran Cave 4
4QpPs	The Psalms Pesher (4Q171/173) from Qumran Cave 4
4QS	The Community Rule (4Q255-64) from Qumran Cave 4
4QTest	Messianic Testimonia (4Q175) from Qumran Cave 4
4Q156	Targum to Job from Qumran Cave 4
4Q157	Targum to Leviticus from Qumran Cave 4
4Q181	The Wicked and the Holy from Qumran Cave 4
4Q274	Tohorot from Qumran Cave 4
4Q280	Curses of Melkiresha from Qumran Cave 4
4Q286-7	Curses of Satan and His Lot from Qumran Cave 4
4Q380	Apocryphal Psalms from Qumran Cave 4
4Q393	A Liturgy or Communal Confession from Qumran Cave 4
4Q424	A Sapiential Work from Qumran Cave 4
4Q504	The Words of the Luminaries (4QDibHam[a]) from Qumran Cave 4
4Q509	Prayers for Festivals from Qumran Cave 4
4Q521	A Messianic Apocalypse from Qumran Cave 4
11QT	The Temple Scroll (11Q19) from Qumran Cave 11
11Q10	Targum to Job from Qumran Cave 11

Bibliography

The following select bibliographical list includes all works cited, discussed or mentioned in the present study.[1]

K. Aland, *Novum Testamentum Graece*, Stuttgart (1979).

M. Baillet, *Qumrân Grotte 4: 4Q482-4Q520*, Oxford (Discoveries in the Judaean Desert VII; 1982).

M. Baillet, J.T. Milik, R. de Vaux, *Les 'Petites Grottes' de Qumrân*, Oxford (Discoveries in the Judaean Desert, III; 1962).

J. Barr, *The Bible in the Modern World*, London (1973).

J.T. Barrera, L.V. Montaner, *The Madrid Qumran Congress: Proceedings of the International Congress on the Dead Sea Scrolls Madrid 18-21 March, 1991*, I-II, Leiden (1992).

J. Barton, *Reading the Old Testament*, London (1985);
Oracles of God, London (1986).

J.M. Baumgarten, *Studies in Qumran Law*, Leiden (1977);
'The 4Q Zadokite Fragments on Skin Disease', *JJS* 41 (1990), pp. 153-165;
'The Cave 4 Versions of the Qumran Penal Code', *JJS* 43 (1991), pp. 268-276.

R.T. Beckwith, 'The Significance of the Calendar for Interpreting Essene Chronology and Eschatology', *RQ* 10 (1980), pp. 167-202.

E. Ben Zvi, 'The Authority of 1-2 Chronicles in the Late Second Temple Period', *JSP* 3 (1988), pp. 59-88.

K. Beyer, *Die Aramäischen Texte vom toten Meer*, Göttingen (1984).

J. Blenkinsopp, *Ezra-Nehemiah*, London (1988);
The Pentateuch, London (1993).

G. Bonani *et al*, 'Radiocarbon Dating of the Dead Sea Scrolls', *Atiqot* 20 (1991), pp. 25-32.

M. Boyce, *The Poetry of the Damascus Document*, Edinburgh (PhD, 1988);
'The Poetry of the Damascus Document and its Bearing on the Origin of the Qumran Sect', *RQ* 14 (1990), pp. 615-628.

G.J. Brooke, 'The Amos-Numbers Midrash (CD 7^{13b}-8^{1a}) and Messianic Expectation', *ZAW* 92 (1980), pp. 397-404;
'Qumran Pesher: Towards the Redefinition of a Genre', *RQ* 10 (1981), pp. 483-503;
Exegesis at Qumran: 4QFlorilegium in its Jewish Context, Sheffield (1985);
Temple Scroll Studies, Sheffield (1989);

---

[1] For further bibliographical information, see the catalogue compiled by Fitzmyer in S. Schechter, J. Fitzmyer, *Documents of Jewish Sectaries: Fragments of a Zadokite Work*, Cambridge (1970), listing relevant works published by 1970; additionally, see J. Fitzmyer, *The Dead Sea Scrolls*, Missoula (1977). Moreover, Broshi, pp. 63-83, records studies produced between 1970 and 1989.

'Psalms 105 and 106 at Qumran', *RQ* 14 (1989), pp. 267-292;

'The Messiah of Aaron in the Damascus Document', *RQ* 15 (1991), pp. 215-230.

M. Broshi (ed.), *The Damascus Document Reconsidered*, Jerusalem (1992).

W.H. Brownlee, 'Biblical Interpretation among the Sectaries of the Dead Sea Scrolls', *BA* 14 (1951), pp. 34-76.

P.R. Callaway, *The History of the Qumran Community: An Investigation*, Sheffield (1988);

'Qumran Origins: From the Doresh to the Moreh', *RQ* 14 (1990), pp 637-651.

J.G. Campbell, 'Scripture in The Damascus Document 1:1-2:1', *JJS* 44 (1993), pp. 83-99.

J. Carmignac, 'Comparaison Entre Les Manuscrits 'A' and 'B' Dans Le Document De Damas', *RQ* 2 (1959), pp. 53-67.

R.H. Charles, *Apocrypha and Pseudepigrapha of the Old Testament*, I-II, Oxford (1912-1913).

J.H. Charlesworth, 'The Origin and Subsequent History of the Authors of the Dead Sea Scrolls: Four Transitional Phases among the Qumran Essenes', *RQ* 10 (1980), pp. 213-233;

The Old Testament Pseudepigrapha, I-II, London (1983-85).

D.J.A. Clines, *The Theme of the Pentateuch*, Sheffield (1978).

D. Coggan (ed.), *The Revised English Bible*, Oxford-Cambridge (1989).

R.J. Coggins, *Introducing the Old Testament*, Oxford (1990).

F.M. Cross, S. Talmon, *Qumran and the History of the Biblical Text*, Cambridge, MA (1975).

P.R. Davies, *1QM, the War Scroll from Qumran. Its Structure and History*, Rome (1976);

'Hasidim in the Maccabean Period', *JJS* 28 (1977), pp. 127-140;

'The Ideology of the Temple in the Damascus Document', *JJS* 33 (1982), pp. 287-301;

The Damascus Covenant, Sheffield (1982);

'Eschatology at Qumran', *JBL* 104 (1985), pp. 39-55;

Behind the Essenes: History and Ideology in the Dead Sea Scrolls, Atlanta (1987);

'The Teacher of Righteousness and the End of Days', *RQ* 13 (1988), pp. 313-317;

'The Birthplace of the Essenes: Where is 'Damascus'?' *RQ* 14 (1990), pp. 503-520;

'Communities at Qumran and the Case of the Missing Teacher', *RQ* 15 (1991), pp. 275-286;

In Search of 'Ancient Israel', Sheffield (1992).

P.R. Davies, R.T. White (eds.), *A Tribute to Geza Vermes*, Sheffield (1990).

M. Dibelius, *From Tradition to Gospel*, Cambridge-London (1971).

D. Dimant, 'Qumran Sectarian Literature: Biblical Interpretation', in M.E. Stone (ed.), *Jewish Writings of the Second Temple Period*, II, Assen-Philadelphia (1984), pp. 503-508.

D. Dimant, U. Rappaport (eds.), *The Dead Sea Scrolls: Forty Years of Research*, Leiden (1992).

J. Duhaime, 'Dualist Reworking in the Scrolls from Qumran', *CBQ* 49 (1987), pp. 32-56.

T. Eagleton, *Literary Theory: An Introduction*, Oxford (1983).

R.H. Eisenman, *Maccabees, Zadokites, Christians and Qumran*, Leiden (1983);
'The Historical Provenance of the Three Nets of Belial: Allusion in the Zadokite Document and Bella/Bela' in the Temple Scrolls', *FO* 25 (1988), pp. 51-66.

R.H. Eisenman, J.M. Robinson, *A Facsimile Edition of the Dead Sea Scrolls*, I-II, Washington (1991).

R.H. Eisenman, M. Wise, *The Dead Sea Scrolls Uncovered*, Shaftsbury (1992).

K. Elliger, W. Rudolph, *Biblia Hebraica Stuttgartensia*, Stuttgart (1967-83).

M. Fishbane, *Biblical Interpretation in Ancient Israel*, Oxford (1985).

J.A. Fitzmyer, *Essays on the Semitic Background of the New Testament*, London (1971);
The Dead Sea Scrolls, Missoula (1977).

V. Gleßmer, 'Liste der Biblischen Texte aus Qumran', *RQ* 16 (1993), pp. 153-192.

S.D. Fraade, 'Interpretative Authority in the Studying Community at Qumran', *JJS* 44 (1993), pp. 46-69.

N. Golb, 'Who Hid the Dead Sea Scrolls?', *BA* 28 (1987), pp. 68-82.

M.D. Goodman, 'Sacred Scripture and 'Defiling the Hands'', *JTS* 41 (1990), pp. 99-107.

J.B. Graber, C.B. Wheeler, *The Bible as Literature*, New York-Oxford (1990).

J.C. Greenfield, 'The Words of Levi son of Jacob in Damascus Document IV, 15-19', *RQ* 13 (1988), pp. 319-322.

B. Grossfeld, *The Targum Onqelos to Deuteronomy*, Edinburgh (1988).

E. Haenchen, *The Acts of the Apostles. A Commentary*, Oxford (1971).

J.H. Hayes, J.M. Miller, *Israelite and Judaean History*, London (1990).

W.L. Holladay (ed.), *A Concise Hebrew and Aramaic Lexicon of the Old Testament*, Grand Rapids/Leiden (1988).

M.D. Hooker, *The Gospel according to St. Mark*, London (1991).

M.P. Horgan, *Pesharim: Qumran Interpretations of Biblical Books*, Washington (1979).

Jewish Publication Society, *Tanakh, the Holy Scriptures*, New York (1985).

G. Jeremias, *Der Lehrer der Gerechtigkeit*, Göttingen (1963).

D. Juel, *Messiah and Temple: The Trial of Jesus in the Gospel of Mark*, Missoula (1977).

J. Kampen, 'A Fresh Look at the Masculine Plural Suffix in CD iv 2', *RQ* 16 (1993), pp. 91-297.

M.A. Knibb, 'The Exile in the Literature of the Intertestamental Period', *Heythrop Journal* 17 (1976), pp. 253-272;
'Exile in the Damascus Document', *JSOT* 25 (1983), pp. 99-117;
The Qumran Community, Cambridge (1987);
'Jubilees and the Origins of the Qumran Community', Inaugural Lecture at King's College London (1989), pp. 1-20;
'The Interpretation of *Damascus Document* VII, 9b-VIII,2a and XIX, 5b-14', *RQ* 15 (1991), pp. 243-251.

H. Kosmala, 'The Three Nets of Belial. A Study in the terminology of Qumran and the New Testament', *ASTI* 4 (1965), pp. 91-113.

A. Laato, 'The Seventy Yearweeks in the Book of Daniel', *ZAW* 102 (1990), pp. 212-225;

'The Chronology in the *Damascus Document* of Qumran', *RQ* 15 (1992) pp. 605-607.

T.H. Lim, 'The Wicked Priests of the Groningen Hypothesis', *JBL* 112 (1993), pp. 415-425.

E. Lohse, *Die Texte aus Qumran*, Darmstadt (1971).

F. García Martínez, 'Qumran Origins and Early History: A Groningen Hypothesis', *FO* 25 (1988), pp. 113-136.

F. Garcia Martinez, A.S. van der Woude, 'A Groningen Hypothesis of Qumran Origins and Early History', *RQ* 14 (1990), pp. 521-542.

B.M. Metzger (ed.), *The Holy Bible. New Revised Standard Version*, New York-Oxford (1989).

J.T. Milik, *Ten Years of Discovery in the Wilderness of Judaea*, London (1959).

C. Milikowsky, 'Again: *Damascus* in Damascus Document and in Rabbinic Literature', *RQ* 11 (1982), pp. 97-106.

P.D. Miscall, *Isaiah*, Sheffield (1993).

D.J. Moo, *The Old Testament in the Gospel Passion Narratives*, Sheffield (1983).

M.J. Mulder (ed.), *Mikra*, Assen-Philadelphia (1988).

J. Murphy-O'Connor, 'La genèse littéraire de la *Règle de la Communauté*', *RB* 76 (1969), pp. 528-549;

'An Essene Missionary Document? CD II,14-VI,1', *RB* 77 (1970), pp. 201-229;

'A Literary Analysis of Damascus Document VI,2-VIII,3', *RB* 78 (1971), pp. 210-232;

'The Critique of the Princes of Judah (CD VIII,3-19)', *RB* 79 (1972), pp. 200-216;

'A Literary Analysis of Damascus Document XIX,33-XX,34', *RB* 79 (1972), pp. 544-564;

'The Essenes and Their History', *RB* 81 (1974), pp. 215-244;

'The Damascus Document Revisited', *RB* 92 (1985), pp. 223-246.

J. Neusner, *Judaism: The Evidence of the Mishnah*, Chicago-London (1981).

E. Qimron, *The Hebrew of the Dead Sea Scrolls*, Atlanta (1986).

E. Qimron, J. Strugnell, *Qumran Cave 4: Miqsat Ma'ase ha-Torah*, Oxford (Discoveries in the Judaean Desert, X; 1994).

C. Rabin, *The Zadokite Documents*, Oxford (1958).

I. Rabinowitz, 'A Reconsideration of 'Damascus' and '390 Years' in the 'Damascus ('Zadokite') Fragments', *JBL* 73 (1954), pp. 11-35.

A. Rahlfs, *Septuaginta*, Stuttgart (1979).

R. Rosenbaum, A.M. Silbermann, *Pentateuch with Rashi's Commentary*, I-II, London (1946).

E.P. Sanders, *Jesus and Judaism*, London (1985).

S. Schechter, J. Fitzmyer, *Documents of Jewish Sectaries: Fragments of a Zadokite Work*, Cambridge (1970).

L.H. Schiffman, *The Halachah at Qumran*, Leiden (1975).

E.M. Schuller, *Non-Canonical Psalms from Qumran: A Pseudepigraphic Collection*, Atlanta (1986).

E. Schürer, G. Vermes, F. Millar, M. Goodman, *The history of the Jewish people in the age of Jesus Christ*, I-III.2, Edinburgh (1973-1987).

D.R. Schwarz, 'To Join Oneself to the House of Judah', *RQ* 10 (1981), pp. 435-446.

O.J.R. Schwarz, *Der erste Teil der Damaskusschrift und das alte Testament*, Diest (1965).

P.W. Skehan, 'The Biblical Scrolls from Qumran and the Text of the Old Testament', *BA* 28 (1965), pp. 87-100.

E. Slomovic, 'Towards an Understanding of Exegesis in the Dead Sea Scrolls', *RQ* 7 (1969-71), pp. 3-15.

J.A. Soggin, *Introduction to the Old Testament*, London (1989).

R.A. Soloff, 'Towards Uncovering Original Texts in the Zadokite Documents', *NTS* 5 (1958-59), pp. 62-67.

H. Stegemann, *Die Entstehung der Qumrangemeinde*, Bonn (1971);
'Das Gesetzeskorpus der <<Damaskusschrift>> (CD IX-XVI)', *RQ* 14 (1990), pp. 409-434;
'The Qumran Essenes - Local Members of the Main Jewish Union in Late Second Temple Times', in J.L. Barrera, L.V. Montaner (eds.), *The Madrid Qumran Congress: Proceedings of the International Congress on the Dead Sea Scrolls*, Madrid 18-21 March 1991, I, Leiden (1992), pp. 83-166.

A. Steudal, 'אחרית הימים in the Texts from Qumran', *RQ* 16 (1993), pp. 225-244.

M.E. Stone (ed.), *Jewish Writings of the Second Temple Period*, Assen-Philadelphia (1984).

F.M. Strickert, 'Damascus Document VII,10-20 and Qumran Messianic Expectation', *RQ* 12 (1986), pp. 327-350.

V. Taylor, *The Gospel according to St. Mark*, London (1952).

J.L. Teicher, 'Die Schriftrollen vom Toten Meer - Dokumente der jüdisch-christlichen Sekte der Ebioniten', *ZRGG* 3 (1951), pp. 153-209.

B. Thiering, 'The Date of Composition of the Temple Scroll', in G.J. Brooke (ed.), *Temple Scroll Studies*, Sheffield (1989), pp. 99-120;
Jesus the Man: A New Interpretation from the Dead Sea Scrolls, London (1992).

E. Tov, 'Hebrew Biblical Manuscripts from the Judaean Desert: Their Contribution to Textual Criticism', *JJS* 39 (1988), pp. 5-37;
The Greek Minor Prophets Scroll from Nahal Hever (8HevXIIgr) (The Seiyal Collection I), Oxford (Discoveries in the Judaean Desert, VIII; 1990);
Textual Criticism of the Hebrew Bible, Minneapolis-Assen/Maastricht (1992).

E. Ulrich, 'Pluriformity in the Biblical Text, Texts Groups, and Questions of Canon', in J.L. Barrera, L.V. Montaner (eds.), *The Madrid Qumran Congress: Proceedings of the International Congress on the Dead Sea Scrolls*, Madrid 18-21 March 1991, I-II, Leiden (1992), pp. 23-41.

R. de Vaux, *Archaeology and the Dead Sea Scrolls*, London (1973).

R. de Vaux, J.T. Milik, *Qumran Grotte 4: II Archeologie et 4Q128-4Q157*, Oxford (Discoveries in the Judaean Desert, VI; 1977).

G. Vermes, *Discovery in the Judaean Desert*, New York (1956);
'Sectarian Matrimonial Halakhah in the Damascus Rule', *JJS* 25 (1974), pp. 197-202;
Post-Biblical Jewish Studies, Leiden (1975);
'The Essenes and History', *JJS* 32 (1981);
'Bible Interpretation at Qumran', *Eretz-Israel* 20 (1989), pp. 184-191;
'Biblical Proof-Texts in Qumran Literature', *JSS* 34 (1989), pp. 493-508;

'Preliminary Remarks on the Unpublished Fragments of the Community Rule from Qumran Cave 4', *JJS* 42 (1991), pp. 250-255;

'The Present State of Dead Sea Scrolls Research', *JJS* 45 (1994), pp. 101-110;

The Dead Sea Scrolls: Qumran in Perspective, London (1994);

The Dead Sea Scrolls in English, London (1994).

J. de Waard, *A Comparative Study of the Old Testament Text in the Dead Sea Scrolls and in the New Testament*, Leiden (1965).

B.Z. Wacholder, 'The < < Sealed > > Torah versus the < < Revealed > > Torah: An Exegesis of Damascus Document V, 1-6 and Jeremiah 32, 10-14', *RQ* 12 (1986), pp. 351-68;

'Does Qumran record the death of the Teacher? The meaning of *h'sp* in Damascus Document XIX,35, XX,14', *RQ* 13 (1988), pp. 323-330.

B.Z. Wacholder, M.G. Abegg, *A Preliminary Edition of the Unpublished Dead Sea Scrolls: the Hebrew and Aramaic Texts from Cave Four*, Fascicle One, Washington (1991).

H. Wansbrough (ed.), *The New Jerusalem Bible*, London (1985).

S.A. White, 'A Comparison of the 'A' and 'B' Manuscripts of the Damascus Document', *RQ* 12 (1987), pp. 537-553.

N. Wieder, 'The Land of Damascus and Messianic Redemption', *JJS* 20 (1969), pp. 86-88.

E. Wiesenberg, 'Chronological Data In The Zadokite Fragments', *VT* 5 (1955), pp. 284-308.

G.H. Wilson, *The Editing of the Hebrew Psalter*, Chico (1985).

M. Wise, 'The Teacher of Righteousness and the High Priest of the Intersacerdotium: Two Approaches', *RQ* 14 (1990), pp. 587-614.

ZEITSCHRIFT FÜR NEUERE THEOLOGIEGESCHICHTE

JOURNAL FOR THE HISTORY OF MODERN THEOLOGY

Edited by

RICHARD E. CROUTER · FRIEDRICH WILHELM GRAF
GÜNTER MECKENSTOCK

The *Journal for the History of Modern Theology* is an academic journal
directed toward theologians, historians, philosophers, and scholars of
comparative religion, as well as representatives of others disciplines related
to cultural studies.
The journal contains articles that deal with the history of theology since the
Enlightenment. Alongside the various types of theology and philosophy of
religion present in Protestantism, the journal shall consider the different
theological and philosophical movements within Roman Catholicism and
Judaism. Its scope is not limited to the history of theology in the
Germanspeaking world, but will include contributions that discuss the
historical processes of theological change that have taken place in other
European countries as well as in North America.
Contributions will be in German or English; a summary (abstract) in the
other language will make it possible to get a quick overview of the contents
of each article.

Volume 2, 1995
Published twice a year with a total of approx. 320 pages.
Complete volume DM 162,−/öS 1.264,−/sFr 156,−; ISSN 0943-7592

Free sample copies available upon request

Price is subject to change

WALTER DE GRUYTER · BERLIN · NEW YORK

TRE Theologische Realenzyklopädie

Studienausgabe Teil I
Bände 1 (Aaron) — 17 (Katechismuspredigt) und Registerband

In Gemeinschaft mit Horst Robert Balz, James K. Cameron, Wilfried Härle, Stuart G. Hall, Brian L. Hebblethwaite, Richard Hentschke, Wolfgang Janke, Hans-Joachim Klimkeit, Joachim Mehlhausen, Knut Schäferdiek, Henning Schröer, Gottfried Seebaß, Clemens Thoma

herausgegeben von Gerhard Müller

20,5 × 13,5 cm. 17 Bände, 1 Index-Band. Etwa 800 Seiten je Band.
Kartoniert DM 1.200,— ISBN 3-11-013898-0 (de Gruyter Studienbuch)

Die TRE-Studienausgabe Teil I umfaßt die Bände 1 bis 17 der THEOLOGISCHEN REAL-ENZYKLOPÄDIE. Erschlossen wird die Studienausgabe durch einen entsprechenden Registerband, der auch Erwähnungen der Stichworte nachweist, die alphabetisch nach den Lemmata „Aaron" bis „Katechismuspredigt" angesiedelt sind (z. B. Zwingli). Die TRE-Studienausgabe Teil I ist damit schon jetzt ein vollwertiges Arbeitsmittel für jeden Theologen.

Um weitesten Kreisen die TRE zugänglich zu machen, wird die Studienausgabe zu einem wirklich günstigen Preis angeboten: DM 1.200,— für 17 Bände plus Register.* Das sind über 13 000 Seiten solidester wissenschaftlich-theologischer Forschung.

Selbstverständlich wird die TRE-Studienausgabe zu einem späteren Zeitpunkt eine entsprechende Fortsetzung finden. In etwa sieben bis acht Jahren wird es von seiten des Verlages ein analoges Angebot geben.

* Die Bände der Studienausgabe entsprechen im Grundsatz denen der Originalausgabe, bei allerdings verkleinertem Satzspiegel. Außerdem mußte aus Kostengründen auf Tafeln und Faltkarten verzichtet werden.

The TRE-Studienausgabe, Part I, contains volumes 1—17 of the THEOLOGISCHE REAL-ENZYKLOPÄDIE. The Studienausgabe is made accessible by means of an index volume, which also points to where the key-words are mentioned. These are arranged alphabetically and go even beyond the headings "Aaron" to "Katechismuspredigt" (catechism sermon) to include, for example, Zwingli. The TRE Study Edition, Part I, is thus already now a high quality working tool for every theologian.

The TRE-Studienausgabe will, of course, be continued in a similar manner at a later time. The publishers plan to present an analogous offer in about seven to eight years.

The volumes of the Studienausgabe basically correspond to those of the original edition. The area of print, however, is reduced. For reasons of cost, tables and folding maps had to be left out.

Preisänderungen vorbehalten

Walter de Gruyter Berlin · New York

GENERAL J